FEMINIST PERSPECTIVES
ON EMPLOYMENT LAW

Cavendish
Publishing
Limited

London • Sydney

FEMINIST PERSPECTIVES ON EMPLOYMENT LAW

Anne Morris, LLB
Senior Lecturer in Law
University of Strathclyde

Thérèse O'Donnell, LLB, Dip LP, Dip IL, M Litt
Lecturer in Law
University of Liverpool

Cavendish
Publishing
Limited

London • Sydney

First published in Great Britain 1999 by Cavendish Publishing Limited,
The Glass House, Wharton Street, London WC1X 9PX, United Kingdom
Telephone: + 44 (0) 171 278 8000   Facsimile: + 44 (0) 171 278 8080
E-mail: info@cavendishpublishing.com
Visit our Home Page on http://www.cavendishpublishing.com

Feminist Perspectives on Employment Law
1. Labour laws and legislation – Great Britain 2. Women – Employment –
Law and legislation – Great Britain
I. Morris, Anne E, 1952– II. O'Donnell, Therese
344.4'1'01

ISBN 1 85941 481 8.   0

1001583621

Printed and bound in Great Britain

SERIES EDITORS' PREFACE

The injustices suffered by women in the world of employment provoked some of the earliest campaigns which might properly be described as feminist. Perhaps it is not surprising, then, that it was in the area of employment law that so much of the earliest feminist legal scholarship was focused and developed. Indeed, employment law has continued to provide a focal point for a large body of critical feminist work. Given the depth and breadth of this scholarship, as well as the introduction of 'protective' legislation as a result of hard fought campaigns, it is surely difficult for even the most conventional of courses in employment law to fail to engage with some of what have come to be seen as 'women's issues'. Yet, whilst feminist work has not been totally ignored, it has undoubtedly been marginalised within the traditional employment law curriculum, ghettoised into those sessions dealing with what are preceived as 'women's issues': equal opportunities, provision for maternity leave, the prohibition of nightwork and so on.

This book is a challenge to that ghettoisation: a refusal to limit the relevance of feminist insight to these issues. Whilst contributors show that there are still important and novel arguments to be made about the traditional topics of concern, they also successfully demonstrate the relevance of gender to every aspect of working life and, indeed, the way that work relates to life outside of the workplace. Intriguing in the present collection is the fact that the chapter on equal opportunities focuses not on unfair dismissal or discrimination in appoinments procedures, but on the mechanics of assertiveness training. Likewise, a chapter on victimisation at work takes not sexual harrassment but bullying as its theme. Another chapter reveals the inadequacy of looking at discrimination at work in terms of a discrete category of gender, and argues the need to take a more holistic approach which is capable of recognising the complexities of multiple discrimination.

Common to all the chapters in this volume is the belief that concern with gender must be pervasive in the study of employment law, rather than being treated as something which can be included as an (optional) supplement to it. Between them, the contributors mount an eloquent plea for the 'mainstreaming' (to coin a phrase) of feminist perspectives.

This volume will make exciting and challenging reading for anyone who is interested in employment law, and a valuable and timely contribution to feminist scholarship in this area. We would like to thank the editors and the contributors for making such an important contribution to the present series, and Jo Reddy at Cavendish for her continuing support of the series.

Anne Bottomley and Sally Sheldon

March 1999

CONTRIBUTORS

Diamond Ashiagbor is currently a Researcher at the European University Institute, Florence. Formerly, she was a Lecturer in Law at the University of Hull.

Dr Alice Belcher, B Soc Sc, M Phil, PhD, FCA, is Senior Lecturer in Law at the University of Dundee. She teaches and writes in the areas of employment law, company law and economics and the law.

Dr Richard Collier, LLB, MA, PhD, is Reader in Law at the University of Newcastle. He is the author of *Masculinities, Crime and Criminology* (1998) and *Masculinity, Law and the Family* (1995).

Joanne Conaghan is a Reader in Law at the University of Kent. Her areas of research include labour law, tort law and feminist legal theory, and she has published widely in all three fields. She is the co-author (with Wade Mansell) of *The Wrongs of Tort* and co-editor (with Anne Bottomley) of *Feminist Theory and Legal Strategy*.

Suzanne Jamieson is a Senior Lecturer in the Department of Industrial Relations at the University of Sydney, where she teaches labour law, discrimination and gender and work.

Anne Morris, LLB, is a Senior Lecturer in Law at the Feminist Legal Research Unit at the University of Liverpool's Faculty of Law. She is the co-author with Sue Nott of *Working Women and the Law* and *All My Worldly Goods: A Feminist Perspective on the Legal Regulation of Wealth*.

Debra Morris is a Lecturer in Law at the University of Liverpool. She is a founding member of the Feminist Legal Research Unit. She is also a Director of the Charity Law Unit.

Sue Nott, LLB, BCL, is a Senior Lecturer in Law and a member of the Feminist Legal Research Unit at the University of Liverpool's Faculty of Law.

Thérèse O'Donnell, LLB, DIP LP, DIP IL, M LITT, is a Lecturer in Law at Strathclyde University and was formerly a member of the Law Faculty at the University of Liverpool. She remains a member of the Feminist Legal Research Unit of the latter.

Jenifer Ross, LLB, MA, Solicitor, is a Senior Lecturer in Law at Strathclyde University. She teaches and writes on labour law, discrimination law and criminal law. In addition to her academic interest in equality and the law, she is a member of the board of directors of the Ethnic Minorities Law Centre in Glasgow.

CONTENTS

TABLE OF CASES

TABLE OF STATUTES

Other Legislation

TABLE OF STATUTORY INSTRUMENTS

TABLE OF EUROPEAN LEGISLATION

TABLE OF ABBREVIATIONS

AC	Appeal Cases
All ER	All England Law Reports
Berkeley Women's LJ	Berkeley Women's Law Journal
C & P	Carrington & Payne
Catholic UL Rev	Catholic University Law Review
Chicago L Forum	Chicago Law Forum
Columbia L Rev	Columbia Law Review
ECR	European Court Reports
EOR	Equal Opportunities Review
F2d	Federal Reporter, Second Series
FLS	Feminist Legal Studies
F Supp	Federal Supplement
Harv L Rev	Harvard University Law Review
ICR	Industrial Cases Reports
IJDL	International Journal of Discrimination Law
ILJ	Industrial Law Journal
Int J Soc L	International Journal of the Sociology of Law
IRLR	Industrial Relations Law Reports
JLS	Journal of Legal Studies
J Policy Studies	Journal of Policy Studies
LS	Legal Studies
McGill LJ	McGill Law Journal
MLR	Modern Law Review
New York U Rev of Law and Social Change	New York University Review of Law and Social Change
NLJ	New Law Journal
OJLS	Oxford Journal of Legal Studies
QB	Queen's Bench Law Reports
SJ	Solicitors Journal
SLS	Socio-Legal Studies

Southern California L Rev	Southern California Law Review
Stanford L Rev	Stanford Law Review
Texas L Rev	Texas Law Review
WLR	Weekly Law Reports
Yale LJ	Yale Law Journal

CHAPTER 1

EMPLOYMENT LAW AND FEMINISM

Anne Morris and Thérèse O'Donnell

The series of *Feminist Perspectives on ...* began with the *Foundational Subjects of Law,* and one of its stated aims was to bring feminist perspectives to bear on areas of the law which had not traditionally been seen as obvious candidates for that kind of analysis.[1] In that sense, employment law might be thought to be different, in that significant chunks of it are recognisably and directly to do with women (sex discrimination, equal pay, maternity rights), and this means that women are at once identifiable as appropriate or 'proper' subjects within that category of legal study. This can, however, be a mixed blessing, since it offers the temptation to 'ghettoise' and assume that there are particular topics ('women's issues') with which feminists should concern themselves (or, indeed, to which they should restrict themselves). Whilst, at the very least, this denies the wider relevance of feminism, it also ignores the fact that a piecemeal approach is not going to achieve the fundamental changes which are necessary if women are to be able to participate fully and equally in society – a participation which requires a just reward for the work they do and the contributions they make, both paid and unpaid. Further, focusing only on the laws which purport to deal with discrimination can encourage the view that, since there are now laws which call for equal pay, outlaw sex discrimination and provide for maternity leave, any lingering 'inequalities' must, by definition, result from the different choices which women make in their lives, rather than from conscious or unconscious bias.

In any event, the aspects of employment law which are most obviously of relevance to women are far from being the whole, or even the bulk, of what constitutes the complex and increasingly wide ranging legal regulation of the working relationship. Indeed, it could be argued that one of the principal defects of the 'discrimination' legislation, which is intended to achieve equality for women in the workplace, is the very fact that it is so readily identifiable and discrete. It is peripheral – a bolt-on rather than a central theme, an afterthought rather than a guiding principle. Just as much in employment law as in other areas, therefore, it is important for feminists to challenge the notion that there are limits to the relevance of feminist perspectives and to reject attempts to restrict feminist scholarship to topics seen as peculiarly appropriate for women (as students and teachers). In many

---

1   Bottomley, A (ed), *Feminist Perspectives on the Foundational Subjects of Law,* 1996, London: Cavendish Publishing.

ways, it is an ideal subject in which to challenge assumptions about the scope of feminist scholarship, because there are few areas of life on which employment law does not impact:

> Work is central to our lives. Paid or unpaid, it is the way in which we meet needs, create wealth and distribute resources. It is a source of personal identity and individual fulfilment, social status and relationships.[2]

This is true for men as well as women but, whilst there are men in low paid, insecure jobs (or no job at all), and whilst there are men who would like to be able to reconcile more easily the demands of work with family responsibilities, it is still women – throughout the world – who shoulder the principal responsibility for the attempt to combine work outside and within the home while being, in general, less well rewarded than men.

The aim of this collection of essays is, therefore, to extend the focus beyond the obvious issues in which feminists might be assumed to be interested, but to do so without ignoring the very real differences which influence the working and family lives of women and men. The volume began to take shape in the months after the General Election of May 1997 and the emergence of a new government with a new(ish) agenda. On the face of it, things began to look up: the government reacted favourably to the Parental and Family Leave Directive and the Part Time Workers Directive, set up the Low Pay Commission, introduced legislation which led to the National Minimum Wage Act, and launched the National Childcare Strategy. A Women's Unit was set up to tackle issues such as the pay and working conditions enjoyed by women. Unfortunately, this had a rather inauspicious start and the Unit was later re-launched under new management, in the person of Margaret (Baroness) Jay, who felt the need vehemently to deny that she is a feminist: 'In politics, feminism is seen as negative, complaining about things; it's perceived to be about separateness. You don't have to be negative like that.'[3]

FEMINIST PERSPECTIVES ON EMPLOYMENT LAW

Such sentiments, coming from the head of the Women's Unit, lead inevitably to the question of what – if anything – feminist perspectives can bring to the category of law termed employment law.[4] The first problem concerns the definition of 'employment law' itself. Whenever, as academic lawyers, we attempt to define the confines of a subject within the curriculum, we invite

---

2   1994 Commission for Social Justice/Institute for Public Policy Research, *Social Justice: Strategies for National Renewal*, London: Vintage, p 151.

3   Sylvester, R, 'What's next for women?' (1998) *The Independent on Sunday*, 8 November.

4   And see Conaghan, Chapter 2, this volume.

disagreement. Few would dispute that employment or labour law deserves its place as an important component of legal studies, but its boundaries are extremely fluid, so much so that it is now a very different construct from, say, 30 years ago.[5] At a very basic level, employment law could be said simply to concern the regulation of the contract of employment between employer and employee. English common law has clung resolutely to the idea that the employment relationship is a mutually agreed contract between two autonomous parties. Of course, this has always been a fiction, since it singularly fails to take account of trade unions and of the abiding imbalance of power between the parties (see, in this volume, Chapters 9 and 5, by Anne Morris and Jenifer Ross, respectively), but it is the contract model and its shortcomings which have shaped modern employment law – together with collective bargaining, on the one hand, and increasing employment protection legislation, on the other. The latter began in the 19th century with laws directed at the protection of the worker at work (for example, the Factories Acts), and in the enjoyment of her wages (for example, the Truck Acts and the Wages Councils), but developed and accelerated in the 1960s and 1970s. As a result of this explosion in national and European legislation, employment law has become a vast and extremely complex subject, so much so that it is very tempting for employment lawyers to focus simply on the workplace and to forget about the life that goes on outside it. Certainly, this is a temptation into which policy makers and legislators have fallen in the past, as may be seen in the various rules which singularly fail to take account of the realities of workers' lives. An obvious example is the maternity rights scheme, under which maternity leave is available. This is welcome (even if largely unpaid and only for 14 weeks) but, at the end of such leave, the worker is expected to return to work, as though she is somehow unaffected by the fact that she now has a dependent child to care for. In other words, giving employment rights (maternity leave) without also ensuring the wider conditions (available and affordable child care) under which they can be meaningfully exercised is a half-hearted measure – and has been recognised as such by the Women's Unit.

A move away from this narrow kind of focus is particularly important for feminists, since one of the tasks of feminism is to challenge the traditional categories of law and to make connections where none have been made before. Contributors to this volume thus look beyond the workplace and ask what changes are needed – and, indeed, whether the kind of change we are supposed to be working towards is possible at all (see Collier). Another task is to highlight the diversity of women, the different discriminations they face, and the different ways in which they experience them (see Ashiagbor). For a long time, women have had to listen to those in power (men) telling them what it is they want and/or need (according to changing fashions and

---

5   As is apparent from a comparison of the content of textbooks today with those of the 1960s.

economic and social conditions) but it is vital that women are able to make known to those who make the laws what it is that they need. There are a number of readily identifiable themes which run through this volume. In particular, a number of contributors reflect in different ways on the promotion, from various quarters, of the idea that we need to have a 'new' relationship between work and family. In addition, and inevitably, given the less than successful record so far, another of the themes is the question of how best to achieve 'equality' for women in paid employment. Underlying all the contributions, however, is the belief that, despite individual successes and changing expectations, there is much that remains to be done and challenged if women are to be able to participate fully in a society which – whether or not it should be – is built around paid (productive) employment. The idea of this volume is not simply to consider women within the workforce or to restrict discussion to sex discrimination and equality measures. The idea is, rather, to bring to bear on the myriad issues raised by the idea of employment a feminist analysis. Women are no longer an adjunct to the study of employment law (if they ever were); they are an integral and vital part of the labour market:

> ... in the longer term, the increased participation of women in the labour force is a critical factor, if not the critical factor, if we are to sustain our living standards and our social systems. In a world with fewer workers and more dependants, we can no longer afford to consign women to a lesser role in the workforce. Unless we tackle the inequalities which persist in the labour market, we will not prosper. It's as simple as that.[6]

The apparent indispensability of women workers is not, however, a sufficient precondition for changes which benefit them (and others). Joanne Conaghan, in a chapter which eloquently lays the theoretical foundations for succeeding chapters, notes the increasing visibility of gender issues, while, at the same time, suggesting that scholars have not yet seriously engaged in the deeper theoretical issues which inform the changes taking place. She signals many of the themes which are the focus of succeeding chapters, including the heterogeneity of women, the problems inherent in a collective bargaining system which traditionally presupposed that workers' interests coincided and, importantly, the 'gendered assumptions which derive from the ideological privileging of productive over reproductive work' (p 40). Whilst acknowledging the criticisms raised by post-modernists of essentialism being an inevitable consequence of standpoint feminism (what is 'woman'?), Conaghan suggests that there are still real benefits to be reaped from women-centred feminist critiques. At the very least, this identifies equality issues as a pervasive rather than a discrete theme and, at best, 'highlights the deep

---

6   Flynn, P, Commissioner for Employment, Industrial Relations and Social Affairs EU-Japan Conference, Brussels, 15 January 1998:
    http://europa.eu.int:80/en/comm/dg05/ speeches/980115pf.html

ideological crisis at the heart of traditional labour law discourse – the collapse of the homogeneous worker and the collective framework which purports to serve him' (p 21).

In considering labour law as an instrument of economic policy, Conaghan suggests that economics and feminist concerns are not necessarily at odds – as seen, for example, in the increased participation of women in the labour market. Nevertheless, the application of economic arguments does not, by and large, benefit women. Thus, the seemingly bi-partisan interest in employment flexibility is flawed if there is only unilateral flexibility to the benefit of the employer (the same notion which preoccupies Jenifer Ross in the context of the contract of employment). Similarly, Conaghan points to flaws in the neo-liberal economic agenda from a feminist perspective, certainly as far as the former's conceptions of law, state and economic organisations are concerned – as is illustrated very clearly in the public sector welfare provision (or lack of it).

The idea that women will voluntarily care for the sick, elderly and other needy individuals – both within and outside their own families – is the theme of Debra Morris' chapter. She focuses on an aspect of women's work which is often overlooked, namely, their work in the voluntary sector and charts the changing face of participation in the sector, from 19th century philanthropy – described (controversially) by Proschaska as an escape from boredom for leisured women – to the commercial reality facing today's volunteers. Whether the voluntary sector is defined 'broadly' or 'narrowly', it involves many billions of pounds and is an important aspect of working lives. Morris points out that, while volunteering may occur only on an occasional basis, other volunteers follow patterns of work more akin to full time employment. Importantly, she considers how gendered such input is: women are involved more at 'grassroots' level and men are more closely associated with management – a distinction which is reflected in the difference in the visibility afforded to the two types of participation. Women's involvement is often considered an extension of their 'naturally' altruistic nature and so, not being 'real work', it is not worthy of payment (compare productive and reproductive work). The increasing formalisation of the sector is most clearly evidenced in several employment tribunal cases discussed by Morris. Such formalisation makes more visible both the volunteers themselves and the potential for their exploitation, and Morris considers issues which arise in the context of paying volunteers (including, for example, the minimum wage). She concludes that a new era of volunteering is emerging and that, in particular, there has been a clear shift from the 'Lady Bountiful' model to that based on a financial rationale – costing out what the service is worth. Generally, this means an enhanced status for volunteers, but this may come at a cost for the service users, for whom the changes may be less welcome.

The diversity of the inequalities found within the labour market are the focus of Diamond Ashiagbor's chapter, which highlights the intersection between gender and race at work. Her main concerns lie with law's current lack of recognition that different types of discrimination can be experienced cumulatively by individuals. It is hidebound by notions of instances of discrimination which are discrete and which fail to address adequately the harms experienced by, in particular, Black and Asian women who have to decide if they are discriminated against for being women or being persons of colour. She discusses the difficulties which feminists face in using the category 'woman' as the foundation for critiques of law, and considers that feminist legal theory and critical race theory must be drawn upon together for a fuller analysis regarding the employment experiences of Black and Asian women. Ashiagbor touches on the concept that social identity comprises a number of strands, with gender and race comprising relevant, but not sole, strands. This approach, which identifies workers as being more complex and having more concerns than crude race or gender discrimination constructs would permit, is a theme also present in Thérèse O'Donnell's chapter, in which she points to workplace bullying as an example of when an individual is treated detrimentally for reasons which can be so complex and manifold that the bully him/herself is incapable of articulating them, but which almost certainly stretch beyond sex and race discrimination. Ashiagbor considers not only the peculiar location of these women in the labour market as a result of both gendered segregation and racial segregation but, also, the feasibility of the anti-discrimination laws being reformulated to answer the challenge presented by discrimination against Black and Asian workers. She views the absence of a single Anti-Discrimination Commission as a key problem in the failure to address cumulative discrimination. She suggests that a one stop agency, which could adopt an 'holistic' approach to multiple discrimination, would begin to recognise the complexities of discrimination which to date have escaped law makers.

Some of these complexities are reflected in Thérèse O'Donnell's chapter, in which she discusses workplace bullying and the absence of a satisfactory legal mechanism to deal with this problem. She considers the emergence of the concept of the workplace bully as a legal actor and the profiling which has taken place in psychological studies of bullies. These studies provide an interesting insight into some of the gender issues present in bullying, and the fine line between assertiveness and aggression. Parallels in the mentality between bullies and other abusive actors are drawn and O'Donnell points out that, while the manipulative nature of sexual abusers or torturers is widely recognised by lawyers, the adult bully addicted to abuse remains something of a shadowy figure. The prevalence of bullying is illustrated by the growth of organisations which seek to support the victims but, at the same time, there remain difficulties in defining bullying – a fact which bedevils this area and which is reflected in the absence of an appropriate law to cope with the problem. O'Donnell analyses the rise and fall of the Dignity at Work Bill 1984, which was anticipated as the panacea to the ill of workplace bullying. Its failure leads to a consideration of the remaining law and its inability to provide a bespoke remedy for victims. Not only do evidential issues concerning potential actions provide huge barriers to victims but, also, the humiliation of admitting to victimhood, the diverse reactions of victims to harassment, and the need to display actual mental injury all operate to disincline complaint and further isolate those who suffer in silence.

Alice Belcher engages with the idea of 'assertiveness' in the form of assertiveness training within the general context of staff development – and the problems which it can highlight. In her analysis, Belcher reflects on the experiences of Scottish universities with interestingly variable results. She suggests that the fluidity of the concepts of staff development, equal opportunities and assertiveness training hamper research into, and the advancement of, these areas and she believes that even more complicated problems arise in the specialist area of women's development training. She concludes that, if the normative connections between the three components are established and work in the way envisaged, then assertiveness training must be included in women's development training. However, in the light of reality, Belcher does question whether assertiveness training is valuable from a feminist perspective and whether it can be counter-productive. She points out its weakness in its inherent dependence for its success on the context in which it operates. Belcher comments on the problems of sexual stereotyping by male colleagues of women's assertive behaviour as 'aggressive' (see the notion of the 'female-boss-as-dragon' in O'Donnell's chapter). Perhaps, argues Belcher, the solution lies in diluting the 'maleness' of the devices, such as assertiveness training, which are used to achieve equality in the workplace, or, at least, in raising the profile of traditionally feminine workplace concerns and of the ways of addressing those concerns. While it is the latter issue of 'feminising' the workplace to which both Anne Morris and Richard Collier turn their attention, with varying conclusions on its viability, Jenifer Ross focuses on the gendered nature of the contract of employment.

Having identified the contract as still being the keystone of the employment relationship, Ross refers to the difficulties inherent in such a contractual characterisation of the employment relationship and expresses concern at the blind acceptance of a notion of equality between the parties. She suggests that the inadequacy of 'the contract' to encompass and reflect modern working life is an inevitable legacy of its focus remaining firmly fixed on the paradigm of the full time working male breadwinner. This is a point taken up in Anne Morris' chapter, which refers to the characterisation of certain workers' benefits as 'women's benefits', and in Nott's chapter when she refers to occupational segregation. Ross outlines some examples of those workers to which the contract is currently blind, including those commonly referred to as 'atypical' workers – in particular, part time workers, homeworkers and volunteer workers. She points to the irony of 'flexible' work being less an issue of flexibility for female workers (for whom it is a Hobson's choice) than a way of retaining real flexibility for employers (a point noted by a number of contributors). In relation to volunteer workers, Ross refers to the expectation of altruism on the part of this group and the notion that this work is done as an expression of civic duty rather than as a form of remunerative employment – a theme echoed in Debra Morris' chapter, where she discusses the multifarious reasons for workers entering the voluntary sector. For Ross, there is a potential for injecting new life into the contract of employment and using it to achieve more for working women by using the influence of anti-discrimination legislation. This influence would come from equal opportunities policies which the judges can – when they choose – consider as more than mere 'mission statements' and which Ross describes as at least a fig leaf of modesty over the vulgarity of indifference to equal opportunities. Essentially, there is no legal barrier to the incorporation of such noble terms into the contract, and using this mechanism may lead to true equality within the employment relationship.

Anne Morris focuses not on the individual contract of employment but, rather, on the collective issue of trade unions and gender equality, in order to discuss the utility of distinguishing between workers' rights and 'women's issues'. She refers to the emasculation of the trade union movement in the last two decades, as well as to the traditional male dominance within the movement. It is this dominance which forms the context for the struggle for feminists in tackling unions' traditional predisposition to downplay or marginalise the concerns of female workers. This institutionalised chauvinism remains, notwithstanding the rise in female membership of unions, which is in indirect proportion to male membership. The changing balance within trade unions, despite women's continuing under-representation at higher levels, has inevitably had an impact on bargaining and has resulted in obtaining benefits which, while welcome, are still seen as 'women's issues' or 'women's rights'. Nowhere is this more clear than in the arena of work and family where, despite neutral terms such as 'parental leave' or 'family friendly policies', there is an implication that, in winning benefits in this area, unions are helping women to do two jobs – the job they are paid to do and the raising of a family. There is no doubt that only women can give birth but, thereafter, the categorisation of child care as a female issue is stunting development in this area. The cosmetic approach is illustrated by the fact that paternity leave may now exist but, while it remains unpaid, is unlikely significantly to alter the balance of child care responsibilities. Similar issues to those which arise in relation to child care arise in relation to care for the elderly. Morris concludes that, whilst it would be too much to move now to a 'non-gendered' bargaining agenda, trade unions must be aware of the consequences of the way they approach bargaining issues and must consider the wider environment in which workers exists – male and female. They do have the means by which to move forward the discussion on the relationship between work and family.

This theme is continued, from a different viewpoint, by Richard Collier, who focuses on the so called 'feminising' of the workplace and, more specifically, on how the 'problematic' male worker fits into this development. He analyses the differing and changing nature of the roles adopted by men and women in relation to home and work but urges readers to view statistics with caution, expressing concerns that there has not yet been the working revolution they suggest. He indicates that, although there may be more women participating in working life, they are not taking jobs previously held by men, nor are many of them making it to the top of their occupational hierarchies. He also urges care in considering that female workers express 'feminine' and males 'masculine' qualities in the workplace and suggests that the new 'service class' supports the theory that the feminised male worker is a product of the late modern capitalist society. Importantly, he refers to legal theory which has suggested that workers do not come to the workplace replete with inherent and complete gender predispositions but, rather, refers to workers as 'active forces' in the social construction of workers as 'gendered subjects'. Collier refers to the UK Labour Government's strategies to engineer a social balance between work and family – two areas which it is assumed are, and which are perceived to be, in competition. In common with Ross and others, Collier considers the emerging notion of 'flexibility' in balancing competing demands, the so-called 'Policies for Working Families' and, in particular, the Parental Leave Directive and the Fairness at Work White Paper. He indicates that, while these initiatives seem focused on a particular balance, they also have an aim of promoting equality between men and women. Collier refers to the difficulties facing the government in de-gendering the worker, a notion which is premised on the assumption that men are to be 'responsible' both as good workers and as 'good parents', and its collision with the dissociation of males from the realm of the familial. The lack of homogeneity amongst 'workers' is again apparent in the point which he makes about the relevancy of the governmental policies being confined to the urban elite, while ignoring the very real struggles of women and men who have no choice but to react to economic circumstances presented to them, and who cannot be perceived to be actively participating in setting the agenda of workplace feminisation. Collier refers further to cross-jurisdictional research which indicates that males do not necessarily take up more extensive child-care responsibilities when accommodating legal provisions are put in place and indeed male acceptance of themselves as domestic actors may only represent a response to circumstances outside of their control. Ultimately, he concludes women still bear the brunt of the burden of combining work and home. The 'good working father' remains, at best, a novelty and, at worst, an anomaly.

Despite the undoubted problems inherent in changing attitudes to work and family life, there is some guarded optimism in Sue Nott's chapter on mainstreaming. She accepts that sex discrimination and equal pay laws reclaimed important legal territory in their times but argues that the time has come to embrace less traditional areas (for feminists) of employment law and – most importantly – to analyse the differential effects as between male and female workers. She contends that to consider areas of law to be gender-blind is simply to perpetuate a legal fiction and she is particularly critical of the traditional use of a male comparator with whom a woman must compare herself (something touched on in Anne Morris' reference to the so called 'pregnancy cases' and in Jamieson's critique of the failure of equal pay laws). Nott also points out that the EU, the body traditionally associated with 'taking up the cudgels' for women workers, has not always accompanied its social policies with stringent laws. The attraction of mainstreaming is that, rather than being a 'bolt-on' strategy akin to anti-discrimination legislation, it provides an opportunity to move from the periphery to the very centre of power, by considering gender impact at the formulation stage of policy. While she cautions against mainstreaming being considered a total solution in itself, its embodiment in PAFT (Policy Appraisal and Fair Treatment) and PAET (Policy Appraisal and Equal Treatment) is encouraging and provides fertile ground for development. Nott makes specific suggestions as to how the impact of these instruments can be heightened and concludes that mainstreaming is *complementary* to other equality strategies. It should not be 'either or ...' but, rather, a part of a strategy which constantly develops ways of coping with imbalance. Moreover, she urges that mainstreaming must be made to work effectively for women (and other target groups) and should not simply become another monument to good intentions.

The potential importance of mainstreaming is apparent from the final essay in this volume, in which Suzanne Jamieson discusses the shortcomings of equal pay legislation, both generally and with particular reference to Australia and Ireland. It is salutary to learn (or to be reminded) that the problems faced by women in the UK are reflected elsewhere in the world. It is particularly important to concentrate on the potential for positive change which may be achieved in new ways when confronted by the inadequacies of the traditional individual route to equality. Jamieson echoes some of the themes identified by other contributors but, in particular, points out the complexities of inequalities and the incoherence, to date, of the State's response to them. Equal pay for women is one of the most fundamental and apparently elusive of rights – indeed in Australia, following the introduction of equal pay laws, the gap is actually widening. Faced with persistent gender segregation in the labour market and with the failure of 'liberal legal strategies', Jamieson raises the question of whether feminists should abandon support for remedies of dubious value or remain engaged and continue to struggle to make the law a more effective weapon in the fight.

CONCLUSION

It is the aim of this collection of essays to open up the category of law which governs employment and to demonstrate that, because work is such an integral part of life, all aspects of life are relevant to work. Because women, have in the past, been denied access to paid employment on the same terms as men, they have suffered far wider disadvantages than 'simply' the wage differentials which appear in the equal pay statistics or in the glass ceiling hampering the prospects of professional women. The unavailability of well (or even adequately) paid employment which takes account of the many different responsibilities which women have in relation to others means that many women are still destined to dependence – on a partner, on the state or on the goodwill of employers, for whom flexibility means the ease with which workers can be laid off,[7] and the poverty wages which such workers are prepared to accept in order to have a job which fits in with their lives. It was unsurprising that the first modern battles in this area were fought in relation to the blatant sex discrimination which existed in the recruitment, promotion and wage rates of women. It would be foolish to underestimate the impact of the legislation passed in the 1970s, which, if it were adjudged to have achieved nothing else, has made women more visible within the workplace. But women are now almost half the workforce and motherhood is not an automatic trigger to long periods out of paid employment. If women are crucial to future prosperity,[8] then the political and the social agenda must reflect that fact. Women are not merely a deviation from the male norm, and feminists must strive to make this understood. Even if the idea of increased male participation in family life and parenting is a fantasy, there is no reason why those (of whatever sex) who do shoulder the major responsibility for care of dependants should not be entitled to real, or 'benign',[9] flexibility at work – in the sense of adequate and fair rewards for part time work (including a recognition of its integral role in the labour market) and increased protection from dismissal (including realistic levels of compensation). With these changes must come a new recognition of the worth of the work which attracts no financial rewards but which is essential to the functioning and the continuation of society.

Law is not necessarily the best instrument for achieving social change, and it certainly is not the only one. Employment, however, is one area in which law has played a vitally important role. Admittedly, the legislation of the

---

7   See Department of Trade and Industry, *The 1998 Workplace Employee Relations Survey – First Findings*, 1998, London: HMSO, p 9: 'numerical flexibility' has increased over the last five years.

8   *Op cit*, Flynn, fn 6.

9   See Alan Howarth, former Employment Minister, speaking at 'The time of our lives', TUC Conference, 1998: see (1998) 82 EOR 17.

1980s shows how the law can be used as a means to narrow protection just as much as to widen it and it is true that the decisions of the national and European courts do not always appear to further the cause of workers' rights or sex equality. Nevertheless, the very diversity of the issues covered in this volume indicates the numerous ways in which the law can impact on women's lives. As feminists, we must also strive to have an impact on the law.

CHAPTER 2

FEMINISM AND LABOUR LAW: CONTESTING THE TERRAIN

Joanne Conaghan

When women, who have always been minor characters in the social and political theory of a patriarchal world, are transformed into major ones, the entire cast, and the play in which it is acting, look very different.[1]

INTRODUCTION

Labour law can be identified as an area where a growing consciousness of gender has produced quite dramatic changes. Over the last 10 years in particular, the strategic deployment of test cases by individuals and groups concerned with advancing women's interests has resulted in the substantial dismantling of key legal assumptions underpinning the labour law conception of the worker.[2] Such developments can be located within a broader shift in focus in labour law away from a preoccupation with collective issues towards a concern with the adequacy and scope of individual legal rights.[3] This, in turn, has generated demand for legal change resulting in achievements for those seeking to improve the legal status of women workers which, while facilitated and, perhaps, in part, presaged by wide reaching demographic changes relating to the gender composition of the workforce and the operation and structure of the labour market, are all the more remarkable given a

---

1   Okin, S, *Women in Western Political Thought*, 1979, Ewing, New Jersey: Princeton UP, p 12.

2   Most notable in this context is the House of Lords' decision in *R v Secretary of State for Employment ex p Equal Opportunities Commission* [1995] 1 AC 1, which held that the hours threshold governing access to employment protection rights was sexually discriminatory, contrary to European law. See, also, *R v Secretary of State for Employment ex p Seymour-Smith* in which the ECJ recently sent back to the House of Lords the question of whether or not the two year qualifying period governing unfair dismissal violated European law (Case C-167/97, decided 9 February 1999). More generally, the legal concept of 'employee' has been strained almost to breaking point by an increasing focus on the legal status of 'atypical' workers, many of whom are women (see, eg, the decision in *Nethermere (St Neots) v Taverna* [1984] IRLR 240 on the employment status of homeworkers), leading courts and tribunals to resort to a number of devices – eg, the 'micro' contract – in order to evidence employment status (*McMeechan v Secretary of State for Employment* [1997] IRLR 353). The government has recently suggested that some, or all, existing employment rights should be extended to cover 'all those who work for another person' – Department of Trade and Industry, *Fairness at Work*, Cm 3968, 1998, para 3.18. See, now, Employment Relations Bill, s 21.

3   Wedderburn (Lord) 'Labour law and the individual: convergence or diversity', in *Labour Law and Freedom: Further Essays in Labour Law*, 1995, London: Lawrence & Wishart, p 286.

backdrop, for the most part, of government hostility towards improved employment protection provision.[4]

The feminist[5] invocation of individual legal rights, combined with the deliberate assault on key labour law concepts, has, arguably, threatened the very bedrock of the framework of labour law as it has traditionally operated in the UK, albeit in association with other destabilising factors. Yet, a feminist presence in theoretical discourse about labour law remains barely detectable. While women workers are no longer invisible in mainstream labour law policy debates, they do not yet occupy any central discursive role in labour law theory. Moreover, while issues traditionally associated with women workers, for example, relating to pregnancy or parenting needs, have undoubtedly assumed a higher profile in the case law and in the dominant literature, they are still largely presented as specialised topics which do not touch the 'essence' of labour law.[6] Even sex equality law, which does not easily lend itself to packaging as a speciality outside the mainstream, particularly given its recent incursions into 'hard' areas such as employment protection[7] and collective bargaining,[8] is still too often regarded as ancillary rather than central to labour law proper.

Increasingly, however, the threatened colonisation of much of labour law by principles of gender equality has forced even the most recalcitrant

---

4   Other significant strategic gains for women in recent years include the successful outcome of the *Webb* litigation *(Webb v EMO Cargo Ltd (No 2)* [1995] 4 All ER 577), concerning pregnancy discrimination, and the development of sex discrimination law to redress sexual harassment at work *(Porcelli v Strathclyde BC* [1986] ICR 564). Britain's membership of the European Community has also produced enhanced legislative protection for women – see, in particular, the Pregnant Workers' Directive (Council Directive 92/85/EEC) – while the election of a Labour Government in 1997 has paved the way for the implementation of the Parental Leave Directive (96/34/EEC) in the Employment Relations Bill, currently going through Parliament.

5   From the perspective of feminist scholarship, 'feminism' may embrace a range of practical and legal engagements not self-consciously styled as such. The deployment of test case strategy by the EOC, eg, may not necessarily be viewed as feminist by those involved but may nevertheless contribute to the furtherance of feminist goals. In this sense, feminist legal thought includes consideration of a broader range of activities than those which might be understood as feminist politically or culturally.

6   A number of student texts in labour law continue to give little or no space to pregnancy and parenting issues: see, eg, Jefferson, M, *Principles of Employment Law*, 3rd edn, 1997, London: Cavendish Publishing; Painter, R, Holmes, A and Migdal, S, *Cases and Materials on Employment Law*, 2nd edn, 1996, London: Blackstone. On the other hand, change is underway: Steve Anderman, eg, has, for the first time in his stimulating text, included a chapter on pregnancy and devoted considerably more attention to gender issues generally: Anderman, S, *Labour Law: Management Decisions and Workers' Rights*, 3rd edn, 1998, London: Butterworths.

7   *Op cit*, fn 2.

8   The impact of equality on collective bargaining has largely occurred in the context of equal pay litigation where the question has arisen as to how far collective bargaining arrangements can justify unequal pay arrangements. See, eg, *Enderby v Frenchay AHA* [1993] IRLR 591; *British Coal Corporation v Smith* [1996] 3 All ER 97. On the potential of collective bargaining as a mechanism for redressing structured pay imbalances, see Fredman, S, *Women and the Law*, 1997, Oxford: Clarendon, pp 242–43.

hardliners to take notice of gender issues. What labour law scholars have *not* done is seriously to engage in the deeper theoretical issues which inform the changes currently taking place. This is in part because of a theoretical lacuna lying at the heart of labour law itself. The legacy of 18 years of Conservative government includes, *inter alia*, the almost total collapse of the traditional analytical framework within which labour law had long been understood and interpreted.[9] Yet, while collective *laissez faire* is no longer adequate as a mode of interpretation, no systematic account has emerged to replace it. Moreover, the continuing failure of labour lawyers to engage with feminist theoretical discourse is largely a product of the way in which the traditional framework defined and marginalised women's issues. Thus, although, as a theory of labour law, collective *laissez faire* has lost much of its explanatory and normative appeal, as an ideology, its influence still lingers over the categories and concepts which form the building blocks of most current attempts to reconstruct labour law theory.

In this context, feminist engagement in the process of theoretical reconstruction could not be more timely. As new and competing discourses scramble to take the place of the old orthodoxy, it seems inevitable that any theoretical approach which is insensitive to the gender dimension in labour law and workplace relations is likely to have limited explanatory and interpretative appeal. Indeed, it can be argued that many of the most dramatic recent developments in labour law mirror the intellectual paths of feminist legal thought – in particular, feminist engagement with the equality principle and the eschewal by many feminists of collectivist politics in favour of an emphasis on group diversity and a recognition and tolerance of difference.[10] It follows that a full understanding of changes in labour law compels some comprehension and awareness of the intellectual and political dilemmas which shape and inform feminist thought. While by no means offering an exhaustive account of the changes which have swept over labour law in the last 20 years, feminism clearly forms part of the narrative which needs to be told.

The object of this essay is to begin this narrative task – to probe the discursive characterisation of labour law from a feminist perspective, with a view to exploring law's role in the social and legal construction of gender relations in and around work. This requires not only an articulation and

---

9   See, in particular, Collins, H, 'The productive disintegration of labour law' (1997) 26 ILJ 295. Other prominent analyses charting the decline of the traditional framework include McCarthy, W, 'The rise and fall of collective *laissez faire*', in McCarthy, W (ed), *Legal Intervention in Industrial Relations: Gains and Losses*, 1992, Oxford: Blackwell; Hepple, B, 'The future of labour law' (1995) 24 ILJ 303. For an excellent general overview, see Deakin, S and Morris, G, *Labour Law*, 2nd edn, 1998, London: Butterworths, Chap 1.

10   See, eg, Young, I, *Justice and the Politics of Difference*, 1990, Ewing, New Jersey: Princeton UP.

application of specifically feminist modes of critique but, also, a close consideration of competing conceptualisations of labour law, past and present. It is hoped that such engagement will facilitate a better understanding of the gender dimension in labour law and its ideological representation(s) and, at the same time, contribute to the necessary task of reconstructing a progressive vision of labour relations and labour law in the wake of the collapse of the *ancien regime*.

LABOUR LAW IN FEMINIST TERRAIN

The project of feminist theory

Despite a popular tendency to assume a single feminist orthodoxy, feminist scholarship is characterised by significant diversity of thought. Feminist theorists approach their studies from a wide range of different political, cultural and philosophical traditions, applying a variety of methodological and epistemological approaches.[11] Not surprisingly, therefore, feminists are often divided over political and legal issues. Within labour law, for example, significant disagreement has arisen over whether, and to what extent, the principle of equality permits the specific legal protection of working women in the context of pregnancy: while some feminists have taken the position that equality is consistent with diversity of treatment where genuine sex based differences arise, others insist that equal treatment compels the *same* treatment of women and men in the workplace, thus requiring the absorption of pregnancy and maternity issues under the general rubric of sickness or disability.[12]

---

11 Feminists seeking to distinguish between different 'feminisms' have adopted a variety of classificatory schemes. Boyd and Sheehy, eg, found their fourfold classification of feminist thought ('liberal feminism', 'integrative or result equality feminism', 'socialist feminism' and 'radical feminism') on fairly traditional political labels (Boyd, S and Sheehy, E, 'Canadian feminist perspectives on law' (1986) 13 JLS 283). Smart, on the other hand, relies upon epistemological diversity, offering a classificatory scheme comprising feminist empiricism, 'standpoint' feminism and postmodern feminism (Smart, C, *Law, Crime and Sexuality: Essays in Feminism*, 1995, London: Sage, pp 4–11). The difficulties associated with identifying and delineating different strands of feminist thought are compounded by the inevitable permeation of patriarchal intellectual traditions into feminist theoretical engagement – see Wright, S, 'Patriarchal feminism and the law of the father' (1993) 1 FLS 115.

12 The debate has taken this particular form primarily in relation to the legal treatment of pregnant workers in the US – see, eg, Williams, W, 'Equality's riddle: pregnancy and the equal treatment/special treatment debate' (1984) 13 New York U Rev of Law and Social Change 325 and Finley, L, 'Transcending equality theory: a way out of the maternity and workplace debate' (1986) 86 Columbia L Rev 1118. To a lesser extent, it has also informed discussion about the scope and content of UK and European law –

Notwithstanding divergences within feminist scholarship, it is, I think, both possible and desirable to identify some common features which distinguish the feminist theoretical project.[13] First, feminist scholars endeavour to highlight and explore the gendered nature of accounts of the social world which posit themselves as neutral and, more specifically, ungendered. Secondly, feminists are concerned to track and expose the myriad manifestations of women's disadvantaged status, and to identify and create conditions leading to desirable social change. Finally, feminist theorists commonly seek to challenge traditional modes of understanding by placing women – their individual and shared experiences – at the *centre* of their scholarship. In summary, feminist theory is predominantly concerned with justice – with identifying and challenging instances of gender based *injustice* and with promoting and realising fairer, more equitable and infinitely more fulfilling social and sexual arrangements.[14]

Although the application of such feminist insights to the world of work has the capacity to transform the terrain of labour law,[15] they come accompanied by theoretical difficulties which currently preoccupy feminist scholarship. Their application to labour law thus presents an opportunity not only to further our understanding of law's role in the construction and regulation of workplace relations but, also, to explore some of the difficulties inherent in the feminist theoretical project by testing the significance and validity of its insights at the concrete level of the world of work.

[continued] see, eg, *op cit*, Fredman, fn 8, pp 183–203 and Conaghan, J, 'Pregnancy, equality and the European Court of Justice' (1998) 3 IJDL 115. More generally, the 'sameness/difference' dilemma has emerged as a predominant philosophical and political focus within feminism, impacting well beyond the issue of pregnancy provision at work. Examples of the voluminous literature include MacKinnon, C, 'Sex equality: on difference and dominance', in *Towards a Feminist Theory of the State*, 1989, Cambridge, Mass: Harvard UP, p 215; Sohrab, J, 'Avoiding the "exquisite" trap: a critical look at the equal treatment/ special treatment in law' (1993) 1 FLS 141; Bock, G and James, S, *Beyond Equality and Difference: Citizenship, Feminist Politics and Female Subjectivity*, 1992, London: Routledge.

13 I draw, in particular, here, from Dalton, C, 'Where we stand: observations on the situation of feminist legal thought' (1998) 3 Berkeley Women's LJ 1 and Lacey, N, *Unspeakable Subjects: Feminist Essays in Legal and Social Theory*, 1998, Oxford: Hart, pp 2–14.

14 My intention, here, is not to 'essentialise' feminism but, rather, to identify and describe some of the more salient features of feminist scholarship without, in any sense, denying both their complexity or inherent contestability. These points are developed further below.

15 'Labour law', here, is construed broadly to include not just the cases and statutes which make up the corpus of relevant legal rules but also the policies and practices which inform and constitute those rules, the ideologies which underpin them and the analyses and perspectives which purport to interpret or explain them, including those from beyond the discipline of law. A major concern of feminist legal theory is to contest the traditional boundaries of labour law, particularly their reliance upon an alleged distinction between home and work as separate and independent spheres of activity – see, further, below.

Feminist dilemmas in labour law

To adopt a feminist perspective is, first and foremost, to bring a gendered perception of social and economic arrangements to bear upon otherwise 'gender neutral' understandings. By highlighting the deeply gendered (albeit largely unarticulated) assumptions which pervade and inform labour law, feminism contributes to a better understanding both of the content of labour law and of its implications for women workers. At the same time, feminism is concerned not just with ensuring that the gendered aspects of labour law are fully recognised and articulated but, also, with exploring how their submergence contributes to the construction and maintenance of arrangements detrimental to women. Implicit in this is some notion of injustice. It is difficult, if not impossible, to enter the world of work without concluding that its arrangements are unfair to women. The evidence is so voluminous and the disparity in the allocation of opportunities and rewards so persistent that, whether or not it can be accounted for in any theoretically coherent sense, the systematic disadvantage of women workers cannot easily be denied.[16] Indeed, many feminist scholars *have* sought to account for such disadvantage, attributing it variously to economic arrangements (including the structure and operation of the labour market), the family, women's biology or (hetero)sexuality.[17] However, there remains little consensus among feminists as to whether, or to what extent, any of these factors is an operating cause of women's poor employment status.

These difficulties are compounded by an increasing trend within feminism away from 'metanarratives' (comprehensive and truth invoking explanations) as coercive and exclusionary. The postmodern recognition that knowledge is necessarily situated and, therefore, that objectivity (in the sense of detached observance) is unattainable renders problematic the making of evaluative pronouncements – for example, that women are oppressed – as such positions generally rely for their validity on the invocation of some notion of objectivity

---

16 This is not to suggest that women's economic situation remains unchanged in the wake of significant economic and social restructuring over the last 20 years. However, although changes in culture and in the economy have brought benefits to some women, the overall picture remains one of continued gender based disadvantage, albeit mediated by variables such as skill, class, age, education and ethnicity – Walby, S, *Gender Transformations*, 1997, London: Routledge. See, also, Brueghel, I, 'Labour market prospects for women from ethnic minorities', in Lindlay, R (ed), *Labour Market Structures and Prospects for Women*, 1994, Manchester: Equal Opportunities Commission, p 54, arguing that the prospects for black women in particular are worsening.

17 For a comprehensive account of competing theories of women's participation in paid work, see Walby, S, *Theorizing Patriarchy*, 1990, London: Basil Blackwell, pp 25–60.

or truth.[18] Similar uncertainty arises with the invocation of specific normative ideals in the context of workplace relations. Assuming that women's poor economic and social status *can* be characterised in normative and ethical terms, what principles or norms does that status offend? While it may easily be asserted that the disadvantages faced by women in paid work violate commonly held principles such as sexual equality, social justice and individual self-realisation, the content of these principles remains contentious and often contextually defined. The terrain of labour law is steeped in contested values and interpretations which throw up not one but a series of conflicting normative frameworks. To what extent, for example, can a consideration of the equity of women's position relative to men's in work be separated from a broader ethical assessment of the work relationship? Surely, the normative values which inform particular understandings of that relationship are an important critical focus for feminists? In other words, invoking justice for *women* workers may engender (or emanate from) a more general ethical preoccupation with justice in the workplace.

There is, then, undeniable uncertainty and contention within feminist theory as to how women's position, at work and in society, should be characterised and understood. However, this is not necessarily a bad thing, producing as it does a healthy theoretical diversity. While some feminists focus on the role of *institutions* or *structures* in perpetuating oppression or disadvantage – the family, the workplace, the labour market, the State – others focus increasingly on the way in which gender relations are *discursively* created and maintained, and in how diverse bodies of knowledge, including law, direct our understanding of these relations. Law's contribution to women's disadvantage is thus both functional and discursive. Not only do the rules and principles of labour law operate directly to regulate working arrangements, which are, to a greater or lesser extent, predicated upon women's economic and social disadvantage, they also operate discursively to construct, inform and authenticate gendered understandings of those arrangements (for example, the idea that women's engagement with paid work is generally subordinate to their need or desire to nurture and procreate), which, in turn, contribute to the maintenance of sexually oppressive practices. Clearly, it is important to address both modes of

---

18 One way of taking a normative stance in relation to legal arrangements without reliance on 'truth' claims involves the application of 'immanent critique', ie, invoking the norms of law itself – justice, fairness, neutrality – and testing law's adherence to them: see Fegan, E, '"Ideology" after "discourse": a reconceptualisation for feminist analyses of law' (1996) 23 JLS 173. There remains, however, the problem of identifying the precise content of such norms. Moreover, such an approach may be seriously deficient in its capacity to bring about desirable social and legal change, as it may result in the dissolution of the concepts being invoked (as, eg, has arguably occurred in the context of the feminist critique of equality). Sooner or later, then, feminist engagement with normative reconstruction seems inevitable. See, generally, *op cit*, Lacey, fn 13, pp 221–49.

operation in any exploration of the relationship between labour law and women's disadvantage.

At the same time, such considerations give rise to a further theoretical problem: the postmodern focus on knowledge as socially constructed (rather than epistemically grounded) calls into question the validity and authenticity of sexual categories in legal discourse. Indeed, postmodern feminists have argued that the categories 'woman' and 'man' should themselves be understood not as biologically or socially fixed but, rather, as the products of discursive engagement, in which case, it makes little sense to speak of 'women's' oppression by 'men', let alone to seek to account for it. The perceived danger here concerns the alleged unifying tendencies inherent in discursive categorisation. To attribute to sexual categories a fixed and immutable content with universal application is, it is argued, to 'essentialise' them, thereby denying both the varied meanings which attach to such categories, depending upon their discursive context, and the diverse identities and experiences of those who are deemed to comprise them.[19] This has particular pertinence in the context of labour law: is it useful (or even meaningful) to be concerned about 'women workers' as a group, or does reliance on such discursive categorisation operate to undermine the manifold differences between them? The interests, for example, of professional women may differ significantly from the concerns of working class women; and ethnicity may also contribute to diverging workplace experiences among women. Whose interests does the feminist legal scholar invoke and represent? Is she, perhaps, too preoccupied with penetrating the glass ceiling and insufficiently concerned with combatting the pervasive evil of low pay? Does her focus on a female paradigm of part time work reflect a failure to appreciate that it may be inappropriate when applied to black and Asian women?[20]

This gives rise to yet a further difficulty for the feminist theorist entering labour law, for how can she espouse and apply a 'woman-centred' approach if there is no agreement as to what constitutes 'woman' for this purpose? *Whose* experience should form the epistemological and critical base of feminist theorising? Can 'standpoint feminism' (as a woman-centred approach is sometimes characterised) avoid the essentialism which is the target of postmodern feminist censure?

---

19 See, eg, Fraser, N and Nicolson, L, 'Social criticism without philosophy: an encounter between feminism and postmodernism' in Nicolson, L (ed), *Feminism/Postmodernism*, 1990, New York: Routledge and Smart, C, 'The woman of legal discourse' [1992] 1 SLS 29. For a critical overview of the anti-essentialist debate, see Brooks, D, 'A commentary on the essence of anti-essentialism in feminist legal theory' (1994) 2 FLS 115.

20 Evidence suggests that women from most ethnic minority groups are more likely to work full time than white women – Bhavnani, R, *Black Women in the Labour Market – A Research Review*, 1994, Manchester: Equal Opportunities Commission, pp 48–50.

There is no doubt that a woman centred approach is very effective in its capacity to challenge and displace dominant discursive understandings. To view labour law through the lens of women's perceived needs and aspirations is radically to refashion it; a labour law which locates women at the margins is fully and fundamentally challenged by a methodology which places them at its centre, producing a picture with very different contours and shades. Issues surrounding pregnancy, parenting and work, for example, emerge from the shadows to assume a much greater practical and legal prominence. The more traditional preoccupations of labour law discourse – the role of the State; the power and legitimacy of trade unions; the scope of managerial prerogative; and the pre-eminence of collective arrangements – are eclipsed. In this brave new world, equality issues emerge not as a discrete specialism within the field of labour law but, rather, as a pervasive theme which penetrates both its inner core and outer reaches. At the same time, attention focuses inescapably on broader distributive concerns, such as low pay and the effects of labour market segregation. Most importantly, however, women-centredness highlights the deep ideological crisis at the heart of traditional labour law discourse – the collapse of the homogeneous worker and the collective framework which purports to serve him.

Given its interpretative power, it would be unfortunate if women-centredness were to be wholly eschewed as a mode of feminist critique. In any case, it might be argued that bringing women to the centre of labour law is not necessarily to deny their diversity; rather, it enables a fuller appreciation of it. While women remain at the margins, it is too easy to depict them as a cohesive group with particular characteristics and needs, thus reinforcing the essentialised male norm in relation to which they are defined and deemed wanting. By focusing on women more closely, we are forced to acknowledge their diversity as well as their commonality. The ideological association of women with part time work, for example, is rendered problematic when women's working arrangements are viewed through the lens of ethnic and racial difference. Similarly, the growing focus on child care as a workplace issue brings to the surface the considerable variations in child care and family arrangements and the cultural, racial, social and economic contexts within which such differences arise.[21] These insights challenge characterisations of women centredness as necessarily essentialist, but they also serve to illustrate

---

21 For a comprehensive account of the factors influencing child care 'choices' in the UK, see Duncan, A, Giles, C and Webb, S, *The Impact of Subsidising Childcare*, 1994, Manchester: Equal Opportunities Commission, pp 3–20. On the use of child care by black women, see *op cit*, Bhavnani, fn 20, pp 55–57. The intersection between gender and race has been an important focus of the anti-essentialist critique, in which concern has rightly been expressed about the exclusionary effects of standpoint feminism in its failure to address or recognise the experiences of black women. See, eg, Crenshaw, K, 'Demarginalising the intersection of race and sex: a black feminist critique of anti-discrimination doctrine, feminist theory and antiracist politics' [1989] University of Chicago Legal Forum 139; Harris, A, 'Race and essentialism in feminist legal theory' (1990) 42 Stanford L Rev 581.

how essentialist assumptions may operate on those to whom they do not properly correspond. In this way, particular female experiences may be of significance to women generally (in the sense of affecting their position), whether or not they actually *have* those experiences. For example, while only some women workers become pregnant, virtually all women workers are, at some point in their lives, affected by the legal, economic or cultural construction of women as potentially pregnant persons. So viewed, pregnancy becomes an issue of relevance to women workers in general, not just to those who become pregnant.

These considerations suggest that the theoretical difficulties which currently beset feminist scholarship – particularly those which arise from the critique of essentialism – while clearly relevant to the articulation of a feminist perspective on labour law, do not, in any sense, preclude it. The key is to treat the insights which derive from feminist debate not as mandates or prohibitions but, rather, as guides to the traps into which the unwitting feminist may fall. In accepting the colonising tendencies implicit in the invocation of the category 'woman', while continuing to see a strategic value in its political and intellectual deployment, such an approach is sometimes characterised as 'strategic essentialism'.[22] However, continued feminist engagement and invocation of sexual categories is, arguably, more than just a strategic ploy: it is, rather, part of a *dialectical* process of critical engagement with categories whose meaning and significance is explored in *contexts* which acknowledge both their power and inherent contestability.[23]

FEMINISM IN THE TERRAIN OF LABOUR LAW

Labour law, whether as a legal discipline or as a field of academic or political debate, provides an excellent example of the constitutive and operative role of gender within a discourse which is, to a large extent, self-consciously blind to its significance. This is especially true of traditional labour law discourse – captured, most notably, in Kahn-Freund's conception of collective *laissez faire*. It is also evident in economic approaches to labour law, particularly (although not exclusively) neo-liberal analyses. However, even when debates are framed in ways which give greater prominence to gender issues – in terms of workers' rights or social justice – there remains a core of underlying assumptions, the gender implications of which continue to be unarticulated and, therefore, largely uncomprehended. Thus, feminism must address and critique not only traditional 'gender-blind' interpretations of labour law but, also, those approaches which purport to acknowledge and accommodate women's needs.

---

22 Spivak, G, 'In a word' [1989] *Differences* 124.
23 See, in particular, *op cit*, Brookes, fn 19, pp 130–32.

It has already been pointed out that the theoretical consensus which governed analyses of labour law for much of the post war era has collapsed in the last 20 years.[24] However, while it may fairly be observed that collective *laissez faire* no longer constitutes either the regulatory system or the dominant ideology within labour law, its influence remains evident in the discursive frameworks which have emerged to challenge it.[25] While this is not the place for a comprehensive exploration of these trends, it is not difficult to identify those which have commanded most attention: on the one hand, the last 20 years have witnessed the hegemonic rise of economic arguments in the context of labour law debate; on the other hand, one can also detect a growing concern to locate and co-ordinate labour regulation within a broader programme of principled social and political reform. Put briefly, current engagement with labour law tends to be informed either by economic concerns, considerations of justice or fairness, or both.[26]

The ideology of collective *laissez faire*[27]

Many of the fundamental features of collective *laissez faire* ideology express a largely hidden gendered content. The dominant assumption, for example, that voluntary collective bargaining is the most effective means of safeguarding

---

24 See *op cit*, fn 9 and accompanying text.

25 Hugh Collins argues that, long after collective *laissez faire* ceased to have any 'purchase on reality', its presence in academic discourse operated to render scholars deaf to the evolution of competing analytical and political perspectives (including, it might be said, feminist perspectives, although Collins does not specifically mention them) – see *op cit*, Collins, fn 9.

26 Collins identifies three competing discourses within current labour law theory: macroeconomic policy considerations; the promotion of political and social rights; and social or distributive justice issues (*op cit*, fn 9). I have effectively collapsed Collins' second and third groupings into an all embracing 'justice' category, although I acknowledge the distinctiveness (but also relatedness) of the discourses as he characterises them. One could, in fact, devise endless classificatory schemes depending upon which features of contemporary labour law one most wished to emphasise. However, my concern is with the gendered assumptions which underpin current ideas, not with how those ideas might best be organised.

27 See, in particular, Kahn-Freund, O, 'Labour law', in Ginsberg, M (ed), *Law and Opinion in England in the Twentieth Century*, 1959, London: Stevens and Kahn-Freund, O, *Labour and the Law*, 2nd edn, 1977, London: Stevens. For analyses and critique of Kahn-Freund's writing, see Wedderburn, L, 'Otto Kahn-Freund and British labour law' and Lewis, R, 'Method and ideology in the labour law writings of Otto Kahn-Freund', in Wedderburn, L, Lewis, R and Clark, J, *Labour Law and Industrial Relations: Building on Kahn-Freund*, 1983, Oxford: Clarendon, pp 29 and 107 respectively. Other prominent scholars in the pluralist tradition include Allan Flanders and Hugh Clegg, authors of the landmark industrial relations text, *The System of Industrial Relations in Great Britain*, 1954, Oxford: Blackwells. For a feminist critique of the pluralist tradition, see Conaghan, J, 'The invisibility of women in labour law: gender-neutrality in model-building' (1986) 14 Int J Soc L 377.

workers' interests[28] problematically presupposes that all workers are, or can be, effectively represented by collective bargaining and that workers' interests largely coincide. Yet the history of the trade union movement graphically reveals their persistent failure to embrace certain categories of workers (largely populated by women) or advance their interests.[29] The pluralist reliance upon a bifurcated model of class conflict, with its implicit conception of homogeneous labour, has obscured both the complexity of conflicting interests characterising workplace relations and the hierarchical context within which such conflicts of interests are routinely played out.

Equally problematic is the pluralist view of law as a largely inappropriate mechanism for the regulation of industrial relations. 'Legal abstentionism' not only fundamentally misconceived the role of the State,[30] it also operated to distort and diminish the significance of legal regulation in the workplace with, *inter alia*, gender implications. Protective legislation, for example, governing the hours of women's work in factories, was traditionally designated as external to the system of collective bargaining and, consequently, never accorded the same legitimacy by pluralist ideology. Yet, for women workers, it was clearly of considerable practical and economic significance.[31] Moreover, the pluralist presumption against law has often operated to *disable* it as a protective mechanism. In the 1970s, for example, when a range of individual legal rights for workers were introduced, they were conceived as 'minimum standards', 'a floor of rights' upon which collective bargaining might build; yet for those workers for whom collective bargaining was not an option, the

---

28 'As a power countervailing management, the trade unions are much more effective than the law has ever been or can ever be', *op cit*, Kahn-Freund, 1977, fn 27, p 10.

29 See, generally, Boston, S, *Women Workers and the Trade Union Movement*, 1980, London: Davis Poynter. Feminist analyses of collective bargaining are better developed in North American than in British legal literature – see, eg, Lester, G, 'Towards the feminization of collective bargaining law' (1991) 36 McGill LJ 1181 and Crain, M, 'Feminism, labor and power' (1992) 65 Southern California L Rev 1819.

30 The pluralist characterisation of the State as a 'neutral' arbiter in industrial relations has been strongly challenged by those emphasising the State's interest in maintaining a particular balance of power in the workplace and the necessary relationship between fiscal policy and the politics of production – see, eg, Lewis, R, 'Kahn-Freund and labour law: an outline critique' (1979) 8 ILJ 202; Hyman, R, *The Political Economy of Industrial Relations*, 1989, London: Macmillan.

31 This legislation was largely repealed by the Sex Discrimination Act 1986. For a feminist analysis of its genesis and early history, see Walby, S, *Patriarchy at Work*, 1986, Cambridge: Polity, pp 100–34. See, also, *op cit*, Fredman, fn 8, pp 67–74, for an analysis of more contemporary feminist debates about protective legislation. It should be noted that collective *laissez faire* ideology was similarly blind to legislative incursions which were not gender related – see, eg, the relative neglect by labour lawyers of statutory incomes policies, observed by Collins, *op cit*, fn 9, p 302.

'floor' was a *de facto* ceiling and an opportunity to deploy law genuinely to supplement the deficiencies of the collective bargaining system was lost.[32]

A final flaw in collective *laissez faire* ideology lies in its representation of the workplace as a largely autonomous, self-governing entity with relatively fixed and uncontested boundaries. In so doing, it presupposes a conceptual and practical separation of the realms of work and family life which is both artificial and misleading. In fact, the spheres of production and reproduction are neither fixed nor separate but constantly changing and interacting.[33] The fundamental dynamics of the workplace – who occupies it and on what terms – are shaped to a large extent by the allocation of power and responsibility within the family. Similarly, the allocation of power at, and over, work contributes to the maintenance of particular relational structures within the family. Yet, it is not just that women's opportunities at work are restricted by their responsibilities at home and vice versa – although this remains an important practical insight – nor is it that the conceptual and ideological separation of work and family, of 'public' and 'private' spheres, obscures this otherwise self-evident truth (which it does).[34] More fundamentally, the reification of a 'natural' divide between the productive and reproductive spheres belies the interconstitutive nature of the relationship between them. To define an activity as 'productive' is also to give meaning to what constitutes 'reproductive' engagement in a context, moreover, in which the characterisation of an activity as productive or reproductive is socially and

---

32 On the exclusion of 'atypical' workers from employment rights, see *op cit*, Conaghan, fn 27, pp 382–83. Most of the relevant provisions, including, for the first time, maternity rights, were introduced by the Employment Protection Act 1975, although some (eg, relating to redundancy pay and unfair dismissal) had already made earlier legislative appearances. The provisions are now largely located in the Employment Rights Act 1996. The 'floor of rights' phrase is attributable to Wedderburn, KW, 'The legal framework of industrial relations and the Act of 1971' (1972) 10 British Journal of Industrial Relations 1.

33 The characterisation of work and family activities in terms of 'productive' and 'reproductive' tasks derives from feminist economics and is part of a broader feminist critique of the failure of traditional economics to recognise or take account of the economic significance of household labour – see, eg, Bakker, I (ed), *The Strategic Silence: Gender and Economic Policy*, 1994, London: Zed; Waring, M, *If Women Counted: A New Feminist Economics*, 1988, San Francisco: Harper Collins. On ways of measuring and valuing women's unpaid work, see MacDonald, M, 'The empirical challenge of feminist economics: the example of economic restructuring', in Kuiper, E and Sap, J, *Out of the Margin: Feminist Perspectives on Economics*, 1999, London: Routledge, pp 175, 181–84.

34 For an analysis of the ideological implications of the work/family dichotomy, see Olsen, F, 'The family and the market: a study of ideology and legal reform' (1983) 96 Harv L Rev 1497. Olsen argues, *inter alia*, that the discursive characterisation of the family and the market in public/private terms reinforces the ideological separation of home and work, carrying with it a series of assumptions about the extent and appropriateness of State regulation in each sphere. The limits of the public/private dichotomy as a mode of feminist critique are explored by Lacey, *op cit*, fn 13, pp 71–86.

politically determined, not naturally arising.[35] It follows that the pluralist conception of collective bargaining as a form of workplace governance is predicated upon a concept of constituency and constituents which is ideologically derived and politically contestable.

One practical manifestation of this conceptual failing has been the traditional adoption by labour law of a paradigmatic worker who is (or was) biographically and empirically male: the full time, long term, generally unionised worker with no domestic responsibilities beyond that of financial provision.[36] This has contributed to the practical exclusion of many women workers from the benefits of collective bargaining and legislative protection.[37] The conceptual separation of work and family has also hampered the effectiveness of legislative efforts to promote sexual equality, by encouraging a focus on workplace practices in isolation from broader social arrangements, particularly those governing the domestic sphere.[38] Although the increasing sophistication of equality jurisprudence has begun to penetrate the boundaries of traditional discourse (by, for example, exposing the interdependence of work and family arrangements),[39] it is only as the 'male norm' of full time, long term employment has broken down, following a growing economic demand for more flexible working arrangements, that labour law has properly begun to recognise and address the situation of the 'atypical' (predominantly female) worker who does not conform to the legally enshrined norm.[40] Thus, it is principally changes in the structure and

---

35 The obvious example here is child care, which, if paid for, is characterised as productive but which is otherwise regarded as reproductive work, although the activity may otherwise be the same. As Rittich observes, 'it is not the internal characteristics of the activity which determine its classification; rather it is the conditions which structure its performance and the existence of direct compensation': Rittich, K, 'Recharacterising restructuring: gender and distribution in the legal structure of market reform', 1998, unpublished doctoral thesis, Harvard Law School, p 50. Rittich emphasises that, although the presence of a monetary transaction is the most frequent determinant of the reproductive/productive boundary, it is not the sole factor, further emphasising its instability (pp 48–59).

36 *Op cit*, Conaghan, fn 27, pp 350–51; see, also, *op cit*, Fredman, fn 8, for a sustained critique of the construction and deployment of the 'male norm' in labour law.

37 Womens' limited access to the benefits of collective bargaining is, in large part, a function of their troubled relationship with the trade union movement: see *op cit*, Boston, fn 29. Although recent years have seen significant improvements in this respect (albeit against a background of declining unionisation), women continue to report difficulties in getting their voices heard in a trade union environment: Rees, T, 'The feminisation of trade unions?', in *Women and the Labour Market*, 1992, London: Routledge, pp 84–107. On the relaxation of legal provisions limiting women's access to employment protection, see *op cit*, fn 2.

38 *Op cit*, Lacey, fn 13, pp 25–27; Conaghan, fn 27, pp 388–99.

39 This is evident, eg, in *London Underground v Edwards (No 2)* [1998] IRLR 364, in which it was held that the introduction of a new rostering system was capable of constituting indirect sex discrimination because of its disparate negative impact on women workers (the applicant's difficulties in demonstrating disparate impact were successfully resolved by the Court of Appeal).

40 On the character, status and gender composition of atypical work, see Dickens, L, *Whose Flexibility? Discrimination and Equality Issues in Atypical Work*, 1992, London: Institute of Employment Rights.

operation of the labour market which have presaged a renegotiation of the productive/reproductive boundary, in the course of which, women's workplace experience has assumed a new prominence and significance. This increased academic and political focus on the plight of atypical workers has also contributed to the further discreditation of collective *laissez faire* as a prescriptive norm.[41]

Labour law as an instrument of economic policy

According to Kahn-Freund, 'the main object of labour law has always been ... to be a countervailing force to counteract the inequality of bargaining power which is inherent, and must be inherent, in the employment relationship'.[42] This view of labour law as a mechanism for ensuring the balanced mediation of conflicts of interest is a far cry from the current political and intellectual focus on labour law as a key instrument of economic policy. Low inflation and enhanced competitiveness and productivity are, increasingly, the standards against which labour regulation is measured and adjusted. Labour law is thus discursively relocated within a normative framework which prioritises the attainment of economic goals.

This approach is, perhaps, most closely associated with the Conservative pursuit of neo-liberal economic and political objectives in the 1980s and early 1990s.[43] Taking the view that existing labour laws, particularly those which enhanced the power of trade unions to engage in collective action, inhibited competition and labour market flexibility, successive Conservative administrations sought to 'free' the market from the 'rigidities' imposed by trade union practices and 'burdensome' employment regulation and to dismantle much of the legal framework designed to facilitate collective bargaining.[44] They also endeavoured to make (more cautious) inroads into

---

41 The demise of collective *laissez faire* as an analytical and prescriptive framework can be attributed to a range of economic, political and cultural factors, including the decline of British manufacturing, the rise of unemployment, the anti-union policies of successive Conservative governments in the 1980s and the cultural triumph of individualist over collectivist social values – see, generally, *op cit*, Deakin and Morris, fn 9, pp 39–56. However, Davies and Freedland argue that a growing concern with industrial justice also called into question the adequacy of collective bargaining, particularly in terms of its ability to protect the interests of certain groups of workers: Davies, PL and Freedland, MR, *Labour Legislation and Public Policy*, 1993, Oxford: Clarendon, p 193.

42 *Op cit*, Kahn-Freund, 1977, fn 27, p 6.

43 On the neo-liberal character of 1980s Conservative policy, see *op cit*, Fredman, fn 8, pp 30–37; Wedderburn, L, 'Freedom of Association and Philosophies of Labour Law' (1989) 18 ILJ 1; and *op cit*, Deakin and Morris, fn 9, pp 40–41, all of whom link Conservative policy to the views of economist and philosopher Friedrich Hayek. In fact, the characterisation of Hayek as neo-liberal (as opposed to conservative) is not without contention, although he is certainly the most persuasive exponent of free market philosophy – see below.

44 For a comprehensive analysis of Conservative labour law policy during this period, see *ibid*, Davies and Freedland, Chapters 9 and 10.

the scope and coverage of individual legal rights, although they were less successful in this (see below).

A concern with the economic implications of labour regulation is not, however, confined to the former Conservative regime. Not only do Davies and Freedland identify it as a prevalent theme throughout the post-war period,[45] but, more recently, economic discourse has been enthusiastically embraced by many progressive labour lawyers, seeking to link high labour standards with improved productivity and competitiveness. For example, Deakin and Wilkinson argue that a low wage economy threatens competitiveness by discouraging investment in new technology, thus allowing 'technologically and managerially backward' firms to remain in business.[46] Karl Klare has contended that workplace democracy is 'good for business' as part of a 'human capital strategy of economic growth'.[47] The need to balance fairness at work with the needs of a competitive economy is also an undisguised feature of the current Labour Government's approach to workplace regulation.[48] More significantly, economic considerations constitute a dominant theme in debates about the legal and political effects of 'globalisation' where the concern is whether, and to what extent, global economic imperatives limit the nation State's power to pursue particular labour policies.[49] In a range of different ways, therefore, labour law has come to be perceived as a function of economic need.

What, if any, are the implications of such an approach for gender relations at work? First, it must be acknowledged that there is no simple correlation between the prioritisation of economic goals and continued gender disadvantage. Indeed, sometimes, feminist concerns and perceived economic needs may converge. For example, the increased post-war participation of women (particularly married women) in paid work, attributable, in large part, to economic and industrial changes (such as the growing demand for labour in the service sector), is generally understood to have advanced women's

---

45 *Op cit*, Davies and Freedland, fn 41.

46 Deakin, S and Wilkinson, F, *Labour Standards – Essential to Economic and Social Progress*, 1996, London: Institute of Employment Rights, p vi. The Institute of Employment Rights is a left leaning 'think tank' comprised of legal scholars, practitioners and trade unionists. Their proposals for the progressive reform of labour law are detailed in Ewing, K (ed), *Working Life: A New Perspective on Labour Law*, 1996, London: Institute of Employment Rights, and supported, *inter alia*, by economic arguments, see pp 22–29.

47 Klare, K, 'Workplace democracy and marketplace reconstruction: an agenda for legal reform' (1988) 38 Catholic UL Rev 1, pp 10–13. Klare's primary focus here is normative but his article provides a good example of the efforts of progressive labour lawyers to beat economists at their own game.

48 *Op cit*, Department of Trade and Industry, fn 2, especially Chap 1.

49 See, eg, Arthurs, H, 'Labour law and industrial relations in the global economy' (1997) 18 ILJ (South Africa) 571.

interests.[50] Yet, in other contexts, women's interests appear to conflict with economic considerations as, for example, in the debate on the legal rights of part time workers.[51]

In fact, this divergence reflects a more fundamental conflict between the pursuit of deregulation and the tenets of sexual equality. The 'deregulation thesis' has been offered at various times to explain and interpret changes in labour law over the last two decades.[52] As a comprehensive explanation, however, it is difficult to sustain as the period in question has, paradoxically, witnessed an *increase* in the range and content of individual legal rights governing work relationships.[53] It has been suggested that the Conservatives' failure to fully effect deregulation derives from an ideological reliance on individualism in the context of decollectivist policies[54] but the limited implementation of deregulation must also be understood against the backdrop of developments in European equality law. In 1986, for example, the UK government was required to amend significant aspects of the Sex Discrimination Act 1975 and the Equal Pay Act 1970, in order to ensure compliance with European law.[55] In 1993, they were similarly required to introduce improved maternity rights as a consequence of the adoption of a new Pregnant Workers' Directive[56] and, in 1995, a House of Lords decision on European equality law precipitated the legislative extension of employment rights to part time workers.[57] In all these instances, individual employment rights were strengthened as a direct consequence of European equality provisions. Moreover, it may be conjectured that the caution exhibited by later

---

50 In fact, this assertion requires qualification: the alleged 'benefits' of increased female labour force participation are greatly dependent upon factors such as class, ethnicity, educational attainment and age – this providing an instance of the difficulties to which a unitary conception of 'woman' may give rise: *op cit*, Walby, fn 16, Chapter 2.

51 See, in particular, *R v Secretary of State for Employment ex p Equal Opportunities Commission* [1995] 1 AC 1, where the government unsuccessfully invoked economic arguments to justify the denial to many part time workers of access to employment rights.

52 See, eg, *op cit*, Ewing, fn 46, pp 21–26.

53 Ryan, B, 'Unfinished business? The failure of deregulation in employment law' (1996) 23 JLS 506.

54 Ryan writes: '... the survival and extension of individual employment rights is intimately linked to the process of decollectivisation. The system of employment rights has been retained in order to smooth the transition to an individualised labour market ...': *ibid*, p 521. See, also, Fredman, S, 'Labour law and ideology in the Thatcher years' (1992) 12 OJLS 24 for a similar analysis of the ideological role of democracy and rights arguments in Conservative labour law policy.

55 Sex Discrimination Act 1986.

56 Council Directive 92/85/EEC. The UK government was generally hostile to the idea of improved pregnancy protection, ensuring that the original European proposals were significantly diluted in their final legislated form – see Conaghan, J, 'Pregnancy and the workplace: a question of strategy?' (1993) 20 JLS 71, pp 82–84.

57 *R v Secretary of State for Employment ex p Equal Opportunities Commission* [1995] 1 AC 1.

Conservative administrations in relation to the introduction of further restrictions on employment rights derived, in part, from an increasing awareness of the potential implications of European equality law.

The increasing encroachment of equality concerns on deregulative policies is a further manifestation of the complex interplay between feminist objectives and social and economic change. While, in the above instance, the goals of equality and deregulation diverged, on other occasions, Conservative strategists usefully allied them, as, for example, in their arguments for the repeal of gender specific protective legislation.[58] Both Conservative and Labour policy makers have, similarly, sought to link the pursuit of labour market flexibility with the need of many women for 'flexible working arrangements' compatible with their domestic responsibilities,[59] although, in this context, commentators have rightly asked: flexibility for whom?[60] What remains clear is that, in the ideological battle being fought, women workers are clearly perceived as a constituency to be won.

The application of economic arguments to the workplace does not, however, work to women's advantage. In particular, there can be no mistaking the generally unfavourable implications of a *neo-liberal* economic and political agenda for women. Most concretely, there is strong evidence to suggest that 'market-friendly' policies, typically characterised by deregulation, privatisation and the prioritisation of efficiency concerns, tend to have an adverse impact on women's employment. This has been observed in the context of economic restructuring in Eastern Europe[61] but there is similar evidence of disproportionate impact closer to home. For example, the removal of wage protection in the 1980s and 1990s, combined with the

---

58 The government's stated objective in repealing the provisions was to get rid of 'unnecessary restrictions and out of date discrimination on women's hours of work': Department of Employment, *Lifting the Burden*, Cmnd 9571, 1985, para 5.10. However, Lord Wedderburn has observed that the repeal of gender specific regulation was 'more concerned to relieve businesses of burdens than proffer real social equality to women': Wedderburn (Lord), *The Worker and the Law*, 3rd edn, 1986, Harmondsworth: Penguin, p 408.

59 See, eg, Hewitt, P, 'Flexible working: asset or cost?' (1993) 14 J Policy Studies 18; Social Justice Commission, *Social Justice, Strategies for National Renewal*, 1994, London: Vintage, pp 159–60. See, also, Department of Employment, *Building Businesses Not Barriers*, Cmnd 9794, 1986, in which the Conservative government sought to justify proposed additional restrictions on access to employment rights by emphasising their advantages to women: 'flexible part time work is particularly welcome to women and, therefore, regulations which tend to reduce its availability place women workers at a disadvantage' (para 7.1).

60 *Op cit*, Dickens, fn 40; Fredman, fn 8, pp 308–16.

61 Kerry Rittich identifies the following typical consequences for women flowing from the implementation of neo-liberal policies in Eastern Europe: 'increased and disproportionate unemployment; loss of income and earning power relative to men; absence of adequate and affordable childcare service; increased care giving and domestic labour; reduced access to health service; and a sharp separation between participation in the formal market and other public activities and family responsibilities': *op cit*, Rittich, fn 35, pp 38–39. See, also, Hopkins, B, 'Women and children last: a feminist redefinition of privatization and economic reform', in *op cit*, Kuiper and Sap, fn 33, p 249.

downward pressure on wages generated by high unemployment, exacerbated the problem of low pay, to the inevitable detriment of women workers.[62] Similarly, the widespread adoption of Compulsory Competitive Tendering (CCT) in the public sector (in combination with other privatisation policies) has generated poorer terms and conditions and increased unemployment, both of which have disproportionately affected women workers.[63] Increased restrictions on local authority spending, in conjunction with government reliance on market mechanisms to generate child care facilities, have resulted in inadequate provision, despite the recent rise in the economic activity of women with small children.[64] Moreover, some groups of women clearly fared worse under Conservative economic policies than others: lone mothers have been particularly hurt by welfare cuts and poor child care provision,[65] while the complex interplay between occupational segregation, gender and ethnicity has generally resulted in disproportionate economic disadvantage for black women.[66]

Moreover, quite apart from such material considerations, neo-liberalism is, arguably, imbued with highly problematic assumptions about law, State and social and economic organisation. For example, the free market emphasis on supply and demand as key determinants of wage levels too often ignores the role of social factors in wage setting, constructing and promulgating a conception of the labour market which is (economically) idealised and separate from the social institutions and values within which it operates. Discrimination is narrowly conceived as 'irrational' decision making, unrelated to differences in the productivity enhancing characteristics of particular workers, the assumption being that where such differences *do* exist and, howsoever derived (for example, as a consequence of unequal access to

---

62 Sanjiv, S and Wilkinson, F, *Low Pay, the Working of the Labour Market and the Role of a Minimum Wage*, 1998, London: IER, pp 27–28. An EOC study in 1994 suggested that the removal of wage protection might not, of itself, significantly affect wage levels; acknowledging, however, that poor enforcement had already precipitated a decline: see Dex, S, Lissenburgh, S and Taylor, M, *Women and Low Pay: Identifying the Issues*, 1994, London: Equal Opportunities Commission, pp 87–88. The National Minimum Wage Act 1998 has been introduced, although its impact on levels of pay remains to be assessed.

63 Escott, K and Whitfield, D, *The Gender Impact of CCT in Local Government*, 1995, Manchester: Equal Opportunities Commission. The gender implications of CCT are also recognised by the House of Lords in *Ratcliffe v North Yorkshire CC* [1995] IRLR 439.

64 *Op cit*, Fredman, fn 8, pp 209–17. See the recent Department of Education and Employment Green Paper, *Meeting the Child Care Challenge*, 1998, (http://www.dfee.gov.uk/Child care), which seeks to improve child care provision through the development of a national child care strategy.

65 As lone mothers are much less likely to engage in paid work (*op cit*, Walby, fn 16, p 54), they are inevitably more dependent on welfare benefits and subsidised child care. Unfortunately, this has spawned a series of policies aimed at controlling lone mothers' access to benefits: Lister, R, *Women's Economic Dependency and Social Security*, 1992, Manchester: Equal Opportunities Commission, pp 44–45.

66 *Op cit*, Bhavnani, fn 20.

educational or training opportunities, or the gendered allocation of labour in the home), they *are* relevant to decision making, regardless of the gendered consequences which may flow from them. In this way, neo-liberalism legitimises market generated inequality.[67]

Inevitably, neo-liberals are sceptical of, if not downright hostile to, equality legislation, viewing it as an unwarranted and unworkable infringement on freedom in market transactions. This is particularly evident in the writing of Friedrich Hayek, in which a commitment to a 'genuine market order' and an antipathy towards 'central planning' lead him to reject State policies designed to secure 'material equality' as intolerably authoritarian, requiring the 'equal submission of the great masses under the command of some elite who manages their affairs'.[68] Even equality of opportunity is unacceptable to Hayek, constituting, he claims, 'a wholly illusory ideal, and any attempts concretely to realise it are apt to produce a nightmare'.[69] Hayek's position on equality flows directly from his understanding of the market as a 'spontaneous' mechanism which produces results not consciously or deliberately planned:

> The postulate of material equality would be a natural starting point only if it were a necessary circumstance that the shares of the different individuals or groups were in such a manner determined by deliberate human decision. In a society in which this were an unquestioned fact, justice would indeed demand that the allocation of the means for the satisfaction of human needs were effected according to some uniform principle of merit or need ...[70]

In other words, because the results of market interactions are *unanticipated*, they carry no moral implications which may be impugned. However, such a conclusion presupposes that the framework within which market interactions occur is neutral – that the set of institutions, practices and rules which govern market transactions are themselves untainted by deliberate moral and political choices, directing particular outcomes and serving particular interests. This assumption directly conflicts with a critical understanding of law as politically and morally imbued; in which understanding, the background rules to market transactions – for example, property and contract rights – have specific distributional consequences.[71] From such a perspective, distributional

---

67 See, generally, Humpries, J and Rubery, J, *The Economics of Equal Opportunities*, 1995, Manchester: Equal Opportunities Commission, especially the essays by Sawyer, M, 'The operation of labour markets and the economics of equal opportunities', p 33 and Humphries, J, 'Economics, gender and equal opportunities', p 55.

68 Hayek, F, *Law, Legislation and Liberty*, 1982, London: Routledge and Kegan Paul, Vol II, p 3.

69 *Ibid*, p 85.

70 *Ibid*, p 81. On Hayek's characterisation of the market as a spontaneous order, see Vol II, chap 10 and Vol III, chap 15.

71 On the distributional consequences of legal rules, see Kennedy, D, *Sexy Dressing, etc. Essays on the Power and Politics of Cultural Identity*, 1993, Cambridge, Mass: Harvard UP, pp 83–111.

concerns cannot easily be distinguished from efficiency considerations (as Hayek's argument suggests), nor can the market be properly understood in isolation from the set of background rules within which its interactions are mediated and directed. Once it is accepted that the market is deeply and deliberately distributive, a political concern with inequality becomes not only legitimate but, indeed, morally imperative.[72]

Thus, 'the market' functions in neo-liberal theory as a discursive technique which justifies particular distributive outcomes by rendering them devoid of political or moral content. Moreover, this ideological exercise is aided by the continued adherence in traditional economic discourse to the productive/reproductive dichotomy, rendering invisible highly gendered redistributive allocations. Consider, for example, the interplay between public expenditure cuts and the role and functioning of the family. The promotion of market-friendly policies is almost always accompanied by an ideological commitment to reducing public service provision (as inefficient) and enhancing the 'private' sphere of market ordering. The ensuing transfer of responsibilities from the public to the private sector inevitably enlists the family (and, therefore, women) in service provision, particularly care-giving and provision for the sick and the elderly. Indeed, it is precisely because the family 'voluntarily' performs services which, in orthodox economic terms, are deemed costless, that it is perceived to be the most efficient provider of these services. So viewed, the family emerges as a necessary corollary to the market by offering a cheap and viable alternative to public service provision. Remarkably, despite this crucial economic role, pro-market economists do not so much make a case for the family as accept its nature and existence as unproblematic.[73] Hayek, for example, assumes that the family does and should engage in reproductive and socialising activities without dwelling too closely on the allocation of responsibility for these tasks or the opportunities this might present for sexual inequality and exploitation.[74] Such wilful myopia is symptomatic of a more general tendency in (neo-)liberal theory to ignore the institutional and structural features of inequality, a tendency which

---

72 Emphasising the distributional consequences of the background rules to market transactions sometimes produces an unbridled enthusiasm for legal change as the key to social transformation. However, while law structures and significantly determines market transactions, the market is not necessarily indifferent to the content of the rules within which it operates. Ideologically, at least, an efficiency or market focus on legal regulation is likely to privilege some legal arrangements over others. See, generally, *op cit*, Rittich, fn 35.

73 *Op cit*, Hopkins, fn 61, pp 250–51; see, also, Waylen, G, 'Women and neo-liberalism', in Evans, J (ed), *Feminism and Political Theory*, 1986, London: Sage, pp 85, 94–96.

74 There are only a few scattered references to the family in *Law, Legislation and Liberty (op cit*, fn 68). In an earlier work, Hayek acknowledges that 'the conditions of domestic service, like all intimate relations, offer opportunities for coercion of a particularly oppressive kind', but concludes that 'the coercion that arises from voluntary association should not be the concern of government': Hayek, F, *The Constitution of Liberty*, 1960, London: Routledge, p 138, cited in Waylen, *ibid*, pp 94–95.

is undoubtedly exacerbated by the discursive separation of market and family. For Hayek, the inequalities which flow from societal arrangements, including a gender division of labour, institutionalised racism and an economic system which presupposes and promotes particular distributional outcomes, become reduced to a series of individual 'voluntary' interactions. In his world, social injustice does not exist and gender disadvantage is merely the random result of market interactions.[75]

If the invocation of economic discourse in its neo-liberal guise rarely serves the interests of working women, what of more 'progressive' economic approaches? Can the language of efficiency ever usefully be turned to women's cause? It has been observed that a number of academics in recent years, recognising the growing influence of economic discourse on labour policy, have sought to make an economic case for higher labour standards by linking them to improved productivity and competitiveness.[76] Economic arguments have also surfaced in debates about sex equality where the costs of continued discrimination have been weighed against the likely benefits flowing from its elimination.[77] While clearly this literature is to be welcomed – in strategic terms, it may often be more effective to make an economic case for equality or justice than a political or ethical one – such a strategy is inevitably double edged, as there is a real risk that the progressive deployment of economic discourse will import, perpetuate and reinforce the same problematic gendered assumptions which characterise neo-liberalism.

One particular difficulty which arises in this context is the (relative) indeterminacy and openness to manipulation of economic arguments. Although presented as scientific, objective and 'real', economic assertions often rely upon assumptions which are unsustainable or, at least, open to argument. For example, in political debate in the US about the economic implications of the proposed Family and Medical Leave Bill (finally enacted in 1993), opponents to the Bill were able to exaggerate its alleged costs by relying upon contentious assumptions about the likely use of leave provision. Moreover, by formulating the debate almost exclusively in terms of the appropriate degree of State intervention in market decision making, they were able to side-step important issues relating to the economic value of care giving

---

75 Hayek argues that social justice is a term 'wholly devoid of meaning or content'. See *op cit*, fn 68, pp 96–100.

76 *Op cit*, fn 46 and 47. In fact, a gender dimension lurks in this argument, in the sense that it is most persuasively deployed in the context of highly skilled, technology driven work and least compelling when applied to 'unskilled', labour intensive work, in which latter context women workers abound.

77 See, eg, Brueghel, I and Perrons, D, 'Where do the costs of unequal treatment for women fall? An analysis of the incidence of the costs of unequal pay and sex discrimination in the UK', in *op cit*, Humpries and Rubery, fn 67, p 155. The collection as a whole explores the possibility of a progressive economic approach to sex equality issues.

in the family.[78] Thus, the political agenda framed the terms of the economic enquiry, inevitably influencing the results.

The political manipulability of economic arguments raises questions about the alleged objectivity of economics as a mode of analysis. Georgina Waylen draws attention to the absence of women, both as researchers and objects of study, in economics and the consequent male bias in terms of methodology, approach and subject matter.[79] Diana Strassmann and Livia Polanyi portray economists as storytellers weaving narratives about human behaviour which form the bases of their theoretical assumptions. These narratives derive from the *knowledge* of the storytellers and 'are situated in the specific experiences and related world views of [the] predominant practitioners [of economics]: white, middle class North American men'.[80] From the 'situated' perspective of the economist narrator, 'work' is something for which you are paid a wage: household labour is not work, producing no recognised economic value, and women who are not 'productive' are economically 'dependent'. Similarly, a 'cost' is viewed as a charge on productive activity: pregnancy and childcare needs constitute 'costs' to employers and the State but not to women; nor are these costs offset by the economic benefits conferred by good parenting.

The economist's perception of a conceptual separation between production and reproduction for purposes of economic calculation thus strongly privileges 'productive' activity, while downplaying, if not ignoring, the economic value of reproductive activity, and accommodating the needs of working parents becomes subject to a set of economic calculations in which 'costs' and 'benefits' are politically construed, not objectively ascertainable. The distinction also generates an ideological and political reluctance to permit reproductive considerations to encroach too closely upon productive concerns, so that those factors inhibiting women's full participation in the productive sphere are deemed to be largely unrelated to the productive enterprise. Not only are women depicted as economically unproductive but their efforts to overcome this designation by participation in the productive sphere are thwarted by an ideological framework which reinforces the obstacles to that participation.

A further problematic dimension of the implicit narrative in economic discourse concerns the gendered conception of human nature and human behaviour underpinning traditional economic analysis. Feminist economists have argued that the economic model of the autonomous rational actor who interacts freely in the marketplace in pursuit of his own self-interest is a

---

78 See Trzcinski, E, 'The use and abuse of neo-classical theory in the political arena: the example of family and medical leave in the US', in *op cit*, Kuiper and Sap, fn 33, p 231.

79 Waylen, G, 'Gender, feminism and political economy' (1997) 2 New Political Economy 205, p 207.

80 Strassmann, D and Polanyi, L, 'The economist as storyteller: what the texts reveal', in *op cit*, Kuiper and Sap, fn 33, pp 129, 143.

masculine construct, deriving from and reinforcing the values and experiences of male economic actors.[81] Not only does such a construct preclude proper consideration of other motivating factors governing human behaviour – for example, altruism or empathy – but it ignores the way in which individual identity and preferences are mediated by multiple experiences and allegiances. The very notion of the universal subject as the basis for economic theorising directly conflicts with a feminist emphasis on the particularity of the subject whose 'situated' knowledge informs and guides decision making.[82]

Of course, this is not to say that individuals cannot, and do not, collectively aspire to a set of shared values or ends. However, in this context, feminists have contended that an economic focus on efficiency as a prescription for making choices in conditions of scarcity is largely misplaced and that economists would do better to concern themselves with the better provisioning of human life.[83] The orientation of traditional economics is revealed as ideological, and its application to labour law thus yields conclusions which, while claiming validity as 'science', are morally and politically contestable. So viewed, the engagement of progressive labour lawyers in economic discourse may be dangerously compromising, as it requires entry into political terrain on terms which include a denial of the politicised nature of the engagement and an ascribed validity to the terms of that engagement on grounds of their alleged neutrality.

Labour law and social and political reform: fairness at work

In May 1998, the Labour Government published a White Paper entitled *Fairness at Work*, outlining their plans for labour law reform and inviting views on how, and to what extent, these might be implemented.[84] The White Paper expresses the government's view that competition and fairness are not only compatible but necessary components of economic growth and that 'a minimum infrastructure of decency and fairness' is a prerequisite to any employment strategy concerned with the development of 'strong partnerships at work'.[85] The proposals include extended access to unfair dismissal with improved mechanisms of redress, a new framework of collective rights,

---

81 *Op cit*, Waylen, fn 79, pp 208–10; Folbre, N and Hartmann, H, 'The rhetoric of self-interest: ideology and gender in economic theory', in Klamer *et al* (eds), *The Consequences of Economic Rhetoric*, 1988, Cambridge: CUP, p 184.

82 *Op cit*, Waylen, fn 79, pp 208–09.

83 Nelson, J, 'The study of choice or the study of provisioning? Gender and the definition of economics', in Ferber, M and Nelson, J, *Beyond Economic Man: Feminist Theory and Economics*, 1993, Chicago, Illinois: Chicago UP, p 23.

84 *Op cit*, fn 2. See, now, Employment Relations Bill 1999.

85 *Ibid*, foreword (by the Prime Minister) and para 1.8.

including a right to trade union recognition, and a set of policies to encourage a more 'family-friendly culture in business' (para 5.3), including reform of current maternity provisions and new rights to unpaid parental leave and leave for family reasons. It is, in many ways, a radical document, not only in bringing the rhetoric of fairness at work back to the forefront of the political agenda but, also, in seeking to change industrial culture from one of conflict to one of partnership and cooperation.

The infusion of a normative or ethical dimension into labour law debate is, however, far from novel. Fairness has always been a consideration within labour law discourse, although, under the traditional collective *laissez faire* framework, the emphasis was on procedural fairness, through the promotion of collective bargaining arrangements, rather than substantive fairness in the form of individual legal entitlements. Davies and Freedland detect an increased emphasis on 'industrial justice' emerging in the 1960s, in part reflecting a civil rights preoccupation with sex and race discrimination but, also, deriving from an enhanced concern with social justice and distributive issues.[86] During the 1970s, many of these concerns found legislative expression in the emergent framework of employment protection and anti-discrimination legislation but, in the 1980s, fairness discourse became harnessed to the implementation of anti-trade union policies, proving particularly successful in the context of government efforts to outlaw closed shop practices.[87] Conservative strategists also made effective rhetorical use of other 'high minded ideals', such as democracy, individual rights and freedom, to bolster and legitimise their legal attack on trade union autonomy.[88]

Thus, in seeking an alliance between economic efficiency on the one hand, and fairness or equity considerations on the other, the current government continues along a path already set by its predecessors, albeit with a somewhat different sense of what fairness or equity in the workplace entails. In fact, the concept of fairness which the White Paper invokes has at least two dimensions. It is concerned, first, with according workers certain minimum rights (including collective rights to facilitate and shore up individual entitlements). This emphasis on rights is closely allied to the idea of responsibilities: if workers are to be accorded rights at work, they must also 'accept their responsibilities'.[89] Rights are, thus, viewed as a means by which industrial conflict can be diminished through the promotion of a culture of co-operation between employers and employees. In addition, *Fairness at Work* is informed by distributive/social justice concerns: it seeks to address problems of exploitation, unemployment and social exclusion. This is most evident in

---

86   *Op cit*, Davies and Freedland, fn 41, chap 5.

87   Unfair dismissal law played a prominent role in the Conservative attack on post-entry closed shops: *op cit*, fn 41, pp 450–54, 473–76.

88   *Op cit*, Fredman, fn 54, p 24.

89   *Op cit*, Department of Trade and Industry, fn 2, para 2.15.

the government's commitment to measures such as the national minimum wage and working time regulation but it is, also, a factor in their promotion of 'family-friendly' policies: reconciling work and family obligations not only improves the quality of family life, it is argued, but also facilitates labour market participation by parents, thus maximising the opportunities to enhance the family income.[90]

As a programme of reform, the government's commitment to family friendly policies may seem very attractive to working women. Of course, questions may still be raised about the adequacy or scope of the proposed reforms: parental leave, for example, is, arguably, of little practical use to parents if it is unpaid; nor does the White Paper expressly address current levels of income protection during maternity leave, which remain, by European standards, low.[91] Moreover, there is no recognition of the obvious need for substantial review of existing equality legislation.[92] But, such reservations about detail aside, should not feminists wholeheartedly welcome the changes in workplace culture which the government seeks to effect?

From a critical feminist perspective, such a question excites no easy answer. In particular, while it should not be assumed that the government's programme is incompatible with feminist objectives, nor should it be assumed to be wholly compatible. 'Family-friendly' does not always mean 'woman-friendly', as the experience of women in Eastern European countries can attest.[93] Indeed, if the object of family-friendly policies is merely to facilitate women's entry to and exit from the workplace without directly addressing the allocation of labour within the family, then such policies are likely to increase the burden which women currently carry, rather than alleviate it. In this context, parental leave arrangements become crucial. The government is right to emphasise the need for a change of culture – employers must recognise that mothers *and* fathers have responsibilities which workplace arrangements should accommodate. But, is there anything in the current proposals for *unpaid* parental leave which is likely to bring about such a dramatic change in culture? To what extent will the government's proposals bring about a change

---

90 'We ... need to ensure that as many people as possible who want to work should have a chance to do so': *op cit*, Department of Trade and Industry, fn 2, para 5.1 (chapter on family-friendly policies). See, also, *op cit*, Department of Education and Employment Green Paper, fn 64, especially the Prime Minister's foreword and chap 1.

91 The White Paper does promise 'a review of existing maternity rights': *op cit*, fn 2, Department of Trade and Industry, para 5.13.

92 The Equal Opportunities Commission has since argued for the wholesale reform of equality law, including the introduction of a single statute to replace the Sex Discrimination Act 1975 and the Equal Pay Act 1970: see EOC, *Equality in the 21st Century: A New Sex Equality Law for Britain*, 1998, Manchester: Equal Opportunities Commission.

93 Kerry Rittich points out that, despite the prevalence of 'family friendly' workplace arrangements in Eastern European socialist regimes, working women continued to shoulder the burden of domestic responsibilities: *op cit*, Rittich, fn 35, p 26.

in the attitude of *fathers* towards their domestic responsibilities?[94] Even the implementation of a radical child care programme is limited in its capacity to bring about the necessary transformation, as it does not address the distribution of responsibility for children between parents. What is, in fact, needed is a change in cultural attitutes towards domestic labour. Yet, despite a recent government emphasis upon the importance of good parenting,[95] the assumptions which underpin the current drive to increase female workforce participation remain wedded to an ideology which denies the value of reproductive work.

This is most apparent in the political and social construction of women who do not engage in paid labour as economically *dependent*. A perception of paid work as the key to women's economic independence, evident, for example, in policy measures designed to get lone parents off benefits and into the workplace, stems directly from a view of reproductive work – bringing up children and related caregiving activities – as economically valueless and non-productive. Thus, the receipt of welfare benefits designates the recipient as *inactive* and, thereby, dependent, despite the reality of daily domestic labour.[96] There can, of course, be no doubt that the lives of many women would be immeasurably improved by better access to paid work; the reality of life on benefit is grim and unappealing. But does the promotion of women's workforce participation really require the ideological reinforcement of the productive/reproductive dichotomy, particularly when it has been shown to pose a major obstacle to that participation? Does a rhetoric which contributes to the continued devaluing of reproductive activity ultimately serve women's interests? After all, as long as such activity remains hidden and economically unacknowledged, how can women hope to have it taken into account, let alone share the burden?

The above analysis suggests that even programmes which purport to promote women's interests may be accompanied by problematic gendered assumptions, which need to be explored. In particular, the discursive construction of the productive/reproductive dichotomy and the consequences

---

94 A recent government survey revealed that women continue to assume primary responsibility for household labour, despite their increased economic activity: see Office for National Statistics, *Social Focus on Men and Women*, 1998, London: HMSO. As *The Guardian* observes: 'while "new woman" has made inroads at the workplace, "new man" has failed to play his part at home': 22 October 1998, p 5.

95 Home Office Consultation Paper, *Supporting Families*, November 1998.

96 For a different view of the economic value of household labour, see, eg, Hutchinson, F, 'A heretical view of economic growth and income distribution', in *op cit*, Kuiper and Sap, fn 33, p 35, exploring the implications for women of the inter-war Social Credit Movement. The economic value of household labour has also been extensively debated within Marxist theory – see, in particular, Vogel, L, *Marxism and the Oppression of Women: Towards a Unitary Theory*, 1987, New Brunswick: Rutgers UP, pp 17–25, 136–75.

which flow from the differential attribution of value or worth to each sphere of activity continue to exercise a tenacious hold upon policy making and theorising.

CONCLUSION

In the course of this chapter, my object has been to engage with both feminist theory and labour law theory with a view to exploring how they might meet and inform each other. I have identified some of the most salient issues currently informing feminist theoretical debate and considered their application to labour law. I have also sought to highlight the more problematic aspects of labour law theory, as it undergoes significant theoretical and ideological reconstruction, emphasising the importance and relevance of feminist insights to that reconstructive process. My focus has been primarily directed at the analytical frameworks within which changes in labour law are located and evaluated. My argument has been that most of these analytical frameworks, even in their most 'feminist friendly' guise, are accompanied by gendered assumptions which derive from the ideological privileging of productive over reproductive work and that those assumptions, to a significant extent unarticulated in labour law theory, remain an obstacle to women's economic and social advancement.

The current emphasis in policy making on the need to reconcile work and family obligations obviously goes some way to addressing the difficulties I have raised. However, it might be argued that even framing the issue in these terms is problematic: the perceived conflict between work and family life is a political and social construct and should be acknowledged as such. Recognising the economic and social value of reproductive work would go some way to achieving this. It would also encourage men to assume a greater share of domestic responsibility.

From such a perspective, it is easy to conclude that the terrain of labour law is much larger than conventional analysis would suggest and that an understanding of the regulation and, indeed, legal construction of work is incomplete without a proper appreciation of the significance of the distinction between reproductive and productive work and the way in which that distinction is perpetuated and reinforced by a range of legal mechanisms including taxation, social security provision and, increasingly, immigration law. In this way, feminist scholarship raises questions not just about the content of law but also about the form in which it is presented and authenticated. As a field of study, labour law is reliant upon a particular perception of social arrangements which is, in turn, derived from a gendered allocation of labour. A woman-centred 'labour' law, on the other hand, might have very different parameters.[97] At the very least, then, feminist engagement with (labour) law requires its fundamental theoretical and conceptual reorientation; at its most radical, feminist theory compels its virtual reconstruction. This is the ongoing project of feminist legal theory.

---

97 See, in particular, here, the pioneering work of the late Tove Stang Dahl in *Women's Law*, 1986, Oslo: Norwegian UP.

CHAPTER 3

EQUAL OPPORTUNITIES, STAFF DEVELOPMENT AND ASSERTIVENESS

Alice Belcher

BACKGROUND

This chapter is an exploration of the linkages between equal opportunities, staff development and assertiveness training. It will be useful, at this stage, to distinguish the normative and positive claims of the chapter. The normative link between equal opportunities and staff development seemed to me to be obvious, in that advancement, in terms of promotion or a shift in career path, presupposes ongoing development. A staff development programme that properly recognises the equal opportunities implications of what is on offer is, therefore, an important part of the implementation of an equal opportunities policy. Equal opportunities and staff development *should* be linked. The normative link between staff development for women[1] and assertiveness training is more tenuous and, for me, more questionable. The issue of whether staff development for women *should* include assertiveness training is discussed in under the heading 'Assertiveness' on p 51. The chapter also addresses the empirical questions of whether equal opportunities and staff development are linked in practice and whether staff development for women and assertiveness are linked in practice.

The methodology for researching this topic is one that I have employed only once before, in my 'Gendered company' article.[2] I began with a personal experience; the experience itself generated ideas; I then pursued various hypotheses in the light of feminist theories, my personal experience and the existing literature. In this chapter, I also include the results of some exploratory empirical research. This research began with my experience of an assertiveness course offered as part of a staff development programme. In my 'Gendered company' article, the narrative of my unpleasant experience was important in, and of, itself. I told the story of my bad day at the Institute of Directors in order to raise consciousness. There is no parallel story to tell of assertiveness training. There is just the fact that, at the end of a day during

---

1   Throughout the chapter, it is women's employment opportunities that provide a focus.
2   See Belcher, A, 'Gendered company: enterprise and governance at the Institute of Directors' (1997) 5(1) FLS 57.

which I should have learnt a new skill, acquired a new weapon and felt empowered, I actually felt like bursting into tears. The negative mood that I experienced on leaving the course was very strong and has been the main impetus for my subsequent investigations of assertiveness and assertiveness training. So, I do not offer this chapter as a dispassionate, scientific account; rather, it is an account which began with, and is heavily coloured by, my own negative experience.

The chapter is structured as follows: first, equal opportunities law, such as it is in the UK, is presented and the normative link with staff development is strengthened (below). Secondly, equal opportunities policies and links to staff development are investigated (p 47). Thirdly, the meaning of staff development and the place of staff development for women are discussed (p 49). Fourthly, ideological and practical difficulties associated with assertiveness training for women are discussed (p 51), and, fifthly and finally, some conclusions are presented (p 59).

EQUAL OPPORTUNITIES LAW

There is no specific UK legislation dealing with equal opportunities policies and/or their implementation. However, the Sex Discrimination Act 1975 makes it unlawful for employers to discriminate on the grounds of sex and/or marital status in relation to most aspects of employment (recruitment, pay, promotion, training, and so on). Positive discrimination, where an appointment to a particular post or a promotion is made on the basis of a factor which is not job related – for example, sex or race – is treated as unlawful under the Act. For instance, in the case of *Jepson and Dyas-Elliot v The Labour Party*,[3] it was held that women only shortlists were unlawful. The UK position appears to accord with the interpretation of the Equal Treatment Directive given by the ECJ in *Kalanke v Freie Hasestadt Bremen*,[4] where it was held that it was contrary to the Directive to give preferential treatment to a woman who was equally qualified with a man, in order to compensate for past discrimination against women in general. Positive discrimination has, however, been adopted in other jurisdictions as a legally plausible method of making equality an achievable reality as opposed to an unattainable ideal. One such jurisdiction is the United States, where the concept of 'affirmative action' is encouraged and, in some cases, enforced in order to 'open the doors of education, employment and business development opportunities to qualified individuals who happen to be members of groups who have

---

3   [1996] IRLR 116.
4   [1995] IRLR 660 ECJ (Case C-450/93). Compare *Marschall v Land Nordrhein Westfalen*, Case C-409/95 [1998] IRLR 39.

experienced long standing and persistent discrimination'.[5] The US approach is based on the radical conception of equality, known as 'equality of outcome', which intervenes to alter the status quo by taking steps to redress previous imbalances. In contrast, the UK approach can be described in terms of a liberal concept of equality which seeks to secure 'equality of opportunity'.

Women seeking equality of outcomes in employment in the UK face the double difficulty of the lack of a specific legal requirement for employers to address the issue of equal opportunities and the fact that positive discrimination is outlawed. Despite this, employers are increasingly adopting and revising equal opportunities policies and, as part of its advisory role, the Equal Opportunities Commission (EOC)[6] conducts research into, and helps to initiate, effective equal opportunities policies. On its current homepage, the EOC describes its understanding of an equal opportunities 'programme'. It states:

> The provision of equal opportunities in the workplace is a legal issue – an equal opportunities programme aims to implement, and complement, the equality legislation and will include any lawful measures contributing to the elimination of inequalities.[7]

The EOC is quite clear that '... a good equal opportunities programme does not simply take steps to avoid blatant, or direct, discrimination' and 'an equal opportunities programme also needs conscious efforts to overcome the effects of indirect discrimination, past and present'.[8] However, the *lawful* measures referred to by the EOC include only those measures specifically permitted under ss 47 and 48 of the Sex Discrimination Act 1975 (as amended by the Sex Discrimination Act 1986). These measures have been labelled 'positive action',[9] as distinct from 'positive discrimination' or 'affirmative action' which are unlawful in the UK. In the framing of ss 47 and 48 of the Act, the overall principle that recruitment and promotion must be on merit, irrespective of sex, was left intact. With positive action measures in place, selection for employment or promotion must still be done on the basis of 'who is the most suitable candidate?' Positive action, therefore, is merely directed at equalising opportunities, in line with the liberal conception of equality. Section 47 of the Act permits training bodies to afford women only access to facilities for training which would help mould them for work in which they are significantly under represented, or to encourage women only to take

---

5   President Clinton, speech on affirmative action, 19 July 1995:
    http://www.washingtonpost.com
6   Established by the Sex Discrimination Act 1975.
7   EOC homepage – http://www.econi.org.uk
8   *Ibid*.
9   The EOC Code of Practice defines positive action, somewhat circuitously, as those measures allowed under the Sex Discrimination Act: EOC Code of Practice for the Elimination of Discrimination on the Grounds of Sex and Marriage and the Promotion of Equal Opportunity in Employment, 1985, para 41.

advantage of opportunities for doing that work.[10] Section 48 contains a similar provision in relation to employers.

The EOC has stated that a good equal opportunities policy will involve identifying positive action measures in order to correct discrimination or under representation. As positive action measures only occur in the context of one sex being significantly under represented, monitoring of the implementation of an equal opportunities policy is recommended by the EOC.[11] It states that:

Sensible monitoring will show, for example, whether members of one sex:

(a) do not apply for employment or promotion, or that fewer apply than might be expected;

(b) are not recruited, promoted or selected for training and development or are appointed/selected in a significantly lower proportion than their rate of application;

(c) are concentrated in certain jobs, sections or departments.

The EOC has also identified some forms of positive action which employers may wish to consider. These include training their own employees for work which is traditionally the preserve of the other sex; positive encouragement for women to apply for management posts (for which special courses may be needed); and using advertisements which encourage applications from the minority sex but make it clear that selection will be on merit and without reference to sex. Other positive action measures which may assist women are: flexitime; career break schemes; workplace nurseries; access to training; access to experience; access to risk taking, monitoring and setting targets for numbers of women in jobs/grades; and women's development training.[12]

To summarise: positive action is all that is allowed under UK and EC law to redress past and current discriminatory unfairness suffered by women. The scope for positive action is not large but it does include training and assistance with access to training. Positive action could mean courses for potential women managers, women only training, and measures which allow access to training, such as child care facilities to cover periods of training, or at least the provision of sufficiently advance notice for child care arrangements to be made. It could be argued that, as equal opportunities should permeate all of an organisation's activities, the link between equal opportunities and staff development needs no further support. In the context of a liberal, rather than a radical, legislative approach to equal opportunities, equal opportunities

---

10 The Sex Discrimination Act 1975 applies to the provision of services and, without s 47, training bodies offering training facilities for women only would be unlawfully discriminating against men.

11 *Op cit*, EOC Code, fn 9, paras 37–40.

12 Willis, L and Daisley, J, *Developing Women through Training: A Practical Handbook*, 1992, Maidenhead: McGraw-Hill, p 3.

policies must, increasingly, be implemented through the training, and the encouragement of training, of (and for) women. This strengthens the normative link between equal opportunities and staff development and makes it more important that staff development for women is designed with proper regard to equal opportunities.

EQUAL OPPORTUNITIES AND STAFF DEVELOPMENT

Having argued that there *should* be a link between equal opportunities and staff development, I now turn to the question of whether that link exists in practice. However, it should be recognised that any weakness in such a link may be due to a general weakness in the implementation of equal opportunities in an organisation, not due to a weakness in this area in particular. Powney and Weiner, in a study of educational institutions, identified a spectrum of institutional adoption of equal opportunities policies and practices as follows:

(1) Equal opportunities is a significant part of the ethos of the institution; for example, reflected in power structures and permeating all institutional activities (ethos).

(2) There is a genuine commitment to good equal opportunities practice (commitment).

(3) The institution is in the process of working towards equal opportunities (predisposition).

(4) There is some 'lip-service' given to equality issues (lip-service).

(5) There is no evidence of any real interest in equal opportunities issues (none).[13]

Farish *et al*, writing in 1995, looked at equal opportunities in colleges and universities and found that developments had been patchy and high expectations of early policy developments had, to some extent, been dashed.[14] Cockburn suggests the following reasons for disappointment with equal opportunities:

> The law is too weak and difficult to use. Organisations taking positive action are too few and their goals and methods too limited. Organisations choose high profile, cost-free measures and neglect the more expensive changes that would improve things for a greater number of women. Policies adopted are seldom implemented. Implementation is not monitored. Non-compliance is not penalised, nor is co-operation rewarded.[15]

---

13 Cited in Farish, M, McPake, M, Powney, J and Weiner, G, *Equal Opportunities in Colleges and Universities: Towards Better Practices*, 1995, Buckingham: Society for Research into Higher Education and Open University, p 4.

14 *Ibid*, p 2.

15 Cockburn, C, *In the Way of Women: Men's Resistance to Sex Equality in Organisations*, 1991, London: Macmillan.

In educational institutions, progress in equal opportunities is associated to some extent with status, with comparatively greater progress being made by smaller, lower status establishments. In particular, it has been observed that the traditional university sector moved comparatively slowly.[16] In order to write this chapter, I attempted to make contact with those responsible for both equal opportunities and staff development at the traditional Scottish universities.[17] In these inquiries, I wanted to find out about the general status and level of implementation of equal opportunities in traditional Scottish universities and to establish whether equal opportunities and staff development were linked in any way. It has not proved possible to make many general statements about the results of my exploratory research. I expected traditional Scottish universities to have been subject to similar social, regulatory, economic and cultural influences and so to be a fairly homogeneous group of institutions. However, in the fields of equal opportunities and staff development, the group was far from homogeneous. An equal opportunities policy had been made by all the universities contacted, but the content of policies was varied. Only one policy included an explicit reference to positive action initiatives. Another referred to the provision of training or access courses for under-represented groups and stated that the provision of opportunities, to transfer between full and part time work – without loss of status or promotion prospects – and for flexible working time and job sharing, was encouraged. In these two universities, equal opportunities monitoring was in place and equal opportunities officers were able to provide well presented, up to date, statistical analyses of promotions and applications for promotion. At the other end of the spectrum, one university does not have an equal opportunities officer because all staff in the personnel department are responsible for implementing the university's equal opportunities policy. The result is that, because most staff in the department are so busy with their designated area of work, equal opportunities gets little attention. At Dundee, the university has an equal opportunities policy. There is also an equal opportunities officer, but this post has been given to a relatively junior member of staff in the personnel department who has a large number of other tasks. Dundee now has an equal opportunities committee, but this was not seen as necessary when the policy was written and had to be campaigned for by staff who had formed a women's group. I found close links between the equal opportunities and staff development functions in the universities with the best general implementation of equal opportunities policies. This suggests that, when the

---

16 *Op cit*, Farish, McPake, Powney and Weiner, fn 13, p 5.

17 I included the following universities in my inquiries: Aberdeen, Dundee, Edinburgh, Glasgow, St Andrews, Stirling and Strathclyde.

implementation of equal opportunities progresses to the higher points on the Powney and Weiner spectrum, the normative link to staff development becomes a positive one.

STAFF DEVELOPMENT AND
STAFF DEVELOPMENT FOR WOMEN

One of the problems I have encountered in my exploration of equal opportunities, staff development and assertiveness training is that the literature on each component often begins by stating that it is difficult to define. The liberal and radical approaches to equal opportunities have already been mentioned and some of the difficulties encountered when deciding what equal opportunities means in practice were described in the previous section. An examination of the literature on staff development reveals parallel definitional problems: for example, in 1978, it was said that:

The trouble is that the phrase 'staff development' is so all embracing that to say one favours and practises it has little more meaning than to say that one favours virtue and opposes sin – it could be anything and everything.

Reporting in 1981, Matheson stated that there had been:

... fundamental disagreements on the meaning of staff development, on what (if anything) distinguishes it from training, on what (if any) philosophies underlie it, on what constitutes its practices and, indeed, on whether it can be meaningfully achieved in practice.[18]

Staff development in the context of universities presents particular problems, and the debates noted by Matheson are not merely academic semantics because:

... acceptance of a concept of staff development, however defined, raises underlying, and sometimes controversial, issues of crucial importance to the survival of staff development as an academically valid and valued activity.[19]

In July 1978, the Co-ordinating Committee for the Training of University Teachers (CCTUT) wrote to 'a number of individuals *actively involved* in staff training and development'. Responses to this survey[20] were not encouraging and included the following:

I am still wary of the notion that staff can/should be 'developed' as people. Many of my academic colleagues would regard efforts to change *them* as impertinent.

---

18 Matheson, CC, *Staff Development Matters*, 1981, London: CCTUT, p 153.
19 *Ibid*, p 153.
20 Reported by Matheson, *ibid*.

'Training' is not a very welcome notion in universities, since it suggests a rather low level, technical school type activity!

By staff development I mean the continuing intellectual growth of every university man [sic] in both his [sic] academic speciality and the way he [sic] communicates to his [sic] students.

Two decades on, we might expect to be able to detect some progress and, indeed, Webb (1996) states that: 'There are many definitions of staff development, but there is also a reasonable degree of convergence.' However, the degree of convergence claimed by Webb is illusory. This is the way he defines staff development:

Staff development is normally considered to include the institutional policies, programmes and procedures which facilitate and support staff so that they may fully serve their own and their institution's needs.[21]

We are back to an 'all things to all people' type of definition that still hides division and diversity. Webb's book is about staff development for academic staff in universities and focuses almost exclusively on teaching and learning. Broader approaches to staff development, that embrace the whole range of university employees and include personal development as well as job specific skills, are excluded from his treatment of the subject in its opening paragraphs. Webb's introduction may appear as a gender neutral definition of how he will approach the subject but, for women, the opportunity to develop themselves and change their career paths is crucial and is an element of equal opportunities. A proper commitment to equal opportunities demands a broad definition of both 'staff' and 'development'. This suggests that there may be an optimum size of staff development function/unit. It needs to be big enough to be able to take a broad approach, but not so large that its parts become professionalised and separated. At Dundee University, staff development may be below the required critical mass. At other Scottish universities, there seems to be more danger of the various parts of staff development becoming so large that connections between, say, teaching and learning, and personal development may be lost.

The next issue is how women's development training fits into the picture. Willis and Daisley, writers with over 20 years' practical experience of women's development training, state:

A common question which arises with this type of training is: 'What about men's development training then?' To which our reply is that there is already an abundance of men's development training happening, because most training in the world of work is designed by men, to address issues defined by men, with courses organised by men, using material developed by men, and attended mostly by men ... In most organisations, training is conducted at times to fit male work patterns, in venues that suit men, with subject matter,

---

21 Webb, G, *Understanding Staff Development* 1996, Buckingham: SRHE and Open University, p 1.

processes and teaching styles appropriate to men. Of course, women attend these courses too, but by definition they will be in the minority and will be in a foreign land. Women at senior levels often report being the only woman on the course.[22]

Women's development training and women only training is usually perceived as resulting from the anti-discrimination legislation. If positive action is defined as any action at all, *short of appointment or promotion*, that enables a woman to be the right person for the job, then women's development training is, by definition, positive action. This does not mean, however, that, wherever there is women's development training or women only training in any form, there is a positive action *programme.* In some organisations, the implementation of an equal opportunities policy included the offering of women's development training. For instance, in 1987, as part of its equal opportunities programme, BBC Scotland held its first women only training course in conjunction with BBC Northern Ireland.[23] At Dundee University, courses for women were proposed – by the same women's group that pushed for the equal opportunities committee to be set up – and are currently on offer to all women employees under the umbrella of the staff development unit.

In the next section, I focus on assertiveness training. Women's development training often includes assertiveness training. A typical range of subjects for women's development training would encompass career planning, assertiveness skills, biography work, goal setting, presentational skills and interview techniques.[24] Also, assertiveness training is often presented as a form of personal development of particular benefit to women. I must acknowledge that my own experience at Dundee University does not fit neatly into my imagined framework. The assertiveness course that I attended found its way into the staff development unit's offering of courses, not through the work of the equal opportunities officer, or at the request of the women's group, but through a proposal which came from the counselling service.

ASSERTIVENESS

The concept of assertiveness training was originated by psychologists working on behaviour therapy and social skills in the US in the 1940s and 1950s.[25] As a therapy, the process of assertiveness training (AT) is viewed as

---

22 *Op cit*, Willis and Daisley, fn 12, p 4.
23 *Op cit*, Willis and Daisley, fn 12, p 55.
24 *Op cit*, Willis and Daisley, fn 12, p 3.
25 Early work includes Salter, A, *Conditional Reflex Therapy*, 1949, New York: Creative Age, and Wolpe J, *Psychotherapy by Reciprocal Inhibition* 1958, Stanford: Stanford UP.

one in which dysfunctional habits or behavioural deficits are replaced by new, better, and more effective behaviours. As with equal opportunities and staff development, there is no clear and generally agreed upon definition of assertiveness, but most behaviour therapists accept a rough statement about self-affirming, direct behaviour that does not attempt to hurt others.[26] The last 30 years or so have seen a growth in assertiveness training as a therapy and seen it move out of the confines of psychotherapy to be marketed as part of personal development. As a philosophy of life, it has been said that:

> Assertiveness training in practice frequently involves [various methods] ... all operating on the belief that 'being assertive' is a rightful, basic human need.

Pattenson and Burns give a more detailed explanation of assertive behaviour:

> Assertiveness is a way of communicating clearly and effectively, particularly in difficult personal, social and professional situations. Elements of assertive behaviour learned through AT include: making clear, specific requests; being able to say 'no'; giving and receiving criticism; managing the expression of feelings, especially anger; receiving compliments; taking the initiative; understanding the non-verbal messages; building self-esteem; and improving self-presentation.[27]

Work is a place where there are often difficult professional situations and some of the difficulties in professional situations arise because they are social and/or personal as well as professional. If assertive behaviour is the answer to interpersonal difficulties at work, it is easy to see the attraction of assertiveness training. The next question to address is how assertiveness training can be connected with women's issues. This can be done in various ways. First, there is the fact that AT has been used widely by women and the majority of participants continue to be women.[28] Secondly, a connection can be made by citing evidence that women tend to be less assertive than men and are therefore (if assertiveness is desirable) more in need of AT. Thirdly, there is a historic link between some of the pioneers of AT and the women's movement in the US in the 1970s. Behaviour therapists at that time:

> ... conceptualized non-assertion as a socially conditioned feminine trait associated with passive, submissive, helpless and altruistic behaviours in women. Assertiveness techniques were utilized in work with women's groups to provide an antidote to the traditional feminine non-assertive programming

---

26 Emmons, ML and Alberti, RR, 'Failure: winning at the losing game in assertiveness training', in Foa, EB and Emmelkamp, PMG (eds), *Failures in Behaviour Therapy*, 1983, New York: John Wiley, p 122.

27 Pattenson, L and Burns, J, *Women, Assertiveness, and Health: A Rationale for the Use of Training in Promoting Women's Health*, 1990, London: Health Education Authority, p 9.

28 *Ibid*, p 8.

... [and] feminist therapists hypothesized that women would use assertiveness to develop their own personal power base in order to confront the male establishment and redress societal inequities.[29]

At this stage, all the normative connections between the three elements (equal opportunities, staff development for women and AT) appear to have been made. Equal opportunities *should* permeate into staff development and into women's development training in particular; and, *if* it works in the ways described above, AT *should* be included in women's development training. Because an assertive person claims rights whilst respecting the rights of others, it has even been stated that 'the essence of assertive behaviour is equality.'[30] This adds the final link that makes the argument circular: a world populated by assertive people *should*, almost by definition, be implementing equal opportunities.

The empirical connections have not followed the same route. The evidence is that equal opportunities in general, and in Scottish universities in particular, are not consistently implemented. Although there has been movement along Powney and Weiner's spectrum, from *none* to *lip-service* and *predisposition*, institutions where there is genuine *commitment* or *ethos* are hard to find. Staff development offerings do include some women's development training, and assertiveness training is also offered in some form. However, the flow from one element to the next is not evident. When Scottish universities were questioned as to their activities in the areas of equal opportunities, staff development and assertiveness training, boxes could be ticked but these activities were not being conducted within the coherent framework I had built in my imagination. My framework for linking equal opportunities to staff development –and, in particular, staff development for women – is not evident in the policies and practices of most Scottish universities, but assertiveness training is being provided, mostly to women and on the basis that it is especially beneficial to women.

In the light of my own bad experience, my thoughts, and some of the more recent literature on the failure of AT, I want to question whether AT is in fact valuable for many women and for the cause of feminism. My doubts about the value of AT for specific women obviously began with doubts about its value for me. However, the literature also describes some failures of AT in practice. For feminists, AT also has some conceptual problems. I shall deal first with the practical, and then with the conceptual, problems.

29 *Op cit*, Emmons and Alberti, fn 26, p 138.
30 Straw, J, *Equal Opportunities: The Way Ahead*, 1989, London: Institute of Personnel Management, p 174.

Practical problems with assertiveness training for women

To begin with, the practical problem of AT for me: I went into the AT session knowing that certain interpersonal situations at work were difficult for me and that I consistently came away from interactions with some individuals thinking that I had got it wrong (again). But, as I stated in my introduction, at the end of a day during which I should have learnt a new skill, acquired a new weapon and felt empowered, I actually felt like bursting into tears. During the training session, we were invited to give examples of our work-related interpersonal problems. I disclosed one of my problem areas to the group, but I was not at all convinced by the suggested handling of the situation. At the end of the day, I felt upset because I had exposed what I perceived as my weakness to a group of strangers, my problems remained unsolved, and I felt that this was my fault for not explaining my problem well enough.

I have tried to analyse this failure of AT. My course was only a one day session, but its curriculum and teaching methods were in line with descriptions of AT I have discovered in the literature. I do not think I went to a substandard course. I have assessed my own level of assertiveness using the Baron Assertiveness Quotient test[31] and, according to my result, I am an assertive person. I have come to several conclusions: first, assertive behaviour will not solve the problems I hoped it would; secondly, my problems are not always, or even often, due to a lack of assertiveness in my behaviour, but are due to the context in which I am trying to operate. Even supporters of assertiveness training are now acknowledging that the effectiveness of assertive behaviour may be context or environment dependent. For instance, Kahn states:

> If assertiveness training is understood in relation to the devaluation and discrimination of women in our society, such training can be a growth enhancing strategy for dealing with social oppression. Factors in the social environment are central to how women perceive themselves and are perceived by others, and the socialization and learning experiences of women must be highlighted in assertiveness training programs. The helplessness and powerlessness that many women feel result from social expectations and real events women experience ... In order for the technical skills of assertive behaviour to make a difference in female experience, women must feel able to act with confidence, and their efforts at self-assertion must be *supported by others' beliefs about women's roles*.[32]

---

31 As reproduced and discussed in Karsten, MF, *Management and Gender: Issues and Attitudes*, 1994, Westport, Connecticut and London: Praeger, pp 142–44.

32 Kahn, SE, 'Issues in the assessment and training of assertiveness with women', in Wine, JD and Smye, MD, *Social Competence*, 1981, New York: Guilford, pp 360–61, emphasis added.

Unfortunately, one of the problems at the heart of discrimination against women is that they are valued by men only when they conform to their allotted sex roles. It is recognised that deviancy from cultural norms for gender appropriate behaviour may result in both negative psychological consequences and in punishment in interpersonal situations. Women who are assertive are often perceived as aggressive by male colleagues. Women face the practical problem that, when they try to apply their assertiveness training skills at work, they are doing so as *double deviants.*

> *Primary deviants* are those who are not members of the dominant class [women]. *Double deviants* are 'uppity' primary deviants. They are not content with second rate status; they want the same opportunities as the dominant group [men].[33]

We should not be surprised by the response of a dominant group threatened by the intrusiveness of the influx of a minority into a majority dominated occupation. Intrusiveness threatens the dominant group, which reacts with increased discrimination against minorities to limit their power gains.[34] I engaged in assertiveness training in the belief that:

> One way to achieve equal power with males is to know how to adopt masculine forms of status and power. The learning of verbal and non-verbal expressions of assertive behavior is one effort toward acquiring equal status.[35]

I have come out of AT questioning that belief. Research has been carried out by psychologists into the question of whether assertion by females is subjected to a different, and more negative, social reaction than assertion by males. Rakos identified over 25 studies assessing the effect of the sex of the asserter on the evaluation of conflict assertion.[36] Conflict assertion means the use of assertive behaviour in a conflict situation. Psychologists conduct their research by setting up scenes or vignettes for subjects to observe and assess. One study found that corporate managers of both sexes valued assertion by females as well as males over self-effacing remarks in work related conflicts.[37] This sort of evidence appears to contradict the hypothesis that assertiveness in women receives negative responses. However, Rakos pointed out that this type of study may have tapped into the abstract value system of the corporate managers, but not into their actual behavioural response.[38] What these subjects say they like in experimental conditions may not receive positive behavioural responses in 'real life'. Overall, Rakos describes the 25 studies as

---

33 *Op cit*, Karsten, fn 31, p 150.

34 *Op cit*, Karsten, fn 31.

35 *Op cit*, Kahn, fn 32, p 361.

36 Rakos, RF, *Assertive Behavior: Theory, Research and Training*, 1991, London and New York: Routledge, p 72.

37 Solomon, LJ, Brehany, KA, Rothblum, ED and Kelly, JA, 'Corporate managers' reaction to assertive social skills exhibited by males and females' (1982) Journal of Organizational Behavior Management 4, pp 49–63.

38 *Ibid*, Rakos, p 75.

exhibiting contradictory research findings, methodological inadequacies, insufficiently researched variables, and a failure to take into account the social and historical nature of the phenomenon being investigated.[39] He concludes that the data, despite all the ambiguities, suggest that the key element in producing a negative reaction to conflict assertion is the asserter's failure to meet a stereotyped expectation.[40] Women are not expected to be assertive and, therefore, experience negative reaction when they behave assertively.[41]

Karsten's approach to the problems for women, in relation to assertiveness, is to acknowledge that assertiveness may be something women can control but that there are other factors they cannot, especially at work. She states:

> Besides avoiding political minefields and practising power-enhancing behaviors, [female] executives must realize that factors beyond their control may create *bureaucratic powerlessness*.[42]

My view is that assertive behaviour by women may not have that much effect in terms of enhancing power and the factors creating bureaucratic powerlessness should not be underestimated. Care should, therefore, be taken not to create an assertiveness expectations gap; that is, a gap between women's expectations of the gains to be made by acquiring assertiveness skills and the gains that such skills can actually achieve, when exercised by women at work.

One of the factors that Karsten describes as creating bureaucratic powerlessness is tokenism. Tokenism is a response by the dominant class (males) to double deviant females. Double deviants are turned into tokens by being sponsored by the dominant group and striking a role model bargain with them. Sponsors convince double deviants that they are better than – and, therefore, unlike – other primary deviants (other women). They also assure them that individualism and merit count, therefore deviants (women) who fail are responsible for their own failure. Double deviants who accept these ideas can be transformed into tokens by agreeing with their sponsors on roles and attitudes. Token females will take the view that sponsors are not prejudiced, and will defend their sponsors, but the sponsor and the token will know that the token cannot completely escape deviant origins and cannot participate completely in the dominant group. Thus, the dominant group retains control.[43]

To conclude, assertiveness training for women suffers from at least two practical difficulties. First, assertive behaviour by women, at least in the

---

39 *Op cit*, Rakos, fn 36, p 84.

40 *Op cit*, Rakos, fn 36, p 90.

41 Women who behave assertively, but are perceived as aggressive, may also be perceived as bullies: see O'Donnell, Chapter 4, this volume.

42 *Op cit*, Karsten, fn 31, p 149.

43 *Op cit*, Karsten, fn 31, p 151.

context of employment, does not work in the same way as assertive behaviour by men because it is perceived differently and often negatively. Secondly, even where assertive behaviour is perceived as appropriate, a patriarchal hegemony operates through such mechanisms as tokenism to maintain control with the dominant group.

Conceptual problems of assertiveness training for women

I now want to argue that assertiveness training for women does not sit comfortably within feminist theories. AT for women is based on the assumption that men tend to be assertive and women tend to have an assertiveness deficit.[44] The suggestion that women suffer from an assertiveness deficit that needs correcting implies that women are flawed. This brings AT for women into the heart of feminist theorising. The feminist psychologist Sandra Lipsitz Bem argues that hidden assumptions, which she calls the lenses of gender, perpetuate male power and oppress women. She states:

> The first lens embedded in cultural discourses, social institutions and individual psyches is the lens of *androcentrism*, or male-centeredness. This is not just the historically crude perception that men are inherently superior to women but a more treacherous underpinning of that perception: a definition of males and male experience as a neutral standard or norm and females and female experience as a sex-specific deviation from that norm. It is, thus, not that man is treated as superior and woman as inferior but that man is treated as human and woman as 'other'.[45]

For feminist writer Jane Ussher, it is the view of women as 'other' that has allowed historically, and is continuing to allow, the mistreatment of women; as witches, as madwomen, and as mentally ill.[46] This may seem a long way from apparently civilised courses run supposedly for the benefit of women, but AT for women does have dangerous theoretical underpinnings. AT for women has been advocated in the context of women's health. At a practical level, it has been argued that women who are trained to be assertive are better able to make and effectively communicate healthy decisions in the areas of birth control, fertility, childbirth, medical treatment, smoking, eating, alcohol, sexual health, etc.[47] At a theoretical level, it has been suggested that assertiveness is healthy; that masculinity is associated with assertiveness; and

---

44   It also assumes that assertiveness can be learnt.

45   Bem, SL, *The Lenses of Gender: Transforming the Debate on Sexual Inequality*, 1993, New Haven and London: Yale UP, p 2.

46   Ussher, J, *Women's Madness: Misogyny or Mental Illness?*, 1991, New York, London: Harvester Wheatsheaf. See, in particular, pp 112–15 for coverage of assertiveness training in the context of a critique of behaviour therapy.

47   *Op cit*, Pattenson and Burns, fn 27.

that masculinity is healthy. In mainstream psychology, the 'masculinity hypothesis' – that is, the hypothesis that the more masculine one is, the healthier one will be – is still a valid research topic.[48] This is another example of male experience and the masculine being treated as the norm and female experience and the feminine being treated as 'other'.

The logic of AT for women is that women will benefit from gaining an attribute which is usually associated with masculinity. This brings the theoretical argument in favour of AT for women close to the feminist discourse on androgyny. Sandra Lipsitz Bem was one of the earliest feminist psychologists. Her theoretical and empirical research on androgyny began in 1973 and, in her book published in 1993, she traces the short history of the rise and fall of androgyny in feminist thought. The good thing about the concept of androgyny was that it challenged long standing assumptions about masculinity and femininity in a new way. It was central to the early feminist critique of the gender polarisation within psychology itself. The concept of androgyny suggested that:

> ... whereas it had earlier been assumed that sex should determine the kind of self-concept an individual should develop and the kind of behavior she or he should engage in, now it was being suggested not only that an individual should be free to have her or his own unique blending of temperament and behavior but, even more important, that the very division of attributes and behaviors into the two categories of masculine and feminine was somewhere between problematic and immoral.[49]

Bem quotes the literary scholar Carolyn Heilbrun, writing in 1973:

> I believe that our future salvation lies in a movement away from sexual polarization and the prison of gender toward a world in which individual roles and the modes of personal behavior can be freely chosen. The ideal toward which I believe we should move is best described by the term 'androgyny'. This ancient Greek word ... seeks to liberate the individual from the confines of the appropriate ... It suggests a spectrum upon which human beings choose their places without regard to propriety or custom.[50]

Bem then relates the three criticisms responsible for the swiftness with which androgyny became a dirty word among feminists: first, throughout the history of Western culture, androgyny had been used as a vision of the perfect man: perfect men would be androgynous, but women would still be androcentically defined in relation to men. Secondly, 'although both men and

---

48 See Arrindell, WA *et al*, 'Gender roles in relation to assertiveness and eysenckian personality dimensions: replication with a Spanish population sample' [1997] Sex Roles 36, pp 79–91 for a very recent example of such work.

49 *Op cit*, Bem, fn 45, pp 120–21.

50 *Op cit*, Bem, fn 45, p 121.

men's activities have been the locus of cultural value in almost all times and places, the concept of androgyny by itself does nothing to point this inequality out'.[51]

> Finally, the concept of androgyny reproduces – and thereby reifies – the very gender polarization that it seeks to undercut. It does this by assuming masculinity and femininity to be conceptual givens, if not set personality structures; by emphasizing the complementarity of masculinity and femininity ... and by focusing attention on the male-female distinction itself rather than on, say, the class or power distinction.[52]

The first two criticisms of androgyny as a concept in which feminists can see salvation can, with very little adjustment, become two feminist criticisms of AT for women. First, because AT for women measures women's assertiveness in terms of the assertiveness appropriate in a perfect man, assertive women will still be androcentically defined in relation to men. Secondly, the concept of appropriately assertive women does, by itself, nothing towards highlighting, or dealing with, underlying inequality.

CONCLUSIONS

This chapter has attempted to cover a great deal of ground and may have raised more questions than it has answered. I approached this subject imagining a logical framework linking equal opportunities, staff development and assertiveness training for women. At the midway point in my theoretical exploration, all the normative connections between the three elements appeared to have been made. Equal opportunities *should* permeate into staff development and into women's development training in particular; and, if it works in the ways described above, AT *should be* included in women's development training. My framework for linking equal opportunities to staff development – and, in particular, staff development for women – was not, however, evident in the policies and practices of most Scottish universities; but assertiveness training is being provided, mostly to women, and on the basis that it is especially beneficial to women. In the last section of the chapter I have questioned whether AT is, in fact, valuable for many women and for the cause of feminism.

In the end, the feminist writers who I have turned to in my questioning of AT for women are radical, rather than liberal, ones. It should not be forgotten that the equal opportunities law that is in place in the UK and the EU is liberal, not radical. Behind my radical critique of AT, in the context of equal

---

51 *Op cit*, Bem, fn 45, p 123.
52 *Op cit*, Bem, fn 45, p 124.

opportunities in employment, there lies a radical critique of the liberal approach to equal opportunities.

I went in to AT on the basis that:

One way to achieve equal power with males is to know how to adopt masculine forms of status and power. The learning of verbal and non-verbal expressions of assertive behavior is one effort to acquiring equal status.[53]

However, Wine and Smye continue:

Other ways to create an egalitarian society are to increase the value of feminine forms or to redefine the forms of social power.[54]

The radical feminist case against AT for women as a solution to women's problems is part of the much wider feminist case against bureaucracy.[55] Perhaps, the final conclusion should be that I went into assertiveness training as a liberal feminist, and came out of this process as a radical feminist.

---

53 *Op cit*, Wine and Smye, fn 32, p 361.
54 *Op cit*, Wine and Smye, fn 32, p 361.
55 See Ferguson, KE, *The Feminist Case Against Bureaucracy*, 1984, Philadelphia: Temple UP.

CHAPTER 4

THE SWEAT OF THE BROW OR
THE BREAKING OF THE HEART?[1]

Thérèse O'Donnell

INTRODUCTION

In the last decade, bullying in its many forms has been recognised as a phenomenon which requires tackling and eradication wherever it occurs, be it in schools, old peoples' homes or the workplace. Critics have challenged the recognition of bullying as merely a fashionable 'nervous' 1990s desire by individuals to take on the status of 'victim'.[2] The evidence of complainants who do not report victimisation for fear of stigmatisation challenges this notion.[3] As Frank Davies, of the Health and Safety Commission, noted, 'some organisations seem to be taking the view that stress is not their problem but an individual's'.[4]

Instances of bullying can often be passed off as simply embodying a 'macho management' approach, which is considered an acceptable management strategy when dealing with employees. It is submitted that the terms 'macho' and 'crisis' are interchangeable, as bullying will often occur when an enterprise or a middle ranking individual feels pressure to survive and aggressively communicates this panic to workers.[5] This chapter will begin by considering definitions of bullying and the worth of existing legal provisions (mainly in the fields of tort and employment law) in tackling

---

1   John Ruskin: 'It may be proved, with much certainty, that God intends no man to live in this world without working but it seems to me no less evident that he intends every man to be happy in his work. It is written "in the sweat of thy brow", but it was never written "in the breaking of thy heart".' Quoted by Lord Rea during the Second Reading of the Dignity at Work Bill, Hansard HL Debs Col 762, 4 December 1996.

2   Frank Furedi (a sociologist at the University of Kent), 'I bully, you bully, we are victims' (1997) *The Independent*, 24 August.

3   See the sex discrimination case of Esther McLaughlin, who was moved from department to department and was given new tasks just as she got to grips with a project. She felt unable to criticise the regime under which she worked, as it could have looked as though she was not capable of performing her job. 'Manager wins record £230,000 in sex bias case' (1997) *The Independent*, 11 December.

4   HSE Press Release: C019:97, 20 June 1997.

5   Possibly, in a 'corporate emergency', there may be a justification for putting an employee under strain if they work in a small organisation, the perception being that a larger employer has a certain amount of cushioning to withstand financial hardship which may not be the privilege of a smaller concern.

workplace bullying; then, the possibility of the resurrection of, and improvement upon, the recent Dignity at Work Bill will be analysed. The final section will reflect upon whether the law is the most appropriate weapon to use in the battle against workplace bullying or if the matter is better dealt with by more informal mechanisms.

In giving a feminist perspective on workplace bullying, several preliminary issues must be addressed. Unlike mainstreaming, which concerns bringing the gender dimension into all issues, with bullying, the issue is about taking gender out of the equation; in a bullying case, a complainant does not have to display particular characteristics (other than having been bullied) in order to bring a complaint. Gender issues remain present in bullying but, rather than relating to the intention of the perpetrator, these are of a more demographic nature, for example: how many victims are women, how many bullies are women and how does bullying manifest itself – is it women bullying women? Those females who have struggled to scale the heights of professions 'the hard way' may be unsympathetic to those displaying 'weakness', particularly if it is due to unreasonable strain at work. The boss may feel that the weakness manifested by the other female employee could reflect on the boss and undermine her own position at work. Thus, the boss contrives to distance the victim as the 'other', either by bullying her herself or by refusing to complain on the victim's behalf, displaying no solidarity with the victim and further isolating her.[6] Lyn Jones parallels this isolation with that reminiscent of the kind experienced by battered women and rape victims before reforms of recent times.[7] Alternatively, the young, enthusiastic recruit, unchallenged by bad experiences, may be seen to be more keen and dynamic than the jaded, older female boss. Dare one say the younger employee might be more attractive? (This notion is present in the subtext of many complaints.) The latter theory is less satisfactory, as its premise is that success excludes beauty. It also relies on the stereotyping of the 'bitch boss' and 'one of the boys' clubbiness.[8] A male judiciary may, in fact, be less sympathetic to a male complainant, on the basis that bullying 'toughens up' a sensitive man and, thus, to complain displays failure and a desire to cling to childish, feminine attributes. A failure to satisfactorily undergo this rite of passage renders the man emasculated and somehow unworthy of a remedy. Indeed, Anthony

---

6   In *Stewart v Cleveland Guest Engineering* [1996] ICR 535, an employee complained about pornographic pictures being displayed by males in the workplace. After her complaint, female employees came forward to say that they had no objection to the display of such pictures.

7   Jones, L, 'Bullying at work', 1997, unpublished article. Lyn Jones is the convenor of Northern Action Against Bullying at Work. See, also, *Jones v The Borough Council of Calderdale* (CA) 5 February 1998 (LEXIS).

8   Some female employees complain that the only employees given any credence are those who can participate in 'locker room' conversations and, if female, are bestowed the honorary title of 'new ladettes'.

Ratcliffe, a teacher bullied by his colleagues, indicated that he was embarrassed to have been bullied by a woman.[9]

It has been suggested by some commentators that a woman's chances of being victimised are greater than a man's because her role has, historically, been seen as less important, especially in the office environment. Existing sex and race discrimination legislation serves a particular purpose in cases where sex or race is a motivating factor in discrimination against individuals. However, sexual and class stereotyping (as in 'old boy network'/ 'old school tie' notions) merely represent tiny ingredients in the complex brew of resentment, fear and antagonism that eventually erupts into workplace bullying. Bullying, by contrast, manifests a whole series of prejudices, which encompass the cultural, educational, sexual, racial, disability based, class oriented, personality dominated, multifaceted world in which individuals live and work. The 1975 Sex Discrimination Act and 1976 Race Relations Act filled legal lacunae of the time. As employment lawyers become more sophisticated in their jurisprudence, and as more psychiatric and sociological expert knowledge emerges, law should reflect such advancement. It is submitted that the process of ensuring dignity at work is a three stage one. The first stage has been achieved with the 1970s legislation, the second stage could come with a Dignity at Work Act similar to the Bill sponsored by Lord Monkswell. Such an instrument would offer a more holistic approach to identifying the complexity of the prejudices which seek to thwart others' dignity. The notion of dignity itself indicates that what sufferers are seeking is nothing more than basic human regard for their physical and mental integrity. Ultimately, a sophisticated piece of legislation recognising these advancements could be produced early in the 21st century which would best articulate how, and why, victims suffer a loss of dignity at work and how this can best be remedied.

THE BULLYING ENVIRONMENT

What constitutes bullying?

One interesting characterisation of bullying is as follows:

> Bullying is like an extra-marital fling – thrilling for those doing it but enraging, humiliating and, sometimes, unbearable for those it is done to.[10]

---

9   'Teacher "bullied by staff" wins £100,000' (1998) *The Times*, 17 July.

10 'The human condition: that little bully – was that you?' (1996) *The Independent*, 20 October.

It is impossible exhaustively to list all forms of human behaviour which could take the form of bullying but the following examples are illustrative: unfair and excessive criticism; publicly insulting the victim; ignoring the victim's point of view; constantly changing work targets or setting unrealistic ones; withholding information in order to embarrass him/her; undervaluing efforts; shouting; and abusive behaviour.[11] A 'bad bosses' hot line was instituted by the Trades Union Congress in 1997 and, after just five days, had received 5,000 calls. At least one company had tried to 'cancel Christmas', refusing to allow employees time off over the festive period. Drivers were being forced to work dangerously long hours, contrary to European law. In creating an overall culture of terror, a female boss in a Scottish financial firm shouted at her subordinate, whom she expected to shout, in turn, at her subordinates.[12] In the extreme cases, involving physical abuse, it has been noted that the horror of an act of violence can be matched by the psychological terror of anticipating it.[13] Frank Furedi suggests that some definitions of bullying[14] appear to include what were formerly called office politics or personality clashes but, now, 'a variety of other acts – indiscreet behaviour, clumsy management styles, the refusal to ask a colleague for a drink – are all potentially the act of a pervasive bully'.[15] Such trifles are not experiences cited by aggrieved employees. Instead, the examples given are more akin to persecution and systematic terror, which even Furedi accepts are genuine concerns demanding action. This was the case with Andrea Harrison, a legal trainee who endured outrageous bullying and sexual harassment from a legal executive in her firm.[16] A particularly disturbing aspect was that, although the senior partner was aware of the activities going on, the bully was a substantial fee earner and it was known that the victim could not leave her job without incurring serious financial damage, as she had funded her own education. The notion of financial power determining the imposition of sanctions is extremely worrying for female employees, who are more likely to be in low paid employment and, in particular, for single mothers with heavy financial burdens.

---

11 Examples referred to by Baroness Gould of Potternewton during the Second Reading of the Dignity at Work Bill, Hansard HL Debs Col 757, 4 December 1996.

12 Examples come from, 'Bullying bosses make working life a living hell' (1997) *The Independent*, 22 December.

13 'Words hurt as much as sticks and stones' (1997) *The Independent*, 31 August.

14 He refers to the MSF (Manufacturing, Science and Finance) Union's definition.

15 *Op cit*, Furedi, fn 2.

16 McCabe, M, 'The legalities of bullying' (1997) 147 NLJ 1699.

How pervasive is bullying?

The National Workplace Bullying Advice Line (NWBAL), founded by Tim Field, author of *Bully in Sight*,[17] was instituted in 1996. By 6 October 1998, it had recorded 2,562 calls relating to bullying. 50% of inquiries come from the public sector, 45% from the private sector and 5% from students and those in the voluntary sector. Approximately 90% of reported examples involved manager on subordinate, 8% peer on peer and 2% subordinate on manager. Interestingly, approximately 75% of callers were female. Field considers that this is because females are more likely to be willing to admit to being bullied and are more likely to be motivated to do something about it. Arguably, they are less ashamed than the male employee, who believes himself to be emasculated by admitting to being a victim of bullying. However, it is submitted that, while females may admit abuse to bodies outside of work, they are no more likely to report bullying to their employers because, as noted, women are generally in more occupationally and financially precarious situations than men. What was not clear from NWBAL's study was whether the women reporting bullying were those in subordinate or senior positions. Perhaps women attempting to crash through a glass ceiling would be even less inclined to admit to bullying than those who had no hope of reaching the upper echelons of their occupations.

The study indicated that over 50% of reported bullies are female. Field suggests that, as teaching, nursing and social work have a higher than average percentage of female managers, then the percentage of female bullies in these jobs seems to be increasing – occupational success causes a metamorphosis into a bully. Special helplines have been set up for those working in the nursing and teaching professions, suggesting that these occupations have been particularly affected by the phenomenon of bullying.[18] Both being publicly funded sectors, it is unclear whether the bullying comes from pressure applied by outside agencies or is initiated by 'insiders'.[19]

Bodies working in the field

A great variety of bodies operate in the field of workplace bullying, their work embracing the political, social and cultural. A few bodies deserve particular

---

17 Field, T, *Bully in Sight: How to Predict, Resist, Challenge and Combat Workplace Bullying*, 1996, Wantage: Wessex Press.

18 'Bullied nurses suffer in silence' (1997) *The Independent*, 21 May; 'Heads "threaten teachers with death"' (1996) *The Independent*, 11 April; 'Head in bullying case took overdose' (1996) *The Independent*, 29 May. See, also, Health and Safety Executive, *Managing Work-Related Stress: a Guide for Managers and Teachers in Schools*, 1998, Suffolk: HSE.

19 Extensive statistics produced by the UK National Workplace Bullying Advice Line can be found at web site http://www.successunlimited.co.uk/worbal.htm

mention.[20] The Andrea Adams Trust was set up by Lyn Witheridge[21] and dedicates itself to raising awareness of – and tackling – bullying, advising and supporting victims of bullying, and, most importantly, assisting them so that they may keep their jobs. The Trust 'does not see those who have suffered workplace bullying as everlasting victims but will help them as they work to regain their self-esteem and survive'.[22]

The Campaign Against Bullying at Work (CABAW) is promoted by the MSF and academic work is carried out at Staffordshire University, which is involved in empirical studies on bullying. The Institute of Personnel and Development carried out a ground breaking study which established that one in eight employees suffered bullying and Unison, which is Britain's biggest union, also revealed that two thirds of its members had either experienced or witnessed bullying. The International Harassment Network, which is the professional body for personnel officers and human resource management, regularly runs conferences focusing on the issues of bullying and, also, runs a National Harassment Helpline.[23] The Suzy Lamplugh Trust assists those suffering from bullying, threats to personal safety and stalking. This blending of bullying and harassment displays an interesting overlap, which will be investigated in the section on 'Protection from harassment law'.[24] Additionally, the more established organs, such as the Commission for Racial Equality, the Equal Opportunities Commission and ACAS are also willing to provide guidance.

---

20 See, also, the Countering Bullying Unit at the University of Wales; Janet Samuel's Imperative Bully Support line; Christina Jones' Imperative Bully Support line; Bully Alert UK; CAFAS (Council for Academic Freedom and Academic Standards); Public Concern at Work; Freedom to Care; Scotland's Workplace Bullying Information Line; Beyond Bullying Association Inc. See, also, the UK Stress Network and its newsletter.

21 Witheridge herself raised an action which went to the EAT concerning redundancy and bullying: *Witheridge v Sun Alliance and London Insurance plc* EAT/144/96; EAT/795/96. Ironically, she had been employed to give counselling and personnel advice to others.

22 http://subnet.virtual-pc.com/~ni407290/andrea-adams/philosophy.htm

23 The ALT runs a telephone line for stressed teachers. The rising profile of bullying is reflected in the fact that branches of USDAW have urged the Executive Council to promote an awareness campaign to highlight the issue.

24 The Health and Safety Executive has also shown an interest in workplace bullying by supplying appropriate guidance to employers: Press Release: E100:97, 12 June 1997. It launched a research project in June 1997 to discover what is meant by occupational stress, its pervasiveness and effect on the health of the population. The team at the University of Bristol will involve 17,000 people in the South West of England and is likely to produce a comprehensive analysis of the problem of workplace stress. The Government also has an inter-agency Group on Mental Health in the Workplace, which has produced a resource pack to help train bosses to manage mental health and stress in the workplace.

Profile of bullies

Bullies often claim not to have intended the dire effects of their activities and this may explain the inability on the part of the bully to feel remorse. Arguably, bullies are indifferent to their victims – both as sufferers and as people. To denude individuals of their identities as human beings results in a continuing spiral of inhumanity. It finds many parallels with the mentalities of torturers and sexually predatory attackers, who view their victims as simple objects of gratification for their pleasure – inanimate objects incapable of feeling pain. Thus, the point of focus should be the impact on the victim, not the intention of the perpetrator. To rely on the evidence of the perpetrator's intention would rarely result in a finding in favour of the victim as proving *mala fides* on the part of the perpetrator would be extremely difficult.

Alternatively, bullies themselves may be viewed as victims, who have been stripped of all sensitivity. Unfortunately, if a child bully is 'successful' in getting his/her way, he/she has no reason to change, and sees bullying as a way of obtaining compliance. No experience of meaningful relationships will occur for (and no reason for constructing them be seen by) bullies, who can obtain their ends by familiar routes.[25] Many bullies exhibit common behavioural traits, and a very small sample may identify some recognisable characteristics in individuals.[26] Bullies tend to be divisive and disruptive influences at work, they have a short term focus to the future and a short term memory of the past and live in a 'bubble of the present'. Bullies can often plagiarise and crave recognition for any task undertaken. They can be bereft of empathy, are unwilling to apologise for mistakes, are quick to blame others, can fail to distinguish between assertiveness and aggression, have mood swings and are uncommunicative and unco-operative. Field has drawn a gender distinction between two different types of bullies, considering that women are divisive and manipulative and tend to leave less evidence of their activities, while men are more overtly hostile.[27] Arguably, such a conclusion tends to accept a 'Lady Macbeth' stereotype of women, in particular of professionally ambitious and successful women. It is certainly true that, in the field of workplace crimes of violence, men have a high profile, committing over 80% of such incidents.[28] By contrast, Peter Randall cites an example of a

---

25 'The human condition: that little bully – was that you?' (1996) *The Independent*, 20 October.

26 These examples are taken from 'The serial bully' at web site http://www.successunlimited.co.uk/serial.htm. This page also gives extensive detail on antisocial personality disorder, narcissistic personality disorder, paranoid personality disorder and the avoiding or acceptance of responsibility.

27 'Beware the bullying female boss' (1997) *The Independent on Sunday*, 13 July. It is unclear whether he was referring to women bullying women, or women bullying men and if it causes a difference in behaviour.

28 Finding from the US Department of Justice and the Bureau of Justice detailed in Randall, P, *Adult Bullying*, 1997, London: Routledge, p 47.

female administrative officer who appeared to extend a 'helping hand' to her assistant, allowing her flexible hours and time off to fit in with child care and ensuring training for her. However, during her appraisal with a senior personnel officer, the assistant was criticised for excessive absenteeism, seeking excessive instruction and favours, allowing her family to take precedence and, interestingly, for being overly familiar with her supervisor. It would appear that the supervisor had allowed the assistant to 'hang herself' in front of her seniors, which certainly hints at the manipulative bully. As far as being more manipulative is concerned, perhaps women would be more likely than men to fall into this category of 'charitable bully'. However, given the paucity of reliable information in this area, any conclusions on gender tendency are flawed. Interestingly, Field says that it is his impression that bullies prefer same sex victims on the basis that one knows one's own gender best, and this creates difficulties of proof under the Sex Discrimination Act.

EXISTING LAW

Vicarious liability at common law

Vicarious liability rests on the premise that an employer is liable for the wrongful acts of an employee. This protects third parties who have suffered through a negligent act of an employee and may choose to sue the insured employer.[29] This option can be open to an employee aggrieved by the action of another employee. A plaintiff must establish that the culprit was 'acting within the course of his employment'. If he/she was off 'on a frolic of his own', then there can be no claim against the employer.[30] The 'nub of the test' is 'whether the unauthorised wrongful act of the servant is so connected with that which he was employed to do as to be a mode of doing it'.[31] Another way of putting it is that an act is within the course of employment if it is 'either (1) a wrongful act authorised by the master, or (2) a wrongful and unauthorised mode of doing some act authorised by the master'.[32] In the context of bullying, an employer may argue that he did not employ someone to bully, he employed them to work a lathe and bullying while working could not be considered to be a method of turning the lathe. Four particular employment

---

29 Employers' Liability (Compulsory Insurance) Act 1969.

30 *Joel v Morison* (1834) 6 C & P 501, p 503.

31 *Jones v Tower Boot Co Ltd* [1997] IRLR 168. See, also, *Bartonshill Coal Co v McGuire* (1858) 3 Macq 300: every act which is done by a servant in the course of his duty is regarded as done by his master's orders and, consequently, is the same as if it were the master's own act.

32 Heuston, REV, and Buckley, RA *Salmond and Heuston on Law of Torts*, 21st edn, 1996, London: Sweet & Maxwell, p 443.

law cases have examined the relationship between common law and employment law standards regarding vicarious liability.

In the case of *Irving v Post Office*, a postman whose job permitted him to write on letters for the purpose of ensuring that they were properly dealt with, wrote abusive and racist remarks on letters addressed to his Jamaican neighbours.[33] The Court of Appeal decided that he was not acting within the course of his employment. His act had been one of personal malevolence; his employment gave him the opportunity for misconduct but this did not mean that misconduct was part of his duties. This position was revisited in the case of *Jones v Tower Boot Co Ltd*,[34] which concerned s 32(1) of the Race Relations Act 1976. The employee in question was aged 16 and had suffered a catalogue of abuse (including physical violence) from his fellow employees. He had been moved after reporting a burning incident but he suffered further abuse and chose to resign. He claimed his employers were liable, on the basis that the abusive employees were 'acting within the course of employment'. The Court of Appeal adopted the view that *Irving* was not to be relied upon, as it did not mention s 32(1) and there was no evidence of it in pleadings before the court.[35] *Irving* simply decided 'course of employment' for common law principles, not for the proper interpretation of s 32(1). The Court of Appeal settled for a 'purposive construction' of the provision and indicated that 'course of employment' should be construed within the natural meaning of those everyday words. A very clear distinction was drawn by Waite LJ, when he indicated that an employer's authority is essential when considering his liability under vicarious liability.[36] By contrast, under s 32(1) of the Race Relations Act 1976, the employer's knowledge and approval are irrelevant to the question of liability.[37] If a common law interpretation were taken, it would mean that the more outrageous the act of discrimination, the less likely it would be considered to be within the 'course of employment'. This was untenable, given the object of deterrence within the 1976 Act and the defence provided for employers.

The Court of Appeal in *Waters v Commissioner of Police of the Metropolis*[38] reached a different conclusion from that in *Jones*. The applicant was a female police officer who alleged that, while off duty, she was seriously sexually assaulted by another off duty (male) officer in the section house. Following an internal police inquiry, no action was taken against the male officer. The

---

33 [1987] IRLR 289.

34 [1997] IRLR 168.

35 *Ibid*, para 20.

36 *Ibid*, para 35, *per* Waite LJ.

37 Other distinctions were also pointed to, such as the greater range of remedies available under statute (eg, injury to feelings) than under common law and the total absence from the common law of a defence of 'reasonable steps' under s 32(3).

38 [1997] IRLR 589.

appellant alleged that, subsequently, she was subjected to harassment, unfair treatment and victimisation. She alleged that this treatment led to ill health, including mental illness and post traumatic stress disorder (PTSD). She raised two claims; one under the head of sex discrimination and one under negligence (see below). Her sex discrimination claim was rejected on the basis that the alleged sexual assault had not been committed in the course of employment. There seems, here, to be a monism between the Sex Discrimination Act and vicarious liability standards, which had been specifically rejected in the context of the Race Relations Act in *Jones*. This is odd, as the two instruments comprise differing aspects of a common code against discrimination. Waite LJ referred to *Jones* and held that – on the basis that both officers were off duty, the alleged perpetrator lived elsewhere and he was a social visitor to her room in the section house with no working connection – there could be no finding of liability.[39]

The case of *Burton and Rhule v De Vere Hotels Ltd* involved waitresses who had been subjected to a barrage of racist abuse during a performance by Bernard Manning.[40] The two waitresses claimed a 'detriment' under s 4(2)(c) of the Race Relations Act 1976, 'detriment' having been defined as putting a worker at a disadvantage. Could the employer, however, be held liable for the actions of a third party? The industrial tribunal was at pains to point out that s 4(2) does not impose strict liability upon the employer and, therefore, it was not enough that the employees suffered racial harassment during their employment. The Employment Appeal Tribunal refused to accept the industrial tribunal's assertion that an employee was required to establish that their employer subjected them to a detriment on racial grounds.[41] It accepted that, in practice, where an employer is shown to have actual knowledge that racial harassment of an employee was taking place, or deliberately or recklessly closed its eyes to the fact that it was taking place, if it did not act reasonably to prevent it, it would readily be found to have subjected its employee to the detriment of racial harassment.[42] However, the court rejected the notion that foresight and culpability were the means by which the employer's duty was to be defined. It felt that, given that the duty in the statute was on the employer not to subject an employee to racial harassment,

---

39 For a highly critical view of this case, see Buckley, L, 'Vicarious liability and employment discrimination' (1997) 26 ILJ 158. Cf *Stubbs v Chief Constable Lincolnshire Police and Others* Case No: 38395/96 (1997). The industrial tribunal in this case concluded that conduct during a party held in a public house could be considered to be within the course of employment. That incident, taken together with a similar previous incident, formed components in a course of conduct undertaken by one of the respondents. See [1999] IRLR 81 (EAT) dismissing appeal.

40 [1997] ICR 1.

41 *ibid*, p 7, para A. For a stinging criticism of this case, see Editorial, 'Did you hear the one about?' (1996) Employment Law Newsletter 1, Issue 8/96, 28 October, p 1.

42 This point was also an element in *Jones v Tower Boot* because the employer had knowledge of the employee's behaviour and allowed it to continue.

the question turned on the meaning of 'subjecting' and it was held that 'subjecting' referred to issues of 'control'; that is, an individual can only allow, or cause, something to happen in circumstances where he/she can control whether it happens or not. The appeal tribunal did not wish to graft tests of foresight from tort on to statutory torts of sexual and racial discrimination and, indeed, indicated its displeasure at this being done.[43] It went on to state that, if a tribunal found that the employer could, by the application of good employment practice, have prevented the harassment or reduced the extent of it, then the employer has subjected the employee to the harassment.[44] Events within the banqueting hall were under the control of the two assistants who, had they been properly instructed by the hotel manager, would have alleviated the situation of the waitresses and, thus, the applicants' claims were successful.

The *Burton* judgment, in respect of actual or deliberate or reckless ignorance, would be particularly helpful as a test within the concept of any statute to be drafted regarding bullying. An employer would be obliged to 'keep his house in order' and could not hide behind 'ignorance'. Additionally, an employer with control could not deny responsibility for putting an employee in a vulnerable situation. While vicarious liability may, at a stretch, protect the vulnerable employee against other employees in the context of bullying, it does not, prima facie, protect against third parties' actions. This gap has been plugged by *Burton* and it is essential for that to be employed in the context of bullying, either by way of development of bullying case law in the future (and see the case of *Chessington*),[45] or in any bespoke legislation. The point has been made that the 'reasonable steps' defence provided in s 32(3) of the Race Relations Act and s 41(3) of the Sex Discrimination Act, taken together with *Jones*, *Burton* and *Chessington*, will require employers to develop an active policy with regard to all forms of harassment.[46] This may, ultimately, lead to a more general harassment code than exists at present.[47]

---

43 The EAT made the point, at [1997] ICR 1, p 10, paras C–D, that lack of possible foresight and the unexpected nature of an event might be relevant to the question of whether an event was under the employer's control. However, foresight of events, or lack thereof could not be determinative of whether the events were under the employer's control. See, for comment, Monaghan, K and Javaid, M, 'No laughing matter' (1997) 147 NLJ 350.

44 [1997] ICR 1, p 10, paras E–F.

45 *Chessington World of Adventures Ltd v Reed* [1997] IRLR 556 followed *Burton*: the employer was held directly liable for a campaign of harassment and ostracism inflicted upon a transsexual employee in circumstances where the employer was aware of, but took no steps to prevent, the behaviour of employees over which the employer could exercise control. In the alternative, it was stated that the employer could have been liable on the basis of vicarious liability.

46 Desmond, H, 'New developments in anti-discrimination law' (1997) 147 NLJ 1216, p 1217.

47 While an employer may be liable for discrimination, employees who aid such harassment may be subject to separate financial liability: *Armitage, Marsden and HM Prison Service v Johnson* [1997] IRLR 162.

Law of negligence

This section concerns the possibility of a bullied employee suing an employer for breach of his duty of care towards that employee. This duty on the part of an employer was established in early case law[48] and has also found expression as an implied term of the contract of employment.[49] While cases regarding physical injury were situations where the proximity of duty, breach and loss were clear (for example, industrial deafness claims), the relationship between these three elements in the case of psychological injury was less certain. This position was clarified in the case of *Walker*.[50] Many bullied employees cite unreasonable working demands, targets and hours being asked of them and it might be of interest to look at cases which have considered issues of so called 'occupational stress'.[51] While there is a certain amount of common ground between the two categories (bullying and occupational stress), they can be conceptually different. Any distinction, inevitably, rests on a clear definition of bullying. If the concept of bullying is extended to ignoring the beleaguered victim's viewpoint (for example, complaints), then this could well result in a monism between the two categories. On a common sense interpretation, it would seem that bullying often involves malevolence, which tends to be absent in occupational stress cases. However, if situations of occupational stress are considered to occur in cases where superiors are concerned only with work targets being met and not with a humane treatment of employees, then such disregard borders on definitions found within bullying. Perhaps a distinction lies in the fact that, with occupational stress, there would seem to be no triumphal afterglow which can be felt by a post-episodic bully – either by way of self-aggrandisement or by projecting a certain self-created image in the eyes of others.

John Walker, a social worker, suffered a nervous breakdown when his case load increased to impossible levels with no extra staffing provision, notwithstanding his attempts to seek extra staff to assist him. After his breakdown, in November 1986, he returned to work in March 1987 but no relief on his workload was forthcoming and he suffered a second nervous breakdown in May 1988. He sued Northumberland County Council. UNISON's solicitors argued that the nervous breakdown was caused by the council's negligence in exposing him to unreasonable stress which could have

---

48 *Wilsons and Clyde Coal Co Ltd v English* [1938] AC 57.
49 *Johnstone v Bloomsbury Health Authority* [1991] IRLR 118.
50 *Walker v Northumberland County Council* [1995] IRLR 35.
51 For a comprehensive overview of the whole area of stress and employer liability, see Earnshaw, J and Cooper, C, *Stress and Employer Liability*, 1996, London: IPD.

been avoided. He won his action and, prior to the council's appeal being heard, the matter settled for £175,000.[52] His employer was liable for the second breakdown because it had knowledge of his first illness and, therefore, his susceptibility, but not for his first breakdown, as it could not be aware of his likelihood to suffer one.

In *Johnstone v Bloomsbury Health Authority*,[53] a senior house officer's contract required him to work a 40 hour week and to be 'on call' for a further 48 hours. Consequently, he claimed that he suffered various adverse effects on his health, including psychological problems. *Johnstone* referred to an implied contractual term requiring his employer not to prejudice his health and safety. Could the express term 'trump' the implied term? Usually, the answer would be in the positive. The majority found that, within the express term, there was a discretion to the employer which then came under the implied term's influence.[54] Interestingly, one of the judges stated that 'those that cannot stand the heat, should stay out of the kitchen', echoing many of the arguments workplace bullying opponents use. Unfortunately, this case, which could have been a landmark occupational stress decision, settled before it reached the stage of a court hearing.

The case of *Ballantyne v Strathclyde Regional Council* (unreported) also involved a social worker under immense stress, less due to overwork and more due to poor treatment at the hands of her superior. She complained about her treatment to the council but its response was long in coming and unsatisfactory. Following this complaint, her life was made a misery by her superior and, as her health declined, Ballantyne sought to keep her employers informed of this. She was eventually off work ill and, although promised an improvement in conditions, when she returned, the situation had not changed. The case settled (for £66,000), on the basis that the council felt that there had been shortcomings in the way Ballantyne was treated.[55] McLean

---

52 'Stressed worker finally wins damages': http://www.unison.org.uk/archive/f32/stress.html

53 [1991] IRLR 118.

54 For comment on the *Johnstone* case, see Dolding, L and Fawlk, C, 'Judicial understanding of the contract of employment' (1992) 55 MLR 562. An unsuccessful attempt had been made to regulate this area in the Junior Doctors (Hours of Work) Bill. See, also, the later decision, *St Budeaux Royal British Legion v Cropper*, EAT, March 1996, Commercial Lawyer 55, where a reduction in working hours was held to constitute a breach of the implied term of mutual trust and confidence because, while the implied term did not override the express term, it did limit employer discretion. This was considered to be a constructive dismissal issue; referred to in Ramage, R, 'Mobbing in the workplace', http://www.law-office.demon.co.uk/mobbing1.htm

55 See McLean, A, 'When stress fractures', *Reparation*, Issue 12, November 1996 and Issue 13, January 1997. This is very similar to the case of Anthony Ratcliffe, who obtained more than £100,000 damages from his former employers. He returned to work after a minor breakdown, then, subsequently, suffered another breakdown. It was claimed that a support plan worked out for him by the council had not been properly implemented. The council did not accept negligence on its part or that a breach of contract had occurred as a result of the head teacher's actions. See 'Teacher "bullied by staff" wins £100,000' (1998) *The Times*, 17 July.

suggests that the possible lines of argument would have revolved around a failure to provide a safe system of work *or* vicarious liability for the senior officer *or* a failure to handle properly the employee's complaints. Unfortunately, none of these arguments were aired for consideration. This has been called a stress case, but it is submitted that, given the type of behaviour to which Ms Ballantyne was subjected, it fits better with the notion of bullying and, at the very least, must be considered as blending elements of both bullying and occupational stress. *Walker* and *Johnstone* show a desire just to 'get the job done' and, therefore, seem more like occupational stress cases.

The problem for the bullied employee is that, for a claim in negligence to succeed, issues of foreseeability must be satisfied. While foreseeability may be present in the professions that routinely deal with traumas such as the Hillsborough football disaster[56] and the Kings Cross fire disaster (although this raises separate problems regarding professional rescuers), the difficulty lies in locating other occupations where workplace stress may be foreseeable;[57] an employer could argue that it cannot foresee what may be an invisible injury. Sometimes, employers may be well aware of the suffering of an employee, as in the case of Andrea Harrison, referred to earlier, where the senior partner 'turned a blind eye' on the basis of financial decisions. Generally, however, it is in the nature of bullying to be covert and it is, very definitely, in the nature of the suffering to be covert. This internalising of suffering raises very interesting questions. It may be said that, if an employee has unreasonable demands made of them then, on a 'reasonable man' basis, harm must be foreseen as a distinct possibility. If we take the situation of an employer who has put an employee in a situation working with someone they know tends to adopt aggressive practices, then, it is submitted, the aggrieved employee has a claim against the employer on the basis of negligence. The employer has the power to place employees in different departments and, so, has control over what the employees are exposed to. As noted, exposing the employer to liability via issues of 'control' has been acknowledged.[58] If the employer does not know of an aggressive atmosphere, then the question is whether the employer 'ought to have known' or if it was part of his duty to investigate the situation. Such an investigation could provide the employer with a defence in any subsequent action. The views of the Health and Safety Executive (HSE) on this point would seem to indicate that an employer is

---

56 Nervous shock resulting from negligence in the context of employment was considered in *Frost v Chief Constable of South Yorkshire* [1997] 1 All ER 540. The decision was reversed in the House of Lords: *White v Chief Constable of South Yorks* [1999] IRLR 110.

57 Studies indicate that military personnel, transport workers, workers in the financial sector, offshore oil and gas industry (among others) can be affected by work trauma. See the HSE Press Release of E82:98, 20 April 1998 detailing the report 'Workplace Trauma and Management' produced for the HSE.

58 *Burton and Rhule v De Vere Hotels Ltd* [1997] ICR 1.

obliged to show some initiative.[59] This will be a question of fact.[60] The other problem can be that – even if an employer makes inquiries of an employee – because of the stigma attached to 'not hacking it', an employee may deny that there is anything wrong and go to quite the opposite extreme to allay suspicions, endangering a future action for a plaintiff.[61] This situation finds parallels in the reactions of rape victims following their attacks. It is now received wisdom that not every victim will physically fight off an attacker, vocally publicise what has happened or weep endlessly. There is a fairly widespread acceptance that any reaction to such an attack is valid and in no way can an unusual manifestation retrospectively belittle the previous incident. Smart[62] comments on Rowland's work in the field of rape trials, which suggests that expert witness evidence on rape responses often help secure convictions.[63] The problem with this strategy is judicial resistance to so called 'psy' (psychiatrists and psychologists) expert witnesses' testimonies. However, this problem is not the one with which to be concerned in the field of looking to employer inquiry as to the wellbeing of employees. Using an expert witness at trial or tribunal stage is locking the stable door too late. Instead, the best use of expert's knowledge can be made by making employers aware of the range of warning signs displayed by a victimised employee. This provides some measure of obligation on a 'bad employer' but protection for a 'good employer', who will make inquiries to check on employee wellbeing. Clearly, a measure of discretion will be inbuilt for the 'good employer' who, having discharged an obligation, can do no more, and there has to be a recognition of the 'stonewall' reaction which an employer cannot be faulted for failing to notice or penetrate. In the case of *Petch*,[64] in the absence of any warning signs of a breakdown or of the workload carrying this risk, then there could be no finding of liability against the employers. Unfortunately, to succeed in a personal injury action, a bullied employee must be suffering from a recognised psychiatric illness, such as post traumatic stress disorder, not merely anxiety and, thus, will be extremely ill. Any remedy in these circumstances can have only a palliative effect.

---

59   The Health and Safety Executive, *Violence at Work – A Guide for Employers*, 1996, Suffolk: HSE, gives practical advice to help employers find out if violence is a problem for their staff and, if it is, how best to deal with it.

60   *Op cit*, Earnshaw and Cooper, fn 51, p 36, state that, in the case of 'eggshell skulls', if there exists a particular susceptibility on the part of the employee, and this could not be foreseen by the employer, then s/he will not be liable. If s/he becomes aware of the susceptibility of the employee, then liability will accrue if it is foreseeable that the employee will suffer such harm.

61   *Petch v Customs and Excise Commission* [1993] ICR 789. This may also raise interesting questions in the context of the defences of *volenti non fit injuria* and contributory negligence.

62   Smart, C, *Feminism and the Power of Law*, 1991, London: Routledge.

63   Rowland, J, *Rape: The Ultimate Violation*, 1986, London: Pluto.

64   *Petch v Customs and Excise Commissioners* [1993] ICR 789.

An attempt was made in *Waters* to reconcile it with the *Frost* decision (subsequently reversed), premised on the idea that there was a duty on an employer to provide a safe system of work (that is, a duty to safeguard against oppressive behaviour and bullying) and to maintain a relationship of trust and confidence.[65] Evans LJ likened the position of an aggrieved employee to that of a citizen who had suffered, on the basis of *Hill v Chief Constable of West Yorkshire*[66] and *Calveley v Chief Constable of Merseyside*.[67] That is, the female officer could not found a claim in negligence against the Commissioner or her senior officers in the circumstances, in so far as she had relied on their responses or failures to respond to the various complaints which she had made.[68] However, such a contention arises from case law concerning police response to civilian complaints about investigations.[69] It is hardly appropriate that the same gloss which was applied to protect against defensive practices regarding the police relationship with the public should be applied to their duty of care to their own employees. It is effectively saying that the police force is in a unique position regarding its employees, in that it owes them no higher duty than that offered to the general public.

An employer has a common law obligation to provide competent fellow employees. If they are incompetent, then an employer may dismiss the culprit. A breach in this case is distinct from that of vicarious liability in that the employee's conduct does not have to fall within 'the course of employment'. Many bullies will often claim that they only intended their insults, jibes and physical assaults to be part of the jokey 'rough and tumble' of life (particularly true in manual jobs). Notwithstanding this, there is still an expectation that an employer will take steps to eradicate prohibited behaviour,[70] although a failure to curb a one-off example of horseplay is unlikely to entail a breach of the employer's duty.[71]

While the Employment Rights Act 1996 contains provisions safeguarding the position of employees who take certain actions on health and safety grounds, the main body of law in this area is the specific 1974 legislation. Under s 2(1) of the Health and Safety at Work Act 1974, employers have a responsibility to ensure, as far as is reasonably practicable, the health, safety

---

65 [1997] IRLR 589, para 57, *per* Evans LJ.

66 [1989] 1 AC 53.

67 [1989] 1 AC 1228.

68 There was also concern about judicial inquiry into police disciplinary affairs. Cf *Bracebridge Engineering Ltd v Darby* [1990] IRLR 289: failure to take a complaint seriously or to make a proper investigation was held to be a fundamental breach of contract by the employer, justifying the employee in resigning and claiming unfair dismissal.

69 *Hill v Chief Constable*; although see, now, *Osman v UK* Case No: 87/1997/871/1083, decision of the European Court of Human Rights, 28 October 1998.

70 *Hudson v Ridge Manufacturing Co Ltd* [1957] 2 QB 348.

71 Jones, MA, *Textbook on Torts*, 6th edn, 1998, London: Blackstone, p 253, referring to *Smith v Crossley Bros Ltd* (1951) 95 SJ 655.

and welfare at work of all their employees.[72] The HSE guidelines on stress at work state that stress should be treated like any other health hazard. Employers should take care over 'the way work is organised, the way people deal with each other at work or from day to day demands placed on their workplace'.[73] This extends to both the physical and mental welfare of employees. For an employer to rebut evidence of non-compliance with a duty under the Health and Safety at Work Act 1974, he must show, on the balance of probabilities, that it was not reasonably practicable for him, in the circumstances, to comply. Under s 2(2)(c), the employer is obliged to provide information, instruction, training and supervision so as to ensure employees' health and safety. As Earnshaw and Cooper point out, this implies that employers must first familiarise themselves with sources of stress at work and the steps that can be taken to alleviate it.[74] Indeed, employer knowledge is a matter dealt with in the Management of Health and Safety at Work Regulations 1992.[75] The Code of Practice accompanying the Regulations states that:

(a)   a hazard is something with the potential to cause harm (this can include substances or machines, methods of work and other aspects of work organisation);

(b)   risk expresses the likelihood that the harm from a particular hazard is realised;

(c)   the extent of risk; that is, the number of people who might be exposed and the consequences for them.

Earnshaw and Cooper make the point that the Regulations will require employers to:

(1)   make themselves aware, through current literature, of the sources of stress at work and of how these may be affecting their own organisation;

(2)   assess risks to the mental health of their workforce;

(3)   make arrangements for putting into practice the necessary preventive and protective measures;

(4)   carry out, where appropriate, a health surveillance;

(5)   give adequate information and training about risks.

The often covert nature of bullying makes this obligation to investigate a particularly onerous one for employers, highlighted by the fact that a failure

---

72   For a consideration of what is meant by 'reasonably practicable', see *West Bromwich Building Society Ltd v Townsend* [1983] ICR 257.

73   Health and Safety Executive, *Stress at Work: A Guide for Employers*, 1995, Suffolk: HSE, cited in *op cit*, Earnshaw and Cooper, fn 51, pp 50–51.

74   *Op cit*, Earnshaw and Cooper, fn 51, p 51.

75   These regulations oblige employers to carry out risk assessments in order to identify hazards and to take appropriate preventative or protective measures to remove or reduce them.

to fulfil a duty under the Regulations will normally attract criminal liability. Many firms have introduced health and safety policy statements which deal with issues of stress, long working hours, working at night and action to be taken in the event of fatigue.[76] While these steps are encouraging in the area of combating bullying, further steps, possibly by legislation, are required.[77]

Dismissal

The dismissal of a bully will usually only be undertaken as a last resort. This remedy is a double edged sword. If an employee is perceived to have caused another employee's dismissal then, perversely, the victimisation may intensify. By contrast, a sacked bully may feel well placed to pursue an unfair dismissal action. Under s 98(4) of the Employment Rights Act 1996, in judging whether an employer acted reasonably or unreasonably in treating as sufficient a reason for dismissing an employee, principles of equity and the substantial merits of the case will be considered. The analysis of a dismissal is a two stage process considering both procedure[78] and substance. A certain latitude is afforded: if a reasonable employer might dismiss, then it will be fair, notwithstanding that not every employer would take the same view.[79] The employer must show that, among other things, he investigated the matter thoroughly, warnings were given (particularly relevant in the case of persistent bullying) and the imposition of the sanction was both proportional and consistent.[80] It may well be that, when a bully is confronted with his/her behaviour and admits that he/she has a problem, such an individual may wish to seek help to alleviate it. Those who believe that bullies are also victims might argue that it would seem harsh to dismiss an employee who wishes to redeem him/herself and, if dismissed, this employee would possibly have a successful claim against his employer. [81]

---

76 Lord Haskel, Hansard HL Debs Col 763, 4 December 1996.

77 In its early days, the Act was a powerful instrument embodying change; however, there have been virtually no prosecutions under it which have resulted in managers going to prison.

78 *Polkey v AE Dayton Services Ltd* [1988] ICR 142; [1987] IRLR 503.

79 *British Leyland (UK) Ltd v Swift* [1981] IRLR 91.

80 Generally, see *BHS v Burchell* [1980] ICR 303 and *Monie v Coral Racing Ltd* [1980] IRLR 464. This is particularly significant where bullying is going at different levels or over a protracted period of time.

81 In extreme cases, an employer may dismiss an employee summarily for gross misconduct. *Refund Rentals v McDermott* [1977] IRLR 59 suggests that, although rare, it is possible to dismiss summarily a long time after the event – this could prove particularly useful in cases of extreme bullying where the victim has been too frightened to speak out.

What of the employee who becomes ill due to bullying and then is dismissed due to ill health? Susan Cochran pursued a personal injury claim against her former firm.[82] Her female boss refused to meet her, criticised her appearance and duplicated her work with another employee. After a while, Ms Cochran became ill and her doctor signed her off work for six weeks, during which time she was sacked. Her boss had claimed that she had been unco-operative and was unable to do her job. She won her unfair dismissal and wrongful dismissal cases when the company settled out of court for about £20,000. The general rule in dismissals due to ill health is that the employer should treat the matter sensitively and sympathetically. It is obliged to make inquiries about how long the illness is likely to last and, if a stress related illness, the employer might ask what caused such a downturn in the employee's health and, thereby, discover bullying. This inquiry must not be lip service and only exceptionally would the absence of consultation allow for a fair dismissal.[83] This is, also, a case where some education of employers or personnel officers as to how to approach the matter delicately with a victim would be useful. A very similar set of inquiries will be required in the context of dismissal for absenteeism. A survey by the Industrial Society found that absence rates in the public and voluntary sector had risen by 25% in the last three years (because of bullying).[84] A failure to make such standard inquiries could ultimately backfire on the employer in an unfair dismissal finding.

Under s 95(1)(c) of the Employment Rights Act 1996, a bullied employee can pursue a claim for constructive dismissal by reason of the employer's conduct. The case of *Western Excavating v Sharp*[85] indicated that, without a fundamental breach of contract, there could be no constructive dismissal.[86] This was problematic for employees: if they were being simply asked to increase their workload, rather than do a 'different' job, this would not come within the definition of constructive dismissal. Alternatively, if an employee endured a variation in their contract for some time, he/she could be deemed to have accepted it and would be debarred from claiming constructive dismissal. However,[87] within an implied term of the employment contract, an employer has a duty to maintain a relationship of mutual trust and confidence with his employees. A breach of the implied term can fulfil the test of *Western*

---

82 'Bullied' (1997) *The Independent*, 2 August.

83 *Eclipse Blinds Ltd v Wright* [1992] IRLR 133.

84 'Like school, only worse: is that your office?' (1997) *The Independent*, 27 April. In the US, it is estimated that workplace aggression caused 500,000 employees to miss 1,751,000 days of work annually. See *op cit*, Randall, fn 28, p 48.

85 [1978] ICR 221.

86 For example, an employer attempting to unilaterally change the terms of the contract by increasing hours or changing duties – changes which are not permitted under the contract. See Pitt, G, *Employment Law*, 3rd edn, 1997, London: Sweet & Maxwell.

87 *Post Office v Roberts* [1980] IRLR 347.

Excavating. Many of the cases which have been successful in this way illustrate bullying, such as swearing at employees[88] and giving an employee a 'dressing down' in front of other employees.[89] Interestingly, the persistent grinding down of an employee's will can be seen in the case of *Lewis v Motorworld*, where an employee withstood constant and unfounded criticism and threats of dismissal from the employer.[90] The Court of Appeal accepted that the cumulative effect of such behaviour could break the implied term, which is, effectively, speaking in the language of bullying.

Prima facie, a bullied employee would seem already to be protected under dismissal law, so why enact a new piece of legislation? Various problems with constructive dismissal as a legal route for bullying victims were pointed out during the Second Reading of the Dignity at Work Bill. First, the employee has to resign, with no guarantee of re-employment. This seems particularly unfair, given that the victim has been persecuted and, additionally, loses his/her source of financial support. Additionally, he/she is doing what the bully wants them to do. This occurred in the case of one individual who, following indirect abuse and, ultimately, physical abuse from fellow employees, called in the police. His employer demanded that he continue working alongside the assailant. He felt he had to resign and, although ultimately successful at a tribunal, while the perpetrators continued working, he was unemployed for two years before finding a new job.[91] Secondly, compensation is limited and, arguably, the test of a breakdown in mutual trust and confidence is still a fairly exacting test, which caters only for situations which employers have allowed, or caused, to spiral beyond the reparable. The point of bullying legislation is to 'nip it in the bud', with constructive dismissal remaining available as a safety net remedy.

Sex and race discrimination law

Many of the cases involving bullying may include an element of sex and race discrimination and, so, are already covered by the 1975 and 1976 Acts. The drawback with using this legislation is that the problem may not be appropriately identified. There are, of course, cases where it is the sex of the worker which is the motivating factor. In one such case (see below), a female was treated badly by her fellow fire fighters because she was a woman. To insist that such cases be treated as 'ungendered' bullying cases is to ignore the

---

88 *Palmanor v Cedron* [1978] ICR 1008.
89 *Hilton International v Protopapa* [1990] IRLR 316.
90 [1985] IRLR 465.
91 'Bullies – not just a problem for kids: a new programme exposes harassment in the workplace' (1997) *The Independent*, 21 August.

source and nature of the problem and, arguably, to deal with it, therefore, inadequately. Conversely, however, where a female employee is badly treated for a reason unrelated to her sex, if she seeks a remedy under the 1975 Act, she is doomed to failure, since she will be unable to prove that she was subjected to a detriment because of her sex.

Tania Clayton was a female fire fighter in Hereford and Worcester Fire Service.[92] Her colleagues mistreated her because she was a female fire fighter. If they perceived her as a threat, they did so on the basis that she was a woman who was good at their job. Their treatment of her[93] was not an 'initiation' into final membership of the watch, it was her passport to leaving the service, that is, an exclusionary practice in both the present and future tenses. Her sex was the whole *raison d'être* for her treatment. To call this bullying in a gender free but personal sense is completely to miss the point. Bullying gets at 'you', the individual, whereas sex, race and religious discrimination targets an individual as a member of a group. It is essential to establish such bigoted reasoning underpinning the perpetrator's actions. With bullying, however, motive should be irrelevant and a tribunal should be concerned only with the fact, manifestation and effect of bullying. A claimant must, otherwise, raise an action on a inappropriate ground, having dubious prospects of success, as shown in the case of Ms Metta MacLeod, a librarian at the University of Glasgow. She could prove bullying but not sex discrimination and so was unsuccessful.[94] It may be argued that to introduce a Bullying Act would provide a two tier system for weak sex and race discrimination claims, so that, if the reason for harassment could not be shown to be either the sex or race of the complainant, a more general (catch all) claim could be lodged. Some critics might argue that an action which depends entirely on the reaction of the victim rather than the motives of the perpetrators is unacceptable as a legal strategy. On the other hand, even in sexual harassment, the harasser may not be consciously aware of his reasons and motive is irrelevant to direct sex discrimination.

Protection from harassment law

Section 145 of the Criminal Justice and Public Order Act 1994 makes it an offence to cause 'intentional harassment, alarm or distress' using threatening, abusive or insulting language or behaviour or using disorderly behaviour.

---

92 'Fire fighter who was harassed wins £200,000' (1997) *The Independent*, 18 March. This was a sex discrimination case; the applicant received the largest non-military settlement ever awarded.

93 Eg, forcing her to sit on a turntable ladder 100 feet in the air and spinning it round for more than an hour, in an attempt to break her confidence.

94 (1999) *The Herald*, 25 February.

Being a criminal sanction, this requires a high standard of proof and, requiring police assistance, is not really an action open to a private individual. Financially, this law provides no remedy for an employee nor a possibility of re-employment. It is also highly unlikely, as it is with the Protection from Harassment Act, that any court would imprison an employee or employer for a breach of the Act, on the basis that it is not really the purpose for which the Act was envisaged.

If an employee inflicts a personal injury on another employee, there seems to be little doubt that the aggrieved employee would be able to pursue a claim for battery against the perpetrator. All that is required is an intention to commit the act – the intention to inflict an injury is not necessary[95] – but the instances of actual physical violence are few; rather, omnipresent tension and constant demands are more likely to be the mechanism for bullying. In the case of verbal taunts, this could be pursued under a claim for assault, providing immediate force is anticipated by the victim.[96] However, it may not be financially worthwhile to pursue a claim against an individual employee and, instead, either the victim may wish to claim against the employer or may wish recognition of the fact that the employer did nothing to ameliorate his situation.

There is evidence that the Dignity at Work Bill was intended as the workplace equivalent to the Protection from Harassment Act 1997.[97] Since the Bill was unsuccessful, is there scope for allowing the Protection from Harassment Act to step into the breach, given that it does not specifically exclude workplace harassment?[98] This Act creates both civil and criminal remedies in respect of a course of conduct which amounts to harassment and which the defendant knows, or ought to know, would amount to harassment. The test for how a person ought to know that a particular course of conduct amounts to harassment is in s 1(2): '... if a reasonable person, in possession of the same information, would think the course of conduct amounted to harassment of the other.'

A 'course of conduct' must involve conduct on at least two occasions[99] but can include speech, which is useful in a bullying scenario. 'Harassment'[100] is

---

95   Wilson v Pringle [1986] 2 All ER 440.

96   Collins v Wilcock [1984] 3 All ER 374.

97   Lord Monkswell, sponsor of the Bill, Hansard HL Debs Col 754, 4 December 1996.

98   Interestingly, Conspiracy and Protection of Property Act 1875, s 7, provides a criminal offence for someone who besieges other people's homes or workplaces with a view to forcing them to do something against their will. The general tenor of this offence would appear to be protection from outside interference rather than 'the enemy within'.

99   Protection from Harassment Act 1997, s 7(3).

100 Ibid, s 8(1). Every individual has a right to be free from harassment and, accordingly, a person must not pursue a course of conduct which amounts to harassment of another and:

   (a)   is intended to amount to harassment of that person; or

   (b)   occurs in circumstances where it would appear to a reasonable person that it would amount to harassment of that person.

not defined in a great amount of detail but is referred to in s 8(3) as 'causing the person alarm or distress', which is fairly open ended. There is a defence for a potential employer in s 8(4)(c): that a course of conduct will not amount to harassment if 'in the particular circumstances' it was reasonable. The legal problems in defining 'reasonableness' need not be stated and may render an employee particularly vulnerable in a struggling enterprise. Damages can also be awarded for any anxiety caused by the harassment,[101] which is particularly significant in the light of the crippling effects of workplace bullying. Injunctions can be awarded under the Act and emergency orders can be obtained quickly, but a considerable amount of evidence is required. Bullying can mean 'one's word against another's' which, it is submitted, will not suffice. Moreover, to continue working in such an atmosphere while an injunction is in place, or proceedings for one are pending, might prove problematic.[102] The Act simply codified the existing common law right which had been recognised in the case of *Khorasandjian v Bush*,[103] where the plaintiff was plagued with unwanted telephone calls, resulting in psychiatric harm. The justification for treating this as a trespass to the person case came from the old authority of *Wilkinson v Downton*.[104] A finding against the defendant was justified on the basis that he had wilfully done an act calculated to cause physical harm to the plaintiff and had caused her harm. Interestingly, in that case, it was stated that it was no answer to say that more harm was produced than had been intended (by the telling of a joke in bad taste) 'for that is commonly the case with all wrongs' and is certainly true in bullying. This, however, still leaves the plaintiff with the problem of being able only to pursue a perpetrator on an individual basis, and not the employer.[105]

There is no doubt that the Protection from Harassment Act had a definite gender dimension as, beyond the realms of the famous, women generally feature as victims of obsessed stalkers.[106] If the Dignity at Work Bill was the workplace equivalent of the former, then a gender dimension is also inherent within the latter. This overlap becomes clear in the *Farley* case cited by

---

101 Protection from Harassment Act 1997, s 3(2).

102 Under s 3(3) and 3(9), breach of an anti-harassment injunction would be contempt of court and a separate criminal offence with police power of arrest. The Act sets up two criminal offences of harassment. The first is a high level offence where, on more than one occasion, the conduct is so threatening that the victim fears for his/her safety. This carries a maximum penalty of five years in prison or an unlimited fine or both. It is an arrestable offence. The second is a lower level offence which occurs when there is harassing conduct on more than one occasion that does not cause the victim to fear violence. The maximum penalty is six months' imprisonment or a £5,000 fine or both. It is an arrestable offence.

103 [1993] 3 WLR 476, which has been overturned, so far as nuisance is concerned, by *Hunter v Canary Wharf* [1997] 2 All ER 426.

104 [1897] 2 QB 57.

105 For an overview of this area and the tort of intimidation, see Conaghan, J, 'Gendered harms and the law of tort: remedying (sexual) harassment' (1996) 16 LS 407.

106 For example, *Khorasandjian* and *Burris v Azadani* [1995] 4 All ER 802.

Randall.[107] Farley had become obsessed with a female co-worker such that his behaviour caused his dismissal. Notwithstanding this, he continued to harass her and eventually, in 1988, went on an armed rampage in his former workplace, injuring four people (including the female) and killing seven others. Farley's action prior to dismissal would seem to be close to stalking and the case would have been, interestingly, analysed as a form of harassing/stalking within the workplace.

Conclusions on existing law

It is clear from the foregoing that, although legal remedies exist for an aggrieved employee, they are hardly tailor-made for the contemporary and future problems facing a victim employee. They, also, have relatively undesirable consequences for the employer, such as having itself or its employees sued or marched off to prison. As Lord Monkswell said, 'the idea of an employee going to his local police station and reporting bullying at work beggars belief, in terms of the way in which employment works'. However, he referred to this unthinkable conclusion in a climate in which the Dignity at Work Bill had a real chance of becoming law. Unfortunately, it fell before the end of the Conservative Government and so has left a gap, which will leave complainants with no option but to tailor their claim to the best existing remedy. For this reason alone, employers may find themselves supporting an Act which, while serving complainants' ends, removes criminal liability. A bespoke Bullying At Work Act, like health and safety legislation, could provide guidelines and defences to 'good employers' and a spur to bad employers to put their houses in order. Although unsuccessful, the terms of the Dignity at Work Bill will provide the template for any future legislation on this area.

SPECIFIC LAW ON BULLYING?

Lord Haskel stated that he was reluctant to impose more regulations on business and industry;[108] but, while internal workplace programmes would be a more satisfactory way of dealing with bullying, such provisions would not take account of the unreasonable employer or employee who refused to

---

107 *Op cit*, Randall, fn 28, p 53.
108 Lord Haskel in Hansard, HL Debs Col 762, 4 December 1996.

implement such programmes.[109] Clause 1 stated that all employees had the right to dignity at work and this right was infringed if:

> (2)　... that employee suffers, during his employment,[110] with the employer harassing or bullying, or any act, omission or conduct which causes him to be alarmed or distressed, including, but not limited to, any of the following:
>
> > (a)　behaviour on more than one occasion which is offensive, abusive, malicious, insulting or intimidating;
> >
> > (b)　unjustified criticism on more than one occasion;
> >
> > (c)　punishment imposed without reasonable justification;
> >
> > (d)　changes in the duties or responsibilities of the employee, to the employee's detriment, without reasonable justification.

The insertion of the phrase 'on more than one occasion' was specifically inserted to avoid the criticism of the Act that many accidentally offensive things said could produce liability under the Bill. However, the activities identified in paras (c) and (d), because they involved discrete situations with specific consequences, did not have to be repeated to fall foul of the Bill. Criticism was made that there was no requirement in the clause that the employer's conduct be unreasonable or that the employee's conduct be reasonable.[111] This was rebutted by Lord McCarthyl, who argued that the issue of reasonableness was dealt with in cl 5, which concerned the employer's defence.[112] Clause 5(1)(a) provided for an employer to have a defence against claims under the Bill if he had a policy and implemented it as outlined in Sched 1 of the Bill. Under cl 5(1)(b), the act or acts complained of would be repudiated by the competent person as soon as reasonably practicable. Finally, cl 5(1)(c) referred to the employer taking all such steps as are reasonably necessary, as soon as is reasonably practicable.[113] Schedule 1 of the Act outlined detailed arrangements for a dignity at work policy.

The Dignity at Work Bill was not perceived as a panacea to the ills of workplace bullying but it was a first step in the recognition of it as an evil upon which the law could intrude. A new piece of legislation gets a comprehensive amount of media coverage, which may, in turn, highlight awareness and concern regarding bullying on a nationwide scale better than

---

109 *Op cit*, fn 108, Col 763.

110 Lord Monkswell made the point that the right of an employee pertained during the employee's employment, rather than in the course of his employment, as he put it, 'to prevent legal difficulties': Hansard, HL Debs Col 453, 20 January 1997.

111 Lord Lucas, Hansard, HL Debs Col 455, 20 January 1997.

112 Lord McCarthy, Hansard, HL Debs Col 456, 20 January 1997.

113 The Dignity at Work Bill, cl 3, extended the right of dignity to contract workers and cl 4 gave the victims the right to pursue their claims to tribunals. Compensation for an aggrieved employee was provided for in cl 6. Clauses 7, 8 and 9 were technical provisions concerning title, interpretation and commencement.

do individual piecemeal programmes run by individual employers. It may also help to 'de-closet' the problem of workplace bullying and may emphasise to individual employees their own right to demand certain initiatives be taken in their workplaces. While legislation is the iron fist, extra-legal mechanisms may provide a velvet glove. It is suggested that both components are essential to a successful campaign against workplace harassment and it is the relationship between these two limbs which is discussed in the next section.

IS THE LAW AN APPROPRIATE MECHANISM FOR RESOLVING WORKPLACE BULLYING?

Pursuing a case can exert a huge toll on an individual in both monetary (there is no Legal Aid for tribunal claims) and emotional terms (the bullying must be relived with legal advisors). While there should be no requirement to resign in advance of pursuing a claim, it is unrealistic to expect an employee to have a meaningful working relationship, in the meantime, with someone they have accused of bullying. The ideal situation may be dealing with the problem 'on site' and resolving issues at an early stage. While it is almost trite to say bullies are weak people who back down when confronted, what is trivialised is the huge leap that it takes for a victim to get to that stage. Complain too early and there is the possibility of being considered to be over sensitive, inadequate or (particularly in the case of women) hysterical, while, if left too late, events may spiral out of control. Conciliation and arbitration implies a uniformity between different companies; and a survey carried out by the IPD in 1996 revealed that those who had raise their grievances at work were generally dissatisfied with the way matters had been handled. A toothless complaints procedure is worse than no procedure at all, as the disappointment in its failure can emphasise the victim's feeling of isolation.[114] Additionally, the notion of in-house mediation is reactive rather than pro-active, which ignores the problems with reporting in the first place. It is, also, possible for a boss to run roughshod over attempts by personnel to mediate.[115] In a small company, there may be no personnel directors or occupational health experts to consult and an employee may have no option but to approach an outside body, such as ACAS. Its input may be refused by an employer without some legal compulsion. Another argument in favour of legislation is that of the negative compulsion of an employer: as the spectre of a tribunal looms, so may the

---

114 *Op cit*, Randall, fn 28, pp 59–60.
115 Case of Susan Cochran, *op cit*, fn 82.

desire for internal conciliation increase.[116] Thus, the short term introduction of a case before a tribunal increases the long term goal of communicative, non-confrontational dialogue between aggrieved and aggressor.

Punitive measures are insufficient in themselves; a climate indicating that bullying is intolerable must be created. There is evidence of a growing awareness of the problem in Sweden, Germany, Denmark, Holland and Norway[117] and this has been hailed as the way forward by Chris Ball, National Officer of the MSF.[118] The point was made by Lord Haskel that the Health and Safety Executive seeks compliance not just by threatening court actions or carrying out inspections but, also, organises seminars, workshops and publicity campaigns designed to inform employers of the regulations and to persuade them that they are good for business. The bully's mindset will not, however, be changed merely by a one day workshop programme on bullying, and bullies must be alerted to the fact that their conduct will not be tolerated at work. How they change their own attitudes remains a matter for which they must take responsibility. It is submitted that the same rationale must underlie a Dignity at Work Act – that is, a multi-faceted approach must be taken, with judicial involvement being a last resort and education being at a premium. A contribution to this educationally and culturally oriented, holistic approach to harassment could be made by a single Discrimination Act overseen by a single Discrimination Commission.[119]

An old joke comments that the notion of dangling a carrot as an incentive to a donkey misses the point. The carrot is not the object of attraction, rather the donkey's motivation arises from a wish to avoid being hit with the stick from which it hangs. Realistically, a court/tribunal action may be the stick with which to persuade employers in the short term, spurring employers to 'clean house' and provide an acceptable working environment for the beleaguered silent sufferers who are, presumably, indifferent to the legal mechanism by which their collective lot is improved. Perhaps, a lesson should be taken from other cultures, if only for the most terrifying of reasons. In Japan, a bullying hotline, pioneered by a union, received 1,045 calls, of which more than half were from women and, in one out of seven cases, employees

---

116 In the case of *Jones v Tower Boot Co Ltd*, it is noted that the RRA and SDA have a variety of functions as educative, persuasive and coercive in the pursuit of the elimination of sex and race discrimination. Such a tripartite thrust should also lie behind legislation concerned with bullying. The point is also made in the *Jones* case, para 38, that provision of a 'reasonable steps' defence will exonerate a conscientious employer who has used his best endeavours to prevent harassment and will encourage lax employers to take the steps necessary to open up the defence to themselves.

117 Possibly signalling the way forward for an EU level standard?

118 http://www.twoten.press.net/stories/96/03/19/headlines/LABOUR_Bullying_Action.html

119 Wintemute, R, 'Time for a single Anti-Discrimination Act (and Commission)?' (1997) 26 ILJ 259.

had either attempted or contemplated suicide.[120] In Russia, a young Russian conscript shot dead three fellow soldiers and a civilian, claiming afterwards he lost his head after persistent bullying.[121] Bearing this in mind, employers may find fines, compensation or anti-bullying policies considerably less daunting.[122]

---

120 'Japan's workers aren't sacked, they're driven to suicide' (1997) *The Independent*, 23 March.

121 'Bullying "drove Russian to kill"' (1997) *The Independent*, 12 January.

122 My thanks go to Mr Alan Sprince and Ms Anne Morris for their helpful comments on earlier drafts of this chapter and to Ms Jenifer Ross for her help with sources. All responsibility for errors remains with the author.

In spite of all the e   the still
central emphasis on collective bargaining and informal sources of
employment rights, it is the contract of employment which remains the legal
foundation of the employment relationship. As such, it operates as a gateway
to many of the statutory employment rights. This chapter will examine the
legal nature of the contract of employment as it has been partly constructed by
gender and as it has continued to develop.

The contract and formal equality

The employment relationship in the UK, as a capitalist economy, is based on
the contract between the worker and the employer. Like all contracts, it is
based on the concept of agreement between two autonomous parties and
represents the ideal of a free and voluntary arrangement between the two.
This ideal is a fiction: economically and legally, the reality of employment
relations is the dominance of capital and the employer. The view that 'contract
is the specifically modern means of creating relationships of subordination'[1]
applies particularly to the contract of employment.

This social reality is reflected in the legal content of the contract of
employment, which, although taking the form of an agreement between
equals, is constructed so as to enshrine the dominance of the employer within
it. The primacy of the employer was emphasised in the 19th century by the
Master and Servant Act 1823,[2] whose one-sided provisions entrenched the
inequality. Servants, but not masters, could be prosecuted for breach of
contract, including neglect of duty. This, along with other statutes which
provided for prosecution for breach of contract,[3] were frequently enforced:
there were an average of 10,000 prosecutions a year in England and Wales

---

1   Pateman, C, *The Sexual Contract*, 1988, Cambridge: Polity, p 118.
2   4 Geo IV c 34, s 3.
3   Act of 1843 (6 & 7 Vict c 40) and 1777 (17 Geo III c 56), which criminalised textile and
    iron workers who failed to finish work on time and failed to return materials.

between 1858 and 1875.[4] They were ameliorated by the Master and Servant Act 1867,[5] and the statutes repealed by the Employers and Workmen Act 1875,[6] having become a dead letter so far as large industrialists were concerned: used by small backward employers but opposed by the growing unions and the newly enfranchised.[7]

While the blunt instrument of the criminal law may have been removed from the inequality of the employment relationship, nevertheless, that relationship is still, essentially, one based on power. The imbalance of power between employer and employee is partly the economic reality of the inequality of the bargaining relationship of the market place, with employment being 'an act of submission, in its operation ... a condition of subordination'.[8] Kahn-Freund here is referring to the relation between an employer and an 'isolated employee' but this is the essence of the contractual relationship, which is always concerned with the employee as an isolated entity, even when incorporating elements into the contract from collective sources. The imbalance of power can also derive from the strength of each party to the contract in relation to the formation of the contract and knowledge of the contract.[9] And, there is an essential legal content to the imbalance: the common law heart of the contract of employment, the implied duty to be ready and willing to work and to obey the lawful orders of the employer, with its corollary the right of the employer to exercise control of the employee. In these three respects, at least, the employment relationship is not an equal one, something the bilateral form of the contract partially conceals.[10]

Employment and gender

If the 19th century origins of the employment relationship are rooted in the economic position of employer and worker, the gendered nature of the concept of employee also derives from the 19th and 20th century view of the labour market. The division of labour between home and work followed on from the collapse of the family system of labour and, with that, came the

---

4   Simon, D, 'Master and servant', in Saville, J (ed), *Democracy and the Labour Movement*, 1954, London: Lawrence & Wishart, p 160.

5   30 & 31 Vict c 141.

6   38 & 39 Vict c 90.

7   *Ibid*, Simon, p 199.

8   Kahn-Freund, O, *Labour and the Law*, 1983, Davies, P and Freedland, M (eds), London: Stevens, p 18.

9   Frug, MJ, *Post-modern Legal Feminism*, 1992, London: Routledge, pp 100–101 (referring not to employment contracts but to standardised commercial contracts). This imbalance was recognised and, to some extent, ameliorated by the House of Lords in *Scally v Southern Health and Social Services Board* [1991] IRLR 522.

10   *Ibid*, Kahn-Freund.

demand for the 'family wage', where a man's wages were viewed as including an amount not just for himself but for his family too. This position was adopted by British trade unions in the second half of the 19th century.[11] Trade union hostility to women in this period was based on two notions: that they undercut men's wages and that they undermined the family.[12] The family wage theory was even explicitly adopted in the legal context of the Australian courts of the early 20th century.[13] While reality has meant that, for many families, either the man's wage was not a family wage or the man was family-less (or the family man-less), the concept and its effects – job segregation and lower wages for women – is one that has endured and has, probably, contributed to the voluntary withdrawal of some women from the labour market.[14]

Another, related, barrier faced by women, in this case predominantly middle class women, was the marriage bar, either forbidding the employment of married women or automatically terminating women's employment in the event of their marriage in certain occupations. In spite of the Sex Disqualification (Removal) Act 1919, which prohibited such discrimination, employment in the civil and other public services was effectively excluded from the operation of the Act by judicial interpretation,[15] an exclusion which continued, in practice, until after the Second World War and was not made illegal in Britain until the Sex Discrimination Act 1975.[16] The work related welfare system also took as its basis the assumption that the primary worker was a man and that married women were (and should be) dependent on their husbands. This approach was still fundamental to the system in the mid-20th century, as it was an important concept in the Beveridge Report.[17] The payment of the 'small' or 'married woman's' stamp – that is, a special reduced national insurance contribution (and correspondingly reduced benefits) only open to women – had been established from the inception of the welfare system[18] and continued until 1975, when formal equality was introduced (though women in the system can, and many do, retain the option to continue with the reduced payment).[19] Similarly, the system for accruing contributory pensions provided that married women could choose to opt out altogether from the system and accrue their (reduced) pension through their husbands'

---

11 Gordon, E, *Women and the Labour Movement in Scotland 1850–1914*, 1991, Oxford: Clarendon, pp 74, 80.

12 *Ibid*, and see Morris, Chapter 9, this volume.

13 *Op cit*, Pateman, fn 1, p 138.

14 *Op cit*, Pateman, fn 1.

15 Fredman, S, *Women and the Law*, 1997, Oxford: Clarendon, pp 80–82.

16 Hakim, C, *Key Issues in Women's Work*, 1996, London: Athlone, pp 123–25.

17 Sir William Beveridge: Social Insurance and Allied Services, 1942, Cm 6404.

18 Unemployment Insurance Act 1920, Second Sched.

19 Social Security Act 1975, ss 5(2), 130(2).

contributions[20] was also abolished as recently as 1975.[21] These measures contributed to reinforcing the supposed subsidiary nature of women's employment.

The notion of the worker, therefore, is a highly gendered one, and this has had an important impact on the way in which certain key aspects of the employment contract have developed.

The contract of employment: gateway to employment rights

The modern history of labour law has tended to be a legislative one, whether in relation to health and safety, discrimination, dismissal or collective matters, largely to counterbalance the dominance of the employer in the contract. This history, however extensive, has not replaced the contract, but the relationship between statute and contract has been an ambiguous one. Employers have had to provide written statements of terms of employment since 1963,[22] but not written contracts, and a body of case law has had to negotiate the relationship between the two.[23] Since the introduction of statutory maternity rights in 1975, it has been open to an employee to rely on either the statutory provision, her contractual provision or a composite right of the favourable aspects of each[24]. One of the most complex and unsatisfactory tensions has been between the right to return to work and the continuation (or not) of the contract of employment.[25] The reasonableness or otherwise of a dismissal (and thus its fairness or unfairness) may be influenced, but not determined, by whether or not it is in breach of contract either by the employee or by the employer.[26] Major aspects of employment are unregulated by statute or are subject to control only in respect of enforcement (or discrimination), leaving the substantive provision to the agreement of the parties – wage levels have been unregulated, but are controlled in respect of non-payment or deductions[27] and discrimination,[28] as have been hours of work. More recent legislation is setting minimum levels in these areas.[29]

---

20 Widows, Orphans and Old Age Contributory Pensions Act 1925.

21 Social Security Pensions Act 1975.

22 Now contained in the Employment Rights Act 1996, s 1.

23 Eg, *Robertson v British Gas Corporation* [1983] IRLR 302.

24 Employment Rights Act 1996, ss 78, 85.

25 The most recent grappling with this issue is *Kwik Save Stores Ltd v Greaves; Crees v Royal London Mutual Insurance Society Ltd* [1998] IRLR 245 (CA).

26 *Westminster City Council v Cabaj* [1996] IRLR 399.

27 Employment Rights Act 1996, Pt II.

28 Equal Pay Act 1970; Race Relations Act 1976, s 4(2)(a); Disability Discrimination Act 1995, s 4(2)(a).

29 National Minimum Wage Act 1998; the Working Time Regulations 1998, SI 1998/1833.

Not only is the contract still important in its own right, it is also a basis both for interpreting the statutory provisions and for giving access to the rights that statutes provide.[30] It is in this last respect that the contract has been particularly crucial. The existence of a contract of employment has acted as a gateway to employment rights, both by denying access to those whose relationship cannot be defined according to the common law concept of contract and by denying access to those whose employment does not meet the statutory criteria of continuous employment. These gateways are of particular interest here, since they have had a disproportionate impact on women and, it can be argued, have arisen because of the gendered nature of the concept of the employee, where the legal construct of contract of employment has been based on a male paradigm: that of a full time permanent worker, a concept which, as we shall see, has been shaken partly because of changes in the nature of work and partly because of challenges to the validity of the use of the contract of employment in this way.

There are, therefore, two major ways in which the concept of the contract has acted to exclude workers from legal protection. The first of these has been by restricting the rights of employees to those whose employment is based on a contract of employment. This is the essence of the common law position, so that, amongst others, the full extent of the employer's duty to take reasonable care for the safety of employees extends to those who are employed under a contract of employment, or who are treated as if they were by the application of the 'control' test,[31] or are considered to be in *pro hac vice* employment of a temporary employer.[32] Statutory health and safety protection also depends on employment status. The key employment section of the Health and Safety at Work etc Act 1974[33] imposes a duty in relation to employees, defined in the Act in relation to a contract of employment,[34] with separate, less extensive duties being imposed in relation to those who are not employees.[35] Many of the duties imposed on employers by the regulations which implemented the EC Health and Safety Directive 89/391 also relate to employees.[36] For example, while the regulations relating to VDUs impose duties on employers in respect of employees ('users') and non-employees ('operators', who are defined as self-employed), more extensive duties relating to eye tests and training apply only in respect of employees.[37]

---

30 For a general discussion of this issue, see Deakin, S and Morris, G, *Labour Law*, 2nd edn, 1998, London: Butterworths, pp 129–31.

31 *Garrard v Southey & Co* [1952] 2 QB 174.

32 *Sime v Sutcliffe Catering Scotland Ltd* [1990] IRLR 228.

33 Health and Safety at Work etc Act 1974, s 2.

34 *Ibid*, s 53.

35 *Ibid*, ss 3, 4.

36 Eg, Management of Health and Safety at Work Regulations 1992, SI 1992/2051.

37 Health and Safety (Display Screen Equipment) Regulations 1992, SI 1992/2792.

Most job protection rights belong only to those employed under a contract of employment. Of the 12 parts of the Employment Rights Act 1996, each part of which provides for one or more sets of employment rights, only Pt 2, relating to deductions from wages, applies to workers employed other than under a contract of employment. The other 11 parts, including the key areas of unfair dismissal, redundancy pay and maternity rights,[38] are restricted, at the time of writing, to those employed under a contract of employment. Even the part relating to shop workers and betting workers and Sunday working, which, on the face of it, appears broader is restricted to such of those workers as are employed under a contract of employment.[39]

The second way in which the contract of employment has acted as a gateway to employment protection rights is through the concept of continuity of employment. Since their inception, the rights to redundancy pay and to return to work after six months of maternity leave have required two years continuous employment as an employee,[40] while the right not to be unfairly dismissed has been dependent on a number of qualifying periods – currently two years.[41] The challenges to the legality of these qualifying periods and the successful challenges to the legality of the long standing requirement for a weekly minimum number of hours continuous employment will be discussed later. The recent introduction of a universal right to maternity leave which is not dependent on the two year qualification has ameliorated part of the problem[42] and it is proposed to reduce the qualification period for unfair dismissal from two years, where it has stood since 1985, to one year, which was its level from 1980 until 1985.[43] However, these qualification periods mean that employers have been free to dismiss employees with shorter time service without fear of legal comeback. A further problem is faced by casual or temporary workers, whose periods of employment, even with the same employer, may be broken and, thus, have to be assessed individually according to the continuity rules.[44]

The contract and 'marginal' workers

These legal/contractual hurdles have had to be overcome by every worker but the greatest problems are faced by those whose form of work does not fit the paradigm of permanent (formerly also full time) employee on a contract of

---

38 Employment Rights Act 1996, Pts 10, 11 and 8.
39 *Ibid*, Pt 4, ss 232, 233.
40 *Ibid*, ss 108, 79(1)(b).
41 *Ibid*, s 155.
42 *Ibid*, ss 71–78.
43 *Fairness at Work*, 1998, Cm 3968, London: HMSO, 3.9–3.10.
44 Employment Rights Act 1996, Pt XIV.

employment. Other forms of work patterns have been variously described, for example, as 'atypical' in a set of draft EC directives on part time, temporary and seasonal employment:[45] describing these work patterns in this way emphasises the point that the traditional model of employment is full time, permanent and unbroken. Another description which contains the same implication is 'non-standard', 'away from standard full time permanent employment forms'[46] but probably the most commonly used description is the euphemistic 'flexible' work. Flexible work is promoted as a key goal, both for the economy and for the individual worker.[47] The euphemism lies not in its flexibility for employers and the economy, but in the extent to which there is truly flexibility for the individual workers who adopt such patterns of employment. There is considerable debate, for example, about the extent to which women adopt part time work in preference to full time work, or homework rather than work outside the home, because they choose to combine work and family to obtain 'the best of both worlds',[48] or because there is no real choice for many women but to accept the poor wages attached to such work because of their child care commitments and the inflexibility of work and child care arrangements.[49]

The definition of flexible non-standard employment adopted by Dex and McCulloch in their analysis of employment in 1994 is to include any part time employment, any temporary employment and self-employment without employees.[50] The percentage of workers (aged between 16 and 64) in non-standard employment was 22% of employed men and 51% of employed women.[51] It may be non-standard or atypical of employment in general but it is a very significant proportion indeed, particularly of women workers. As they point out, employment amongst those younger than 16, or older than 64, constitutes a much higher percentage in addition.

A number of approaches have been used to analyse the subsidiary nature of non-standard employment. Employment may be seen as 'primary' or 'secondary' in relation to the family income, where the secondary partner's contribution is insufficient to sustain the family. Since many women with child care or other family commitments work part time, part time women

---

45 Draft Directive on the approximation of laws relating to working conditions; draft Directive on the approximation of laws relating to distortions of competition; draft Directive on improving the health and safety at work of temporary workers (1990).

46 Dex, S and McCulloch, A, *Flexible Employment in Britain: A Statistical Analysis*, 1995, Manchester: EOC, p 1.

47 See, eg, *op cit, Fairness at Work*, fn 43.

48 *Op cit*, Hakim, fn 16, p 71.

49 *Ibid*, Dex and McCulloch, pp 14–15; Phizacklea, A and Wolkowitz, C, *Homeworking Women*, 1995, London: Sage, p 123.

50 *Ibid*, Dex and McCulloch, p 33.

51 *Ibid*, Dex and McCulloch.

workers are often viewed as essentially secondary.[52] Another important concept which relegates non-standard employment to a subsidiary position is that of 'marginal' employment – marginal, that is, to the market, usually because the hours worked are very small, or the work pattern is casual, seasonal or temporary[53] – 'relatively less visible or more difficult to count because it is part time, seasonal, irregular or combined with domestic work'.[54] These concepts are acknowledged by EC law and have provided a justification for excluding certain categories of worker from the protection of the Social Security Equal Treatment Directive[55] and the Part Time Workers Directive.[56]

First, in *Nolte v Landesverischerungsanstalt Hannover,*[57] the European Court of Justice refused to follow the Advocate General's opinion and held that German legislation refusing to admit people in 'minor' employment to the contributory social security system was justified. Under this scheme, workers were in minor employment when they worked fewer than 15 hours a week and earned no more than one-seventh of the monthly reference wage (the average wage). Mrs Nolte, who had worked for 10 years as a part time cleaner, had been refused a disability pension because she had made no contributions. The Court rejected the extreme position of the German Government, that such people should not be considered part of the workforce at all, since their earnings were not sufficient to satisfy their needs, but accepted its argument that the exclusion from the contributory scheme was justified, so as to encourage the creation of this kind of employment (by removing financial barriers).

Secondly, and ironically, the Framework Agreement on part time work, implemented by the Part Time Workers Directive 97/81, allows governments to exclude casual workers from the definition of protected part time worker entirely,[58] while the equal treatment of part time workers is subject to the possible justification of special conditions on objective grounds. The sort of objective grounds contemplated relate to time worked and an earnings qualification.[59] Thus, the concept of minor/marginal/secondary employment is live in relation to employment as well as social security.

There can be no doubting the gendered nature of non-standard work. The figures analysed by Dex and McCulloch showed that women made up the majority of part time jobs (between 828,000 and 1,045,000 men, compared with

---

52   *Op cit*, Hakim, fn 16, pp 65–74.
53   *Op cit*, Hakim, fn 16, pp 20–44.
54   *Op cit*, Hakim, fn 16, p 20.
55   EC Directive 78/7.
56   EC Directive 97/81.
57   [1996] IRLR 225.
58   EC Directive 97/81 Framework Agreement, cl 2.
59   *Ibid*, cl 4.

between 4,644,000 and 4,956,000 women, the variation depending on whether the figure was based on self-definition or hours worked)[60] and, in 1997, 81% of all those of working age who worked part time were women (44% of women in employment and 5% of men in employment);[61] women also made up the majority of temporary employees (728,000 women to 650,000 men) and of casual workers (135,000 women to 80,000 men) and a substantial proportion of seasonal workers (31,000 women to 40,000 men).[62] According to officially compiled statistics, there are more men than women working at paid employment at home[63] but a marginally greater percentage of women workers than men workers work at home,[64] while the majority of women home based workers are in part time temporary contracts, with the majority of men in full time permanent contracts.[65] The membership organisation National Group on Homeworking estimates that most homeworkers are married women who are mothers of two or more children and that one of every two UK homeworkers comes from an ethnic minority.[66]

However, it is not just in statistical preponderance that non-standard employment takes on its gendered content but, also, in the underlying social and ideological nature of the division between work and home. Because of this separation and the traditional allocation of employment to the male sphere of responsibility and of family and home to the female sphere, work which is more easily combined with family responsibilities is viewed as being a female pattern of working and as a secondary or marginal one.

Forms of employment relationship: contract of employment

There are, broadly, two forms of employment relationship adopted in UK legislation: the contract of employment and the worker's contract. The former is the basis for the majority of employment protection rights[67] and the latter is included in an expanded definition of employment, in relation to deductions

---

60 *Op cit*, Dex and McCulloch, fn 46, p 37.

61 Labour Force Survey 1997, reported in (1998) 79 EOR 30.

62 *Op cit*, Dex and McCulloch, fn 46, p 37.

63 *Op cit*, Hakim, fn 16, pp 36–38.

64 Felstead, A and Jewson, N, *Homeworkers in Britain*, 1996, London: HMSO, p 14: this is based on the 1991 Census returns; Hakim's and Dex and McCulloch's are based on the 1994 Labour Force Survey.

65 *Op cit*, Hakim, fn 16, p 38.

66 National Group on Homeworking: Submission to Low Pay Unit on the National Minimum Wage, 1997.

67 Employment Rights Act 1996, Pts 1, 3–12, s 230.

from wages,[68] equal pay[69] and sex[70] and race[71] discrimination. While the concept of a worker's contract is broader than that of a contract of employment, nevertheless, it is not inclusive of all forms of employment relationship.

The approach used by the courts to determine whether or not an employment relationship is a contract of employment has been notoriously vague and contradictory, in a number of ways. The issue has been viewed as, primarily, one of fact,[72] so that different tribunals or courts could legitimately arrive at different decisions providing they guided themselves by an accurate statement of the law. The predominant test of employment is the 'multiple' test, which balances a number of different factors without clarifying the weight to be given to each one.[73] At the same time as using the multiple test, the courts are also inclined to identify an underlying theme, on the one hand, such as whether the person is working for their own business or their employer's[74] or, on the other hand, to look to a basic contractual test that there is 'mutuality of obligation' between the parties.[75] Mutuality has never been adopted as the sole test of an employment contract but, where it has arisen, it has taken on a central position, similar to that which control used to have under earlier tests. Until recently, it appeared to be conclusive of the issue: that is, not a factor to be weighed in the balance along with other factors[76] but an 'irreducible minimum of obligation on each side'[77] – that is, the obligation to pay wages by the employer and the obligation to provide her own work and skill by the employee. The problem with mutuality of obligation is that, as with so many of the tests adopted, it is, ultimately, a circular test. The essential difference between a contract of employment or service and a contract for services is that, whereas the latter is a contract to perform certain services, the former is a contract to place the employee's work and skill under the control of the employer. Thus, mutuality of obligation may define a contract but it also describes what can be expected of the parties to it once it has been established.

---

68 Employment Rights Act 1996, Pt 2.

69 Equal Pay Act, s 1(6)(a).

70 Sex Discrimination Act 1975, s 82(1).

71 Race Relations Act 1976, s 78(1).

72 *O'Kelly v Trusthouse Forte plc* [1983] IRLR 370; *Lee v Chung* [1990] IRLR 236.

73 *Market Investigations Ltd v Minister of Social Security* [1969] 2 QB 173.

74 *Market Investigations Ltd v Minister of Social Security; Lane v Shire Roofing Co (Oxford) Ltd* [1995] IRLR 493, which saw the ultimate question as 'whose business was it?'.

75 *Clark v Oxfordshire Health Authority* [1998] IRLR 125.

76 *Ibid*, p 128.

77 *Nethermere St Neots Ltd v Taverna and Gardiner* [1984] IRLR 240, p 245.

The emphasis on mutuality of obligation has had the greatest impact on casual workers and homeworkers (who are considered separately below). Casual workers agree to work when required: in theory they may never be required to work, nor can they be forced to work when they are required. This has meant that it has been almost impossible for casual workers to establish the existence of an overall contract of employment because there appears to be no overall mutuality of obligation. For these contracts, the multiple test seemed to become a two stage test, in which it was necessary, first, to pass the hurdle of mutuality of obligation before moving on to balance the other factors present in the contract. For casual workers, too, the problems created by the need to establish an employment contract are compounded by continuity requirements. For unfair dismissal and redundancy protection, the worker must not only be an employee but an employee continuously employed for two years. It is, therefore, not sufficient to establish current status: it is necessary to show sufficiently long term status, as well, to meet the qualification demands of the right sought. While it might be sufficient in some cases to establish that the casual worker was employed under a contract of employment for one specific engagement with the employer – where, for example, all that is being claimed relates to that one engagement (such as payment)[78] – in cases where the worker is claiming, for example, unfair dismissal or a redundancy payment, it would be the overall position which would generally be relevant. The length of the specific engagement(s) could be crucial, as was the case in *Clark v Oxfordshire Health Authority*.[79] This case concerned the dismissal of Mrs Clark, a nurse, who had been employed in a nurse bank over a period of three years as a staff nurse and who worked as she was called upon to fill temporary vacancies. To qualify for the right not to be unfairly dismissed, she had to have been continuously employed in a contract of employment for two years. The Court of Appeal overturned the Employment Appeal Tribunal's finding that there was a 'global' contract for the three years of her employment, holding that there was no mutuality of obligation overall, and remitted the case back to the tribunal to reconsider it in the light of her specific periods of employment by the Authority.

However, in a subsequent case, the Court of Appeal, by majority, have moved away from a mechanical application of the mutuality concept and adopted an approach which looks promising, in terms of allowing casual workers the protection of a contract of employment. In *Carmichael v National Power plc*,[80] Mrs Carmichael and Mrs Leese complained that they had not received the statutory written statement of particulars of employment. They were employed as station guides on a 'casual, as required' basis and both the industrial tribunal and the Employment Appeal Tribunal held that there was

---

78 *McMeechan v Secretary of State for Employment* [1997] IRLR 353.
79 [1998] IRLR 125.
80 [1998] IRLR 301.

no mutuality of obligation and, thus, no contract of employment. The reasoning was simply that there was no enforceable contractual obligation to offer work and no enforceable contractual obligation to accept it when offered. Using a different contractual approach, the majority of the Court of Appeal held that this was confusing enforcement of the contract with its terms. While it might not be possible for either the women to enforce an offer of work or the employer to enforce a requirement to work (and, of course, no employer can force any employee to work), this did not necessarily mean that the contract between the parties was not a contract of employment. There was, they held, an implied term of that contract that the employers would provide a reasonable share of what guiding work would become available from time to time, while the workers had a corresponding duty to accept work when offered, subject to reasonableness. Having decided that the 'irreducible minimum' obligation was present and that there had been no other reason advanced by the employers for denying them the status of employees, the court held that the overall contract was one of employment. This decision seems to have application to other general agreements to do casual work, including that involved in the earlier decision of *Clark v Oxfordshire Health Authority*.[81] The only suggestion made there for what, in the absence of obligations to give and perform work, would suffice for mutuality was the obligation to accept work, on the one hand, and the obligation, on the other hand, to pay a retainer.[82] This is far in excess of what was demanded by the much more realistic and flexible approach taken in the more recent case.

Forms of employment relationship: the worker's contract

Where the concept of employment is extended beyond that of the traditional contract of employment, the definitions contained in the different statutes are not the same. The definitions of the term 'worker' in the Trade Union and Labour Relations (Consolidation) Act 1992[83] and the Employment Rights Act 1996[84] are virtually identical: using the shorter version in the 1992 Act, a worker includes not only someone employed under a contract of employment or a contract of apprenticeship but, also, someone employed under 'any other contract whereby he undertakes to do or perform personally any work or services for another party to the contract who is not a professional client of his'. The term 'worker' is not used in the Equal Pay, Sex Discrimination or Race Relations Acts but the concept of employment is extended to include

---

81   [1998] IRLR 125.

82   *Ibid*, p 130.

83   Trade Union and Labour Relations (Consolidation) Act 1992, s 296(1).

84   Employment Rights Act 1996, s 230(3).

anyone employed under 'a contract personally to execute any work or labour.'[85] Since the latter definition does not exclude employment by a client, it is wider than the definition of worker.[86] The extended definition gives an important, if limited, protection for those who are genuinely self-employed or whose contracts do not meet the legal tests of an employment contract. Only employees are covered by the maternity provisions of the Employment Rights Act 1996[87] and the protection against dismissal because of pregnancy or childbirth.[88] In *Caruana v Manchester Airport plc*,[89] Ms Caruana, a self-employed researcher working under a series of fixed term contracts for Manchester Airport, challenged a decision not to renew her contract when she announced that she was pregnant and would be taking maternity leave. She was successful in her claim that she had been directly discriminated against on the ground of her sex; her contract came within the extended definition of employment in s 82(1) of the Sex Discrimination Act 1975 and the fact that it was fixed term did not remove it from the protection afforded by both EC and UK law.

Although there is an expanded concept of employment, there have been a number of restrictive interpretations, both of s 82(1) of the Sex Discrimination Act 1975 and s 78(1) of the Race Relations Act 1976 and of s 9 of the Sex Discrimination Act 1975, which protects contract workers against discrimination by principals to whom they are contracted. Two appeal cases, in particular, take a very technical approach to the issue, applying a narrow contractual framework rather than trying to fulfil the intention of the Act. In *Rice v Fon-a-car*,[90] the taxi firm respondents had required one of their drivers to dismiss a relief driver they had allowed him to employ when they discovered that the relief was a woman. Because there was no contractual obligation to supply a relief driver (simply permission to do so), the Employment Appeal Tribunal held that she had not been employed as a contract worker and could not make use of s 9 of the 1975 Act. In *Mirror Group Newspapers Ltd v Gunning*,[91] the respondent group had refused to allow an agency agreement for the distribution of newspapers to be transferred to the daughter on the death of her father, the former holder of the agency. Ms Gunning claimed that the refusal was on grounds of her sex. The industrial tribunal, supported by the Employment Appeal Tribunal, held that the agency agreement came within the definition of employment under s 82(1) of the 1975

---

85 Equal Pay Act 1970, s 1(6)(a); Sex Discrimination Act 1975, s 83(1); Race Relations Act 1976, s 78(1).

86 *Mirror Group Newspapers Ltd v Gunning* [1986] ICR 145, p 156.

87 Employment Rights Act 1996, Pt 8.

88 *Ibid*, s 99.

89 [1996] IRLR 378.

90 [1980] ICR 133.

91 [1986] ICR 145.

Act, since the agreement required the holder to be directly involved in the day to day supervision of the work. Without, at any point in either of the judgments, considering what the purpose of the legislation was, the Court of Appeal decided that the agreement was outside the statutory definition. Not only did they not agree that the contract obliged the holder to supervise the work personally but they additionally held that, in any event, such an obligation would not be sufficient: there would need to be an obligation to do, personally, the actual labour. Nor would an understanding that she would do at least part of the work herself suffice. This they expressed as requiring that the 'dominant purpose' of the contract be the personal provision of the work or services. In this case, the dominant purpose was the securing of an efficient system of newspaper distribution. This tends to miss the point that most contracts are not undertaken primarily for the purpose of the labour involved – if I employ a sculptor to sculpt me a statue, an example given of personal labour in the case, I am doing it for the purpose of having a statue sculpted, not providing an opportunity for the sculptor to labour. In a different context, the Court of Appeal has more recently refused to apply a 'dominant purpose' approach in relation to s 7 of the Race Relations Act 1976,[92] which applies to 'work for a [principal] which is available for doing by [contract workers] who are employed not by the principal himself but by another person, who supplies them under a contract made with the principal'. In *Harrods Ltd v Remick*,[93] three black and Asian women working for concessionaires in Harrods raised race discrimination actions against the store for refusing or withdrawing store approval from them. The Court of Appeal rejected an argument that, since the 'dominant purpose' of the contract between the concessionaire and Harrods was to market goods rather than to supply labour, the contract was not one to which s 7 applied, the court refusing to read restrictive words into the statute. Although the contracts referred to in s 78(1) and s 7 of the Race Relations Act 1976 (s 82(1) and s 9 of the Sex Discrimination Act 1975) are different, the whole approach of the Court of Appeal in this later case is more focused on the aims of the legislation, refusing this and another ground of appeal based on the traditional concept that Harrods did not, contractually, have control over the concessionaires' employees, on the basis that, if the grounds of appeal were right, 'these ladies will be victims of injustice without redress. The legislation will have failed to achieve the purpose set for it by paragraph 25 of the White Paper'.[94] Rigid adherence to traditional contractual doctrine can stand in the way of justice.[95]

---

92 The equivalent of s 9 of the Sex Discrimination Act 1975.

93 [1997] IRLR 583.

94 *Ibid*, p 585.

95 As was pointed out ([1997] IRLR 583, p 585), this is the purposive approach which was also applied in *Jones v Tower Boot Co Ltd* [1997] IRLR 168.

There has been varying success for those who have tried to argue that volunteers' contracts should be accepted as either contracts of employment or extended employment contracts.[96] While there has been at least one successful English tribunal case under s 78(1) of the Race Relations Act,[97] Scottish tribunal decisions have tended to distinguish that case on the basis that, in it, a formal service agreement had been entered into with the organisation (Relate) which was completely dependent on volunteers for its operation.[98] In a recent tribunal decision, not only did the tribunal rely on *Mirror Group Newspapers Ltd v Gunning*[99] and find that the 'dominant purpose of the agreement was not to bind the applicant personally to execute any work of labour ... the dominant purpose was to set out terms which, if voluntarily observed, would enable the respondents' work to be carried out',[100] but it, also, quoted approvingly the approach of another English tribunal decision which found that there was no employment relationship: 'A volunteer means just that. It is a word which is very often used to distinguish circumstances in which there is no consideration for a contract. One is merely taking on an obligation as a volunteer for moral, social or philanthropic purposes.'[101] It is particularly disappointing that in Scotland, where (unlike England) there is no doctrine of consideration in the law of contract, there should be adherence to such an inflexible doctrine.

There are, therefore, two problems with defining an employment contract: first, there is the need to fit the contract into the form of a standard contract of employment to attract all employment protection rights; and, secondly, where that does not apply, there is the problem of fitting the contract into an extended employment contract. There can be no justification for distinguishing between the two forms of contract. This is recognised in the National Minimum Wage Act, which gives the same protection against dismissal for the assertion of statutory rights as employees, with employees being protected by a new s 104 of the Employment Rights Act and workers having their own equivalent remedy under the new Act. The removal of the restriction of all existing employment protection rights to employees was being canvassed at the time of writing:[102] extending protection to all workers, not just those whose employment fits a traditional gendered work pattern, is

---

96 For a discussion of voluntary work, see Morris, Chapter 6, this volume.

97 *Armitage v Relate and others* (unreported, COIT 43538/94).

98 *Houlihan v Aberdeen City Council* (unreported, SCOIT S/841/96): Sex Discrimination Act 1975, s 82(1); *Ditta v Lothian Victim Support and Victim Support Scotland* (unreported, SCOIT S/400794/97): the Race Relations Act 1976, s 78.

99 [1986] ICR 145.

100 *Ditta v Lothian Victim Support and Victim Support Scotland* (unreported, SCOIT S/400794/97).

101 *Parmar v Portsmouth Citizens Advice Bureau* (unreported, COIT 15030/951).

102 Employment Relations Bill, cl 21: Regulations may extend categories entitled to employment protection.

long overdue. At the same time, the alternative – the worker's contract or the extended employment contract – is bogged down in traditional contract doctrine. A more inclusive approach is necessary.

Homeworkers

The contractual approach to the employment relationship has particularly disadvantaged home based workers, quite apart from isolation, poor wages and health and safety problems.[103] The irregular nature of some of the work means that there may be difficulties in establishing the necessary mutuality of obligation over a sufficient period. This is most likely to affect women home based workers. Although homeworking is a female pattern of work, it was noted[104] that more men than women are reported to work at home. However, amongst these home based workers, a majority of men were in full time, permanent contracts, while a majority of women were in part time, temporary contracts. Thus, it is women homeworkers who are likely to be faced with problems of regularity and, thus, of mutuality of obligation.

While this means that there must be uncertainty over any homeworking arrangement which does not contain an obligation to provide and do work or to do work and pay a retainer, the Court of Appeal, long before *Carmichael v National Power plc*,[105] was prepared to interpret long term contracts for homeworking, in the light of a course of dealing over a number of years between women homeworkers and their employer which implied an obligation on the employer to offer work[106] and the worker to accept it. This approach is, in itself, uncertain: it does not protect the worker who has not built up sufficient years of service and, since the status of the contract is dependent on sufficient regularity of dealings, it is probably only in retrospect that its nature will ever be clear, in any event.

The second legal difficulty is that it is an essential part of the contract of employment that it is to perform personal service, while this is also basic to the concept of the worker's contract or the extended employment contract provided for in legislation. Central to the homeworking contract, on the other hand, is the performance of the work and, although the majority of homeworkers do not apparently have help with their work, a substantial minority do.[107] This takes homeworking not just out of the protection offered to employees but, also, out of that offered to workers as well.

---

103 *Op cit*, Phizacklea and Wolkowitz, fn 49; *op cit*, Felstead and Jewson, fn 64.

104 See, above, fns 63–66.

105 [1998] IRLR 301.

106 *Nethermere St Neots Ltd v Gardiner and Taverna* [1984] ICR 612; *Airfix Footwear Ltd v Cope* [1978] ICR 1210 (EAT).

107 *Op cit*, Felstead and Jewson, fn 64, p 37.

In relation to low pay, there has been acknowledgment of the particular exploitation faced by homeworkers and, in order to extend the remit of Wages Councils to them, a specific definition of homeworker was included in the legislation.[108] This expanded definition dealt with both problematic issues: first, because Wages Council Orders were not restricted to employees and, secondly, by declaring that a homeworker's contract did not have to meet the general definition of a worker's contract, which included the requirement to perform services personally, though any helpers were restricted to two individuals. The National Minimum Wage Act 1998 also provides an extended definition to include homeworker.[109] It is not just in relation to wages that protection is required, and any review of the general applicability of employment legislation should ensure it is as inclusive as possible.

Part time and non-continuous employment: the impact of indirect discrimination

Two things have happened – which have been speeding up more recently – in relation to non-standard employment in the last two decades. First, there has been an increase in the number and proportion of part time workers, both women and men. It has been argued that the 'feminisation' of the workforce has meant an increase not in full time, permanent jobs, but in part time, particularly short hours, work.[110] At the same time, there has been an increase in the percentage of male part time workers, although it is still the case that the vast majority of part time workers are women.[111] Recession and rising unemployment have, also, meant that there has been an increase in short term working among men, with the difference in length of tenure of job between men and women narrowing markedly.[112] In fact, part time work, in particular, has remained a predominantly female mode of employment but there is a definite, and partially justified, perception that there is a general increase in 'flexible' non-standard modes of employment.

Secondly, there has been an attack on the discriminatory nature of many employment rights as they affect women, particularly under Art 119 of the Treaty of Rome and EC Equal Treatment Directive 76/207. A major success was the successful challenge of the discriminatory continuity of employment provisions, which required employees to work 16 hours a week to obtain the

---

108 The last before their abolition was the Wages Act 1986, s 26.

109 National Minimum Wage Act 1998, s 35.

110 *Op cit*, Hakim, fn 16, Chap 3.

111 Labour Force Survey, 1997, reported in (1998) 79 *Equal Opportunities Review* 30; *op cit*, Dex and McCulloch, fn 46, Chap 3.

112 *Op cit*, Dex and McCulloch, fn 46, Chap 4; *R v Secretary of State for Employment ex p Seymour-Smith and Perez* [1995] IRLR 464 (CA).

rights to redundancy pay and not to be unfairly dismissed within two years of starting employment with their employer, while those who worked between eight and 16 hours had to work for five years for the same rights, and those who worked fewer than eight hours a week could never obtain either right. The decision of the House of Lords in *R v Secretary of State for Employment ex p EOC*[113] came after a considerable line of cases which had asserted that (dependent on statistical proof in each case) treating part time workers less favourably than full time workers could be indirect sex discrimination, subject to justification on objective grounds.[114] In this case, the statistical proof was accepted that the majority of part time workers were women (87% at that time): the only issue was whether or not the government's political justification of the discriminatory provision, that an increase in employment protection rights would lead to a reduction in the number of part time jobs, amounted to a legal justification. Amongst other arguments, evidence that, in other EC countries, where there was no such discrimination, there had been an increase in part time work at least as great and, in some cases, greater than in the UK convinced the House of Lords that the discrimination had not been justified[115] and the provision was declared to be in breach of Art 119 in the case of the right to redundancy pay and of the Equal Treatment Directive 76/207 in the case of the right not to be unfairly dismissed. The legislation was subsequently amended to remove the hourly requirement altogether,[116] benefiting not only those who previously had to work five years to obtain these rights but also those who worked fewer than eight hours a week who, previously, had not been protected at all. It made pointless those decisions about contractual hours which had been based solely on attempting to evade responsibility for statutory rights. This was a step in advance of the existing EC proposals for protecting part time workers,[117] which proposed to exclude those who worked fewer than eight hours a week from its scope, a restriction omitted from the eventual Part Time Workers Directive 97/81 enacted in 1997.

An attack on the two year qualification period, also based on indirect sex discrimination, is (at the time of writing) in limbo, although the result of the case may be academic, as the government has indicated that it intends to reduce the qualification period to one year. However, there are a number of outstanding claims waiting for a ruling from the referral by the House of Lords to the European Court of Justice (ECJ) in *R v Secretary of State for*

---

113 [1994] IRLR 176.

114 Eg, *Jenkins v Kingsgate Clothing Productions* [1981] ICR 653; *Bilka-Kaufhaus GmbH v Karin Weber von Hartz* [1987] ICR 110.

115 *R v Secretary of State for Employment ex p EOC* [1994] IRLR 176, p 182.

116 Employment Protection (Part Time Employees) Regulations 1995, SI 1995/31.

117 Draft Directive on the approximation of laws relating to working conditions; draft Directive on the approximation of laws relating to distortions of competition; draft Directive on improving the health and safety at work of temporary workers (1990).

Employment ex p Seymour-Smith and Perez.[118] Ms Seymour-Smith and Ms Perez claimed that the two year rule indirectly discriminates on grounds of sex and the ECJ was asked a number of questions, mostly concerned with how to prove disparate impact in indirect discrimination and how to justify it. The statistical basis of the claim had been contested, but the Court of Appeal accepted that the figures showed a clear, persisting difference between the numbers of men and women who could meet the two year requirement.[119] The Secretary of State's argument that to increase the qualification threshold would lead to a decline in employment opportunities, was rejected by the Court, since it was an assertion not backed by empirical evidence.

The ECJ has effectively left it to the House of Lords to decide whether the qualification period is discriminatory, although the only comment in the judgment on the specific statistics (para 64) was that they did not appear on the face of it to show that a considerably smaller percentage of women than men can meet the requirement. Even if the House of Lords decides that figures do show a considerable difference, either in particular years, or as a 'lesser but persistent and relatively constant disparity over a long period' (para 61), the case illustrates the serious problems in relying on equal treatment legislation for development of the law to protect those involved in non-standard forms of employment, useful as it has been in certain cases. Proof of indirect discrimination requires relevant statistics in every case, which must show that, in the particular employment, there is a clear and considerable disparate impact on women. Where general legislation is challenged, the appropriate figures are global but, in individual indirect discrimination cases, particular figures must be gathered, and tailored to the particular sector (and/or locality). In any case, figures may change over time, as in *Seymour-Smith and Perez*, where, although there was a consistent and, despite comments of the ECJ, striking gender difference in length of service from 1985 to 1991, when the women began their action (in 1991, 74.5% of male and 67.4% of female employees had more than two years service), in the two subsequent years, the difference had narrowed markedly, a fact which gave the Court of Appeal some anxiety.[120] The use of statistics and the response to apparent change in these is flawed in a number of ways. First, while percentages may be close, the actual numbers may be extremely large. Secondly, total figures may mask different gender experiences. For example, although statistics indicate that more men than women are involved in home based work, the sectors of such work, the work patterns and contractual forms involved are different for men and women.[121] Thirdly, it is the mode of

---

118 [1997] IRLR 315 (HL); C-167/97, 9 February 1999 (ECJ).
119 [1995] IRLR 464, p 476.
120 *Ibid*, p 476.
121 See, above, fns 63–66.

working (part time, temporary or home based) that is significant, and which can be characterised as gendered in mode, because of the perception of non-standard working as associated with women as secondary earners with a marginal commitment to work outside the home. Men who take on that mode of working whether from choice or lack of alternatives also require protection.

Another problem with relying on indirect discrimination is the use of the justification defence. After the Court of Appeal decided in 1995 that the essentially rhetorical argument used by the government to justify its setting of the qualification at two years was unsubstantiated by evidence, the ECJ accepted an unsubstantiated 'aim' of government as a justification of social policy which treats 'marginal' workers less favourably than the rest of the working population.[122] Excluding those working under 15 hours a week and receiving less than one-seventh average earnings from various benefits was held to be justified by the aim of fostering a demand for such employment without the need for evidential proof that the aim would be fostered by the policy. While continuing to acknowledge governments' broad margin of discretion in implementing Community law, the ECJ has now emphasised that this cannot frustrate fundamental principles and that mere generalisations will not be evidence of justification (paras 74–76). This should be sufficient to enable the House of Lords to uphold the Court of Appeal's more robust approach.

Extending rights through specific legislation, such as the Part Time Workers Directive 97/81 or the Part Time Employees Regulations 1995, is a more direct and, ultimately, more effective way of tackling the problem. Nevertheless, the role played by anti-discrimination laws in extending protection should not be overlooked. Nor is it only women who have benefited, although it is only women who can initiate change using them. Part time male workers and male workers without two years continuous employment are able to take advantage of any declaration that the discriminatory legislation is contrary to EC law, established because of discrimination against women.[123]

The development of the contract of employment

Although the contract of employment is still grounded in its 19th century origins, there is one way in which the concept of the contract has developed to bring it (whether or not kicking and screaming) more into line with late 20th

---

122 *Nolte v Landesversicherungsanstalt Hannover* [1996] IRLR 225; *Megner and Scheffel v Innungskrankenkasse Vorderpfalz* [1996] IRLR 236.

123 *Davidson v City Electrical Factors Ltd* [1998] IRLR 108 (male employee with one year's service entitled to have his action for unfair dismissal sisted pending the outcome of *ex p Seymour-Smith and Perez*); *Hammersmith and Fulham London Borough Council v Jesuthasan* [1998] IRLR 372 (male part time employee dismissed before the 1995 Regulations were introduced entitled to take advantage of the decision in *ex p EOC*).

century attitudes to employment and the relative rights and obligations of employer and employee. The mutual duty of trust and confidence which has always imposed extensive duties of loyalty and confidentiality on the employee has developed to impose a range of duties on the employer. It has been suggested that this obligation 'will come to be seen as the core common law duty which dictates how employees should be treated during the course of the employment relationship'.[124] The duty on the employer is not to 'conduct itself in a manner calculated and likely to destroy or seriously damage the relationship of confidence and trust between employer and employee'.[125] This duty is an important development in the contract of employment, which recognises, increasingly, the rights of employees by imposing duties on the employer, often under the umbrella of the mutual duty of trust and confidence. An important part of this development has been the recognition of harassment and the interlinking of contractual principles and sex discrimination law to the benefit of both.

Much of the early impetus for the development of this duty came from unfair dismissal law and the concept of constructive dismissal, although its development has come through a number of different strands.[126] The 'contractual' test was eventually approved, so that it is only where the employer is in serious breach of contract, rather than behaving unreasonably, that an employee is entitled to resign without notice and raise a complaint of unfair dismissal.[127] That this is not simply for breach of an express term of the contract was acknowledged from the start: breach of an implied term of the contract can also ground constructive dismissal. Lord Lawton, in *Western Excavating (ECC) Ltd v Sharp*, felt it 'unnecessary and inadvisable' to give a general explanation of what conduct on the part of the employer might amount to breach of contract but he was able to give one example: 'Sensible persons have no difficulty in recognising such conduct when they hear about it. Persistent and unwanted amorous advances by an employer to a female member of his staff would, for example, clearly be such conduct.'[128] The recognition of sexual harassment not only as sex discrimination but as breach of contract owes much to this single example of Lord Lawton's.[129]

This interlinking has taken another important form. While employers' vicarious liability for discriminatory treatment in general, and harassment in particular, has been important, the development of a duty to treat complaints

---

124 Brodie, D, 'The heart of the matter: mutual trust and confidence' (1996) 25 ILJ 121, p 125.
125 *Woods v WM Car Services (Peterborough) Ltd* [1981] IRLR 347, approved in *Malik v BCCI* [1997] IRLR 462.
126 See *ibid*, Brodie.
127 *Western Excavating (ECC) Ltd v Sharp* [1978] ICR 221.
128 *Ibid*, p 229.
129 Cited in, eg, *Begg and Mair v Singh* S/67/88 and S/68/88; *Gordon v James Jappy t/a Paper Leaf* S/148/89.

seriously, introduced primarily in the context of sexual harassment cases, has a general application for all employment grievances. In *Bracebridge Engineering Ltd v Darby*,[130] where Mrs Darby's complaint to the company that she had been sexually assaulted by a chargehand and manager was not treated 'with the seriousness and gravity which it should', this failure of the employer was viewed as a breach of the mutual obligation of trust, confidence and support and the obligation not to undermine the confidence of the female staff – an obligation which, 'in a case of this nature, where sexual discrimination and investigation are concerned ... is an extremely important one for the female staff'.[131] It is a fairly small step from acknowledging that importance to acknowledging the importance of taking all employee complaints seriously, whatever aspect of work relations or environment they are concerned with.[132]

Another possible revitalising of the contract of employment, helped by the influence of anti-discrimination legislation on the practice of employers and workers' representatives, may lie in the potential impact of equal opportunities policies. While not a statutory requirement, the publishing of such policies is recommended in the CRE and EOC Codes of Practice in Employment[133] and is a matter of routine in larger organisations, frequently applying to a range of possible discriminatory factors, not only the statutory ones of race, sex and disability. Publishing an equal opportunities policy does not, however, guarantee that the employer's practice reflects the policy and there is even evidence to suggest that 'equal opportunities employers' may do worse than those who do not issue formal statements, at least in relation to ethnic minority job applicants.[134] These statements, at their worst, are a fig leaf to cover indifference to equal opportunities.

There have been two reported cases where there has been an attempt to rely on the terms of such a policy as terms of the contract of employment. In both cases, this was in relation to non-statutory grounds of discrimination, in one age[135] and in the other sexual preference,[136] where there is at present no statutory right to non-discrimination. Although, in *Secretary of State for Scotland v Taylor*, the EAT found that the company's equal opportunities policy had not been breached on age grounds because Mr Taylor, a prison

---

130 [1990] IRLR 3.

131 *Ibid*, p 6.

132 *WA Goold (Pearmak) Ltd v McConnell* [1995] IRLR 516; *Waltons and Morse v Dorrington* [1997] IRLR 488.

133 CRE Code of Practice for the Elimination of Racial Discrimination and the Promotion of Equality of Opportunity in Employment, 1983, 1.1; EOC Code of Practice for the Elimination of Discrimination on the Grounds of Sex and Marriage and the Promotion of Equality of Opportunity in Employment, 1985, para 33.

134 Cardiff Business School, 'Racial discrimination in speculative application: new optimism six years on?', 1998, referred to in (1998) 81 EOR 11.

135 *Secretary of State for Scotland v Taylor* [1997] IRLR 608.

136 *Grant v South-West Trains Ltd* [1998] IRLR 188.

officer, had reached the new retirement age (55) and the anti-age discrimination part of the policy could not be assumed to have been intended to apply to retirement, the court did, nevertheless, accept the tribunal's finding that the terms of the policy had been incorporated into Mr Taylor's contract of employment. Both IT and EAT rejected the employer's argument that the policy was a 'mission statement' and, as such, unenforceable. Quite the opposite decision was reached in *Grant v South-West Trains Ltd*, in which Ms Grant challenged the decision not to grant her female partner the same travel rights as those awarded to the opposite sex partners of other employees, on the basis that the refusal was contrary to the company's equal opportunities policy. Not only did the High Court hold that the terms of the policy could not over-ride the explicit reference to 'opposite sex' but it, also, held that the policy itself was in 'general, even idealistic' terms and, so, was non-contractual. The policy committed the company to 'ensuring that all individuals are treated fairly and are valued irrespective of disability, race, gender, health, social class, sexual preference, marital status, nationality, religion, employment status, age or membership or non-membership of a trade union. No one is to receive less favourable treatment on any of the above grounds'. In Mr Justice Curtis's view, not only was it general and idealistic but 'it also covers such matters as 'health and social class', which would be alien to employment contractual law'.[137] Why these would be any more alien than religion or disability or any of the other grounds is not clear. Indeed, class may be thought to be the essence of the matter. Neither case report makes it clear how the respective policies were introduced. Mr Justice Evans relies heavily, in support of his judgment, on how the policy was introduced (as much as its content) and the fact that it was not introduced through the machinery of collective bargaining, which would have indicated contractual intent. Taking both cases together, there seems no barrier to the incorporation of such general and idealistic terms into the contract (non-discrimination in itself being a very basic form of idealism), so long as the necessary intention can be inferred, either from their source in collective bargaining arrangements or in the terms of the policy itself – including more specific commitments to a discrimination-free promotion system, for example, rather than the simple assertion at which so many policies excel.

CONCLUSION

Not only is the legal concept of the contract of employment based on the inequality between the employer and worker, it also reflects the gendered nature of work and social attitudes. An employee has been seen as, typically, a full time permanent worker with continuous employment. Other patterns of

---

137 [1998] IRLR 188, p 189.

work have been viewed as, essentially, secondary or marginal, largely because they are perceived as being linked with the female sphere of commitment, primarily to family and home rather than work. This has determined the nature of, and rights accorded to, employees' contracts and those of workers more generally.

While the feminisation of the workplace may have involved as much of an increase in part time work (a traditional female pattern of work) as any greater involvement of women in the workplace, there has also been a change in men's work patterns: an increase in part time work, and less security of employment. To a lesser extent than is often perceived, there has, therefore, been some fracturing of the common view of the paradigm employee. At the same time, legal attitudes to the contract have been under challenge from a sex discrimination standpoint, while courts have, to a limited extent, shown themselves more willing to adopt less traditional approaches to analysing the contract. However, these are only first steps towards a broader, more inclusive approach to employment relationships and employment rights which, at the moment, large numbers of women workers stand outside. Changes in the definition of employment and related changes to the terms of employment, through the implied terms or the incorporation of terms, are modernising influences on the contract which would benefit all workers – men and women – by including them, rather than leaving them marginalised and excluded from fundamental legal rights.

CHAPTER 6

VOLUNTEERING:
A NICE LITTLE JOB FOR A WOMAN?

Debra Morris

INTRODUCTION

It is remarkable how little has been written on the effect of gender on the character and composition of the voluntary sector.[1] In attempting to remedy this, this chapter will argue that, while the nature of the voluntary sector has traditionally been female gendered, it is undergoing a period of change, brought about through the formalisation of the sector itself.

It will be seen that, throughout history, women have volunteered. Voluntary work has often given women a place in society which would otherwise have been denied them. Women have readily risen to the challenge of helping out on the ground, but their organisations have often been run by men. This is still true, to some extent, and evidence will be examined which proves that more men than women tend to manage voluntary bodies. Being seen as largely 'women's work', voluntary work (and paid social work) has mainly been devalued in society and taken for granted. Major changes in the voluntary sector occurred in the 1990s, due to the shift in welfare provision from the State to the voluntary and private sectors, and the consequent changes in the funding of voluntary bodies. These changes have resulted in the role of volunteers in the delivery of welfare services being increasingly formalised. At the same time, the professionalisation of the voluntary sector, and the increased bureaucracy that this entails, is fashioning a more prominent face for the sector and for the volunteer, in particular. It will be seen that there is increased legal encroachment into the regulation of volunteering. Whilst the advantages of this phenomenon are recognised, to some extent, the demise of the 'feminine form of philanthropy'[2] is also lamented.

---

1   Prochaska notes, 'Many issues raised by the expansion of philanthropy have been treated with considerable insight. But at least one question has largely escaped the historian: the role of charitable women among the "Fathers of the Victorians"': Prochaska, FK, 'Women in English philanthropy 1790–1830' (1974) 19 International Review of Social History 426.
2   Butler, J, *Woman's Work and Woman's Culture*, 1869, London: Macmillan, p xxxvii. Discussed below.

THE VOLUNTARY SECTOR

Before focusing on the role of women in the voluntary sector, this section will consider the broad nature of volunteering and the voluntary sector in general. The extent to which people volunteer and their reasons for doing so will be examined. It will be seen that whilst, in the past, the typical female volunteer complied with the 'Lady Bountiful' image of being middle-aged and middle-class, changes in social conditions may (rightly) result in shifts in these perceptions.

Volunteering is the commitment of time and energy for the benefit of society or the community. It is undertaken by choice, without concern for financial gain. Voluntary work has been defined as unpaid work (except for expenses), done through a group or on behalf of an organisation of some kind but not for a trade union or political party.[3] Not all volunteering occurs in the voluntary sector. Volunteers may offer help through the aegis of a statutory body as well as a voluntary organisation. However, a key defining feature of many organisations in the growing and dynamic voluntary sector is that they rely on voluntary activity.

One of the voluntary sector's main characteristics is its heterogeneity, reflecting the diversity of the social conditions with which it is engaged. It includes organisations of all sizes, involved in all manner of activities, carried out in a great number of different ways. They may be established using a variety of legal forms and are subject to a wide range of regulations and regulators. The pluralistic nature of the voluntary sector has given rise to many attempts to define its boundaries. The ongoing work co-ordinated by the Johns Hopkins University at Baltimore, USA on the scope, structure, history, legal position and role of the non-profit sector in a broad cross section of countries has identified a broad and narrow voluntary sector.[4] The broad sector definition, which is used for international comparison purposes, includes all organisations that are: formally constituted; independent of government and self-governing; not directly run by a for-profit agency or the State; and not distributing any profits or delivering financial services. The narrow sector definition, which, the researchers argue, fits more comfortably with the public's view of what constitutes voluntary action, excludes organisations which are: insufficiently altruistic; do not deliver public benefit; and are not fully independent. The number of voluntary bodies in 1990 is estimated, using the broad definition, at 378,000–418,000. Using the narrow definition, the estimates decrease to 200,000–240,000. The total operating

---

3 Goddard, E, *Voluntary Work*, 1994, London: HMSO.
4 See, eg, Kendall, J and Knapp, M, *Voluntary Sector in the UK*, 1996, Manchester: Manchester UP. In particular, see Chap 4.

expenditures in 1990 for the broad and narrow voluntary sectors is estimated at £26.4 billion and £10.0 billion, respectively. Similarly, the broad and narrow voluntary sectors' operating income is estimated at £29.5 billion and £12.3 billion, respectively.[5]

Not all voluntary organisations satisfy the legal definition of 'charity'[6] in English law. Some may have non-charitable objective but may still be voluntary organisations – not for profit, independent and voluntarily managed. These may include friendly societies, campaigning groups, etc. A registered charity is a voluntary organisation which has objects that satisfy the legal definition of charity and is registered with the Charity Commission, a government department accountable to Parliament through the Home Office, which registers, supports and monitors charities in England and Wales. This is the part of the voluntary sector about which most is known, quantitatively, due to the registration requirements. The total number of registered charities on the register at the end of December 1997 was just over 184,000.[7] Of these, about 28,000 were subsidiaries or branches of other charities. This means that there were about 156,000 'main' charities on the register. Some groups may be exempt or excepted charities and are, therefore, not on the register. Others may have charitable objectives but may not have been registered. Many charities on the register are very small organisations, and the financial wealth of registered charities, measured by their annual income, is concentrated in just a few very large charities. At the end of 1997, 91% of main registered charities had an income of less than £100,000 and approximately 75% of these had a gross income of less than £10,000. The largest 251 charities attracted approximately 40% of the total annual charitable income.[8]

Some very large and formal voluntary organisations will be staffed entirely by paid employees, with the only voluntary element being the unpaid board of management. At the other end of the scale are organisations run entirely by volunteers. Research undertaken by the National Council for Voluntary Organisations (NCVO) in 1998 found that less than 25% of general charities employ paid staff.[9] It is estimated that general charities have over 3 million volunteers and that they contribute the equivalent of almost 1.6 million full time jobs. The research places an economic value on this activity at £12 billion, of which £8 billion is either in terms of direct service work or administrative support. The remaining £4 billion relates to fund-raising.

---

5   Source of this information is *op cit*, Kendall and Knapp, fn 4, Chap 4.
6   For a 'modern' classification of the English definition of charity, see *Income Tax Special Purposes Commissioners v Pemsel* [1891] AC 531.
7   Charity Commission, *Annual Report 1997*, 1998, London: HMSO, para 60.
8   *Ibid*, para 61.
9   Hems, L and van Doorn, A, *NCVO Survey of Job Roles and Salaries in the Voluntary Sector 1997/1998*, 1998, London: NCVO.

The work done by volunteers covers almost the entire range of social provision and provides opportunities for the exercise of widely differing skills and abilities and for every level of responsibility and initiative. At one end of the scale, there are highly trained and experienced volunteer project managers, often retired from government or industry, running large programmes.[10] At the other end of the scale, occasional volunteers might bake cakes or lick stamps. In between, volunteers may serve extensively in 'befriending' and supporting those in need, or organise or participate in fund-raising efforts. Volunteers may have direct contact with service users of any age, or they may undertake work in which personal contacts are slight or non-existent, though its purpose is still that of helping other people. Time given can vary from occasional involvement in specific events (such as serving on a stall at an annual fund-raising bazaar), to several hours each month or week, to the equivalent of working full time. There are some organisations, like the marriage guidance charity Relate, or the Citizens' Advice Bureau, for example, which are highly specialised and seek only volunteers who are able and willing to be trained for, and to undertake, a particular type of skilled work.

In the UK, there is a rich tradition of voluntary activity, whereby individuals come together to meet social or economic need, without calling on the State. In the welfare state, volunteers provide support to overburdened services, complementing the work of paid staff. As members of voluntary organisations, they have continued to compensate for gaps in the existing statutory services, providing those services which can more appropriately be given by volunteers. The State, through statutory bodies, has an awareness of its own need for voluntary reinforcements.[11] The *Compact on Relations between Government and the Voluntary and Community Sector in England*, published in November 1998, specifically recognises that the government and the voluntary and community sector fulfil complementary roles in the development and delivery of public policy and services, and that the government has a role in promoting voluntary and community activity.[12] Voluntary activity provides a means by which the community itself can participate in discovering and meeting the needs of its members, and

---

10 Note the role of the Retired Executive Action Clearing House (REACH) – an organisation that finds voluntary jobs for people with managerial or professional experience. A similar scheme is the Retired and Senior Volunteer Programme (RSVP).

11 Under the previous Conservative Government, see, eg, Volunteering Unit, *Make a Difference: An Outline Volunteering Strategy for the UK*, 1995, London: Home Office. Under the present Labour Government, in October 1997, David Blunkett, the Secretary of State for Education and Employment, launched a radical new programme called Millennium Volunteers to provide volunteering opportunities for young people.

12 *Getting it Right Together: Compact on Relations between Government and the Voluntary and Community Sector in England*, Cm 4100, November 1998, London: Home Office. Parallel compacts have also been developed in other parts of the United Kingdom.

formulate its own definitions of welfare. The wider the field of recruitment for volunteers, the more significant this function becomes.

The impulse to serve as a volunteer is strong and widespread. In 1998, the Institute for Volunteering Research published the third national survey of volunteering.[13] For the purposes of the survey, volunteering is defined as 'any activity which involves spending time, unpaid, doing something which aims to benefit someone (individuals or groups), other than, or in addition to, close relatives, or to benefit the environment'. It was found that, since 1991, when the last survey was conducted, the rise in volunteering had flattened out, so that, in the previous 12 months, just under half the population had volunteered at least once. This represents a total number of 21.8 million volunteers in the UK, giving a total of 88 million hours per week.

Questions about volunteering were also included in the General Household Survey in 1992.[14] Under a narrower definition of voluntary work,[15] almost a quarter of people aged 16 and over said that they had done some kind of voluntary work in 1991. The average time spent on voluntary work was about four hours per week, which, if totalled across the population, suggests that, according to this survey, 20 million hours are spent volunteering each week.

The motives, conscious and unconscious, which prompt people to volunteer are complex and subtle. Any attempt to isolate particular reasons invites over-simplification. Perhaps the safest generalisation that can be made is that every volunteer is motivated by a mixture of altruism and self-interest.[16] Volunteers help themselves as much as their community or environment. In return for giving their time, they often gain an increased sense of self-esteem, while developing skills and talents. For example, some may make new friends and relieve loneliness. Others may suddenly have more time on their hands and feel a need to have a structure in their lives following retirement or child rearing, or they may be moved by a particular cause. Volunteering allows ordinary people to help others – it fulfils the need that many have to be needed. One tangible motivating factor may be a desire to gain experience before applying for paid employment. A recent study of voluntary work by unemployed people found that reasons for doing voluntary work while claiming benefits included improving job prospects. Some saw voluntary work as a stepping stone to employment: helping to increase confidence, motivation to look for a job and a feeling of being 'job

---

13   Davis Smith, J, *The 1997 National Survey of Volunteering*, 1998, London: National Centre for Volunteering. (Hereafter referred to as the 1997 survey of volunteering.)

14   *Op cit*, Goddard, fn 3.

15   Voluntary work was defined as unpaid work (except for expenses) done through a group, or on behalf of an organisation of some kind, but not for a trade union or political party.

16   This is confirmed in the 1997 survey of volunteering: *ibid*, Davis Smith.

ready'.[17] This is especially so for young people not settled in their career or mothers contemplating re-entering the employment market.

Voluntary work is, theoretically, an option for everyone, regardless of age, gender, race, ability, health, background or any other label. Historically, however, organised voluntary work has been the prerogative of the upper and middle classes – there was a commonly held view that the typical volunteer was a middle-aged, middle-class married woman. Long standing traditions or perceptions are not changed overnight, but there are signs that the range of social backgrounds is getting wider.[18] Moreover, the availability of different sections of the community for voluntary work is affected by both changing work patterns and wider social changes, including: the increased use of family planning and the concomitant tendency towards later child bearing; the increase in single parent families; more part time employment of mothers; the movement of mothers into full time work; shorter working hours in some occupations; earlier retirement, often resulting in earlier promotion to responsible and demanding work; and increased longevity and the consequent increased need to care for elderly relatives. Many of these factors particularly affect female volunteers.

WOMEN AND THE VOLUNTARY SECTOR

Some of the most basic caring tasks in human society, such as child rearing and looking after the sick and elderly, have traditionally been carried out through the use of voluntary activity; traditionally, through female voluntary activity. Many of the images, values and typical activities of the voluntary sector are 'female' and 'soft'. They are rooted in the traditional assumptions of a woman's place being at home or engaging in 'good works'. Voluntary work naturally fits in with the very powerful social expectations of the maternal role of a woman, governed more by her emotions than by rational thoughts.

A historical perspective

When commenting on the years 1790–1830, Prochaska noted that, for women, philanthropy was an escape from boredom – 'it was outdoor relief for leisured

---

17 Elam, G and Thomas, A, *Stepping Stones to Employment: Part Time Work and Voluntary Activities Whilst Claiming Out-of-Work Social Security Benefits*, DSS Research Report No 71, 1997, London: TSO.

18 See Joseph Rowntree Foundation, *Involving Volunteers from Underrepresented Groups*, Social Policy Research Findings 105, 1996, York: Joseph Rowntree Foundation.

women'.[19] This caricature of 'Lady Bountiful', filling her time by helping the poor because she had nothing better to do is a recurrent theme in the literature.[20] McCarthy notes how this has stigmatised and trivialised women's philanthropy.[21] Even as late as the early 1970s, one American writer was of the view that wealthy women volunteer mainly due to their need to leave the home and 'see the world'. Gold states:

> ... many women form structures disguised as 'causes' and 'needs' in order to fulfil their powerful social needs for adult contact ... the loneliness they feel in their well furnished homes and apartments, empty until 3pm or dinner, is assuaged by their involvement with the self-created 'work' that women without special training can do.[22]

However, Summers, in her work on women's philanthropy in the 19th century, finds this line of reasoning 'belittling and insulting'.[23] She concludes that there must have been (and, I suggest, there still is) some positive motivation for their voluntary activity. A more compelling and more modern reason why women involve themselves with voluntary work may be the lack of availability of satisfying part time work for women.[24] Whilst fulfilling their need to be needed,[25] voluntary work allows women to be involved in interesting and useful work outside the home. It can also be their first step back to paid employment, providing a much needed boost to their confidence after years of domestic work.

Throughout history, women have played a central role in the creation of voluntary organisations. Similarly, the voluntary sector has done much to enlarge the public domain of women by broadening their horizons. Historians relate that, barred from other areas of (masculine) civil life, women founded and actively shaped some of the first charities, settlements and social welfare programmes. Paradoxically, at the same time, voluntary work confirmed women's 'rightful' domestic status. Charity begins at home, and women, regarding voluntary work as a natural extension of their domestic role as

---

19 *Op cit*, Prochaska, fn 1, p 441.

20 See, for example, Prochaska, FK, *Women and Philanthropy in Nineteenth Century England*, 1980, Oxford: Clarendon.

21 McCarthy, K, 'Parallel power structures: women and the voluntary sphere', in McCarthy, K (ed), *Lady Bountiful Revisited: Women Philanthropy and Power*, 1990, New Brunswick: Rutgers UP.

22 Gold, D, 'Women and Voluntarism', in Gornick, V and Moran, B (eds), *Woman in Sexist Society*, 1971, New York: Basic, p 388.

23 Summers, A, 'A home from home – women's philanthropic work in the 19th century', in Burman, S (ed), *Fit Work for Women*, 1979, London: Croom Helm, p 38.

24 This is also acknowledged by Gold, *ibid*.

25 Simey talks of the '... hunger of the idle woman to be valued as an individual': Simey, M, *Charity Rediscovered. A Study of Philanthropic Effort in 19th Century Liverpool*, 1992, Liverpool: Liverpool UP, p 65.

wives and mothers, were often the first to identify the social welfare needs of women and children and to respond to them through a wide range of charitable activities.[26] The voluntary nature of the work automatically overcame the opposition of those who disapproved of women earning a living. In the early 1800s, the sort of voluntary work that women were engaging in all around England included work in 'lying-in charities, asylums for the deaf, blind, destitute and insane, soup kitchens, village shops, libraries, chapels, schools, and hospitals'.[27] Prochaska notes that women 'deemed such duties their particular calling. Compassion and tenderness were, after all, considered to be peculiarly feminine virtues'.[28]

Involvement in voluntary work gave many women, for the first time, some power outside their homes. This was especially the case for 'correctly behaved' young ladies for whom 'money-raising efforts provided a heaven sent excuse for all manner of activities which would otherwise have been forbidden'.[29] More importantly, Beveridge notes:

> When Elizabeth Fry, in February 1818, was summoned to give evidence to a Committee of the House of Commons on the Prisons of the Metropolis, she was [quoting from Whitney][30] 'the first woman other than a queen to be called into the councils of the Government in an official manner to advise on matters of public concern'.[31]

It was not just in England[32] that women were enhancing their own social role and making a significant contribution to the development of society through their voluntary work. McCarthy, commenting on an international study looking at women and philanthropy, said, 'often denied access to political participation and barred from remunerative occupations until well into the 20th century, middle-class women donors, volunteers and organisational entrepreneurs nevertheless left their imprint on national legislation and institutions in a variety of countries'.[33] However, it has been noted:

---

26 See, eg, Koven, S, 'Borderlands: women, voluntary action and child welfare in Britain, 1840 to 1914', in Koven, S and Michel, S (eds), *Mothers of a New World. Maternalist Politics and the Origins of Welfare States*, 1993, London: Routledge, where the author looks at the history of child welfare in Britain from the mid-19th century until World War I and explores how, through voluntary work, women gained power and political expertise.

27 *Op cit*, Prochaska, fn 1, p 431.

28 *Op cit*, Prochaska, fn 1, p 431.

29 *Op cit*, Simey, fn 25, p 63.

30 Whitney, J, *Elizabeth Fry: Quaker Heroine*, 1937, London: George G Harrap, p 215.

31 Beveridge, W, *Voluntary Action*, 1948, London: Allen & Unwin, p 126.

32 For an overview of the social achievements of women through voluntary work in Liverpool in the 19th century, see *op cit*, Simey, fn 25. In Victorian England, Liverpool's efforts at resolving social problems were often regarded as pioneering examples for the rest of the country.

33 McCarthy, K, 'Women and philanthropy' (1996) 7 Voluntas 331.

The irony, of course, was that, when many programs designed and run by women obtained social respectability, they were taken over by men. In addition, women were often denied access to paid jobs within the new agencies, although their volunteer labor was always of great importance.[34]

Once State funding and supervision were provided, what began life as initiatives run by women on a voluntary basis became bureaucracies staffed by men on a salary. Koven notes that, in the late 1800s, 'even single-sex organisations, like women's settlements, had close ties to male supporters and operated within larger social and political structures dominated by men'.[35]

Women as (invisible) volunteers

This image of the voluntary sector of the past is mirrored in the results of current surveys of volunteering,[36] which reveal that, although men and women are now equally likely to volunteer, women are much more likely than men to be involved in fund-raising and in delivering direct services, whilst men are more likely than women to be involved in the financial or strategic role of serving on committees. In law, the board of management of a voluntary body plays a crucial role. Managers, who may be called trustees, are under onerous obligations (both fiduciary and statutory) and are responsible for the general management and control of the voluntary body.[37] They make policy and present the face of the voluntary body to the outside world. With registered charities, for example, their names have to be held at the Charity Commission, together with the registration documents. They are the people in power. Their image is typically male and based on the male productive role, which emphasises visibility, independence and economic power. The volunteers providing services, more of whom are female than male, on the other hand, remain invisible, working behind the scenes.

As well as the surveys on volunteering, other sources confirm that, at the management level, men outnumber women in the voluntary sector quite significantly. For example, in a survey undertaken for the NCVO in 1991, it was found that men (63%) outnumbered women (37%) at both national and local levels on boards of trustees.[38] A more comprehensive survey

---

34 Burbridge, L, 'The occupational structure of non-profit industries: implications for women', in Odendahl, T and O'Neill, M (eds), *Women and Power in the Nonprofit Sector*, 1994, San Francisco: Jossey-Bass, p 123.

35 *Op cit*, Koven, fn 26, p 98.

36 See *op cit*, Davis Smith, fn 13, and *op cit*, Goddard, fn 3.

37 In the context of charities, see Charities Act 1993, s 97, for a definition of a charity trustee.

38 Ford, K, *On Trust: Trustee Training And Support Needs*, 1992, London: NCVO.

commissioned by the NCVO in 1994[39] has done much to uphold the stereotype of trustees being white, middle-class, middle-aged and male. By contrast, women, people with disabilities, people from non-professional backgrounds and people from ethnic minority communities all tend to be under-represented at the decision making level within voluntary bodies. It was found that, of the one million charity trustees in the UK, 65% were male. Nearly 50% of men were trustees of more than one organisation, compared with 35% of women. Reflecting the American experience,[40] it was also discovered that a higher proportion of male trustees than female trustees held some sort of office on the board. Long standing allegations that an 'old boys' network' exists linger and job allocation along stereotypical gender lines is evident. Far more men occupy the influential position of chair,[41] while far more women carry out the task of honorary secretary. Men are also likely to be trustees of national organisations, while women are likely to be trustees of local branches of national organisations. This may suggest that, as organisations become more 'powerful', in the sense that their budgets grow and more professionals are involved, boards of trustees become increasingly male.[42] As part of the NCVO survey in 1994, organisations were asked if they had an equal opportunities policy in relation to membership of their governing body and, if so, was it designed to assist any particular category. 52% had an equal opportunities policy and, of those, 23% were designed to assist a particular category.[43] Cancer Research Campaign, a national charity, is a prime example of a male dominated organisation. In 1997, its highest governing body, the council, had 14 members but included only two women. The charity's director of communications explained:

> ... the council reflects the 'way of the world', which is male dominated. With representation from the world of business, commerce and science, it is hard to find women who fit the bill.[44]

It could be said that the voluntary sector, therefore, is traditionally 'gendered female': there is a large 'workforce' of female volunteers undertaking individual acts of charity, generally regarded as 'women's' work', that is routine and largely devalued, yet these women are dominated by a male

---

39 See Sargant, N and Kirkland, K, *Building on Trust. Results of a Survey of Charity Trustees*, 1995, London: NCVO.

40 See, in general, Odendahl, T and Youmans, S, 'Women on nonprofit boards', in *op cit*, Odendahl and O'Neill, fn 34.

41 A survey undertaken in 1998 ascertained that 72% of all chairs of trustees are male: the Association of Chief Executives of National Voluntary Organisations, *Gender and The Chief Executive in the Voluntary Sector*, 1998, Middlesex: ACENVO.

42 See, to similar effect, observations in *op cit*, fn 40, where Odendahl and Youmans suggest that women may lose control of boards as boards become more powerful.

43 Gender (58%), race (53%), disability (32%) and age (16%) were the most frequently mentioned categories.

44 'Taking more women on board', *Third Sector*, 24 July 1997.

power structure, responsible for planning and managing the sector and making decisions about resource allocation.

The evidence suggests that women are more likely to be stuffing envelopes than serving on voluntary boards of management, the latter being one of the key aspects of voluntary bodies. Aware that ethnic minority women, in particular, are under-represented on voluntary boards, the NCVO, in partnership with the Commission for Racial Equality, have begun to address this issue. This is being done mainly through developing and disseminating good practice in this area and through the development of programmes to encourage the recruitment and support of under-represented groups. In particular, a resource and seminar programme was developed in 1997,[45] in order to generate ideas on how to achieve fairer representation. It has been noted that views are mixed on the role of women and how they should be recruited. Some organisations do not see it as an issue, whereas others want their boards to be more diverse but need more guidance.[46] Some of the negative images of volunteering which have been proffered by respondents in the 1997 survey of volunteering[47] suggest that there may be barriers discouraging women from becoming involved. These barriers include the 'culture' of many committees, which may be perceived as unwelcoming to anyone who does not 'fit' the typical stereotype of a trustee. For example, 36% of non-volunteer respondents said that they were discouraged from volunteering by 'all the associated bureaucracy'.[48] The sort of cultural and organisational features that might deter women include: the way trustees are recruited and selected; attitudes towards diversity; the role of the chair; the use of jargon in meetings; the timing of meetings; and the non-payment of expenses.[49] It could be suggested that one of the main deterrents to acting as trustee for women is the competing demands on their time. Being a trustee does not simply entail attending monthly meetings. NCVO research shows that trusteeship can demand a considerable time commitment, with one in five trustees in their survey giving at least one day per week to their duties and a further 40% giving one day each month.[50] As more women attain the levels of competence and business skills frequently sought by the larger charities, so their professional working days grow longer. Many of these women also have domestic commitments, which eat into their 'free time', greatly restricting the opportunities for responsible trusteeship.

---

45 See NCVO, *Governance in Focus: A Race and Gender Perspective. An Executive Summary*, 1997, London: NCVO.

46 *Op cit*, Cancer Research Campaign, fn 44.

47 *Op cit*, Davis Smith, fn 13.

48 *Op cit*, Davis Smith, fn 13.

49 *Ibid*, NCVO.

50 See *op cit*, Sargant and Kirkland, fn 39.

The value of 'women's (voluntary) work'

Some American commentators suggest that many tasks now performed in the voluntary sector settings are economically devalued in society because the skills that the jobs require are taken for granted and treated as invisible, largely due to the fact that the work is often performed by women.[51] In short, women's voluntary work outside the home is regarded in the same way as their work within the home. It has less status accorded to it than work undertaken in the business sphere. In effect, work that is not done for pay does not really exist. The very fact that it is women who do this work makes it appear unskilled and undemanding. In turn, the fact that women are sufficiently talented to make it *appear* unskilled and undemanding does not help their cause. Paying for this work, or even noticing its existence, deviates from the illusion that it is 'natural'. It is presumed that the skills and talents required to carry out these tasks are natural attributes of women, deserving no special credit. Brown and Smith go so far as to say, concerning women and their natural role as carer: '... the act of *not* caring would be seen as a defection from normal and loving relationships.'[52] Research on paid informal care schemes revealed (unsurprisingly) that carers are predominantly women.[53] According to one organiser:

> It's not just that caring is traditionally women's work and so fewer men apply. When a man does apply, you do feel, I think, that you've got to be extra-careful – caring men attract suspicion in a way that caring women don't.[54]

The entry of more women into the paid labour market, burdening women with a double agenda of family and work responsibilities, has severely reduced the pool of 'traditional' volunteers. Nevertheless, Brown and Smith point out[55] that, whilst women's paid employment status outside the home is incompatible with full time caring, women are still portrayed as behaving unnaturally if they do not adopt the caring role.

Another typically female voluntary activity which is taken for granted is organising and hosting social events with the aim of fund-raising. Such events may be gala balls, luncheons, garden fêtes or the like. This is another area where women's work is invisible and devalued, again on the assumption that it is the sort of thing that women do naturally, and, therefore, without much

---

51 See, eg, Steinberg, R and Jacobs, J, 'Pay equity in nonprofit organizations: making women's work visible', in *op cit*, Odendahl and O'Neill, fn 34.

52 Brown, H and Smith, H, 'Women caring for people: the mismatch between rhetoric and women's reality?' (1993) 21 Policy and Politics 186.

53 See Morris, Chapter 9, this volume.

54 Leat, D and Gay, P, *Paying for Care*, 1987, London: Policy Studies Institute, p 22.

55 *Ibid*, Brown and Smith, p 187.

effort on their part. One American academic has termed this 'sociability work', defined as 'the creation of an ambience by those who provide some kind of hospitality'.[56] Daniels argues that the effort that goes into this activity can be dismissed as 'merely' sociable interchange, related to women's gender roles and natural propensities, requiring no real skills. She says that, by dismissing this effort, the importance of planning, experience and ability in making such functions a success, together with much hard work, is overlooked.[57] Not only is this work invisible to the general public, it is even devalued by the women who do it. Daniels noted that 'women may even be apologetic about the time they give to the promotion of sociability. A few go further, to disavow or deride this activity'.[58]

The fact that women care naturally is used to explain the low wages of *paid* workers in the voluntary sector.[59] Professional nurses and child-minders, for example, are simply extending their natural family role as nurturer, so do not need to be paid very well for doing it. Comparisons across sectors suggest that, for most job roles, salary levels in the voluntary sector are below the market average. For example, figures produced in 1998[60] show that salaries for voluntary sector staff are up to one-fifth lower than the national average. Research undertaken by the NCVO in 1998 found that 75% of paid workers of general charities are female.[61] Due to uncertainties in funding, working in the voluntary sector, often on fixed term contracts, can be precarious. The NCVO research[62] found that general charities employ a large number[63] of casual workers, subject to zero hours contracts which do not specify particular hours of employment. Under zero hours contracts, workers are permanently 'on call' but are only paid for the time worked. Under such conditions, strong commitment to the ideals of the voluntary sector may lead to many paid workers being taken advantage of. For example, some paid workers in the voluntary sector are now even being asked to work some 'voluntary hours' as part of their job.[64] One in 10 organisations in the 1998 NCVO survey reported that some of their paid workers took a 'salary sacrifice' (that is, work for a lower salary than the post is graded) and four out of five organisations

---

56 See Daniels, AK, 'Good times and good works: the place of sociability in the work of women volunteers' (1985) 32 Social Problems 363.
57 In this, she compares such work with housework and home making.
58 *Ibid*, Daniels, p 370.
59 *Op cit*, Steinberg and Jacobs, fn 51, p 90.
60 Reward Group, *Charity Rewards Review 1998/99*, 1998, Staffs: Reward Group.
61 *Op cit*, Hems and van Doorn, fn 9.
62 *Op cit*, Hems and van Doorn, fn 9.
63 9.1% of all paid workers employed by general charities are casual workers.
64 See 'Charity boosts hourly rate', *Third Sector*, 5 March 1998, commenting on Cancer Research Campaign's advert looking for a part time assistant manager to work 12 paid hours and four voluntary hours per week! See below on minimum wage.

reported that some paid staff worked additional hours on an unpaid, voluntary basis.[65]

THE CHANGING FACE OF VOLUNTEERING

The formalisation of voluntary work

There has been a gradual change, accelerated in the 1990s, in the State funding of voluntary organisations providing social welfare services. In the past, they were awarded unrestricted grants to further their activities. Now, many social welfare voluntary organisations enter into contracts, often with local authorities,[66] in which the voluntary organisations agree to provide specific services in exchange for payment from the local authorities. At the same time as the occurrence of this shift from grants to contracts, the role of local authorities, especially in the field of community care, has been shifted from the traditional one of provider to that of contractor.[67] These developments mean that, now, voluntary organisations are delivering more core welfare services and are being funded to provide such services by contract, rather than by grant. The implementation of the National Health Service and Community Care Act 1990 exemplifies this 'mixed economy of welfare' policy in practice, whereby the State increasingly withdraws from the direct provision of care and, instead, purchases welfare services from other providers, including voluntary organisations. This new basis of funding of social welfare has been described as the 'contract culture' and this new climate of contracts is giving rise to a fundamental shift in the values and culture of volunteering. The expansion and increased professionalism in the voluntary sector (both partly, but not wholly, due to the contract culture) have also had their parts to play in changing the role of volunteers. As the emphasis on good management and effective organisation within the voluntary sector has grown, a by-product has been an increased formalisation for volunteers.

In some respects, the previously fragmented and marginal voluntary sector has assumed some of the negative bureaucratic features of the statutory system. As voluntary bodies are engaged in more formal commitments for service delivery, they have to operate to formalised standards, which clearly affect volunteers. The problems posed for volunteering by contracting were

---

65 *Op cit*, Hems and van Doorn, fn 9.

66 Voluntary organisations are also supplying services, under contract, to other bodies, as well as local authorities. These include health authorities, training and enterprise councils (TECs), trust hospitals and even private companies.

67 The authority's role is also sometimes described in the literature as that of 'purchaser', 'enabler', 'procurer' or 'commissioner'.

first documented by Hedley and Davis Smith in 1994.[68] Their study concluded that, although contracts can offer advantages in terms of security of funding, the contract specifications seldom made explicit reference to volunteers, either as workers or as management committee members. A later study, by Russell and Scott,[69] whilst confirming that volunteers generally tend to be invisible in contracts, found that the workload, level of responsibility and skills required of volunteers have increased significantly as a result of the development of contracts, particularly for those on management committees. There is some evidence that, in some organisations, volunteers are being replaced with paid staff.[70] Alternatively, where organisations retain their volunteers, the role of volunteers in service delivery has become increasingly formalised and tighter management control is being imposed over them.[71] Tighter job descriptions, formal review and appraisal systems and even disciplinary procedures are all, now, becoming commonplace for volunteers. The 1997 survey of volunteering showed some evidence of this.[72] For example, the survey found that the proportion of volunteers working to a job description had increased from 12% in 1991 to 17% in 1997 and the number of volunteers being called for interview has doubled over the period to 14%. A further move towards formalisation is seen in the practice of screening volunteers. As volunteers are treated in the same way as employees for the purpose of police checks, vetting of volunteers undertaking work with children, young people or vulnerable adults is now commonplace. This practice will increase when Pt V of the Police Act 1997 comes into force. Employers will then have wide access to police records through the Criminal Records Agency and, therefore, police checks will become *de facto* obligatory for some types of voluntary work. This may deter volunteers who do not wish to subject themselves to such checks. It may also cost volunteers money. It is expected that an enhanced criminal record certificate will cost around £10. At present, there is no provision for free checks for volunteers.[73]

There is even a rather widespread phenomenon of paying 'volunteers'.[74] This carries potential for legal implications which could change the face of volunteering. The Commission on the Future of the Voluntary Sector warned in 1996 that 'in the eyes of the law, volunteering may be becoming

---

68 Hedley, R and Davis Smith, J, *Volunteers and the Contract Culture*, 1994, London: Volunteer Centre UK.

69 Russell, L and Scott, D, *Very Active Citizens? The Impact of the Contract Culture on Volunteers*, 1997, Manchester: Manchester UP.

70 *Ibid*, Russell and Scott.

71 *Ibid*, Russell and Scott.

72 *Op cit*, Davis Smith, fn 13.

73 There is simply a statutory power allowing the Secretary of State, by regulation, to exempt certain groups from paying any fee: see, eg, Police Act 1997, s 115.

74 See the results of a survey discussed in Blacksell, S and Philips, D, *Paid to Volunteer. The Extent of Paying Volunteers in the 1990s*, 1994, London: Volunteer Centre UK.

indistinguishable from paid work and, thus, subject to the full panoply of employment legislation'.[75]

Exploitation of volunteers

The object of making greater use of voluntary help should always be to extend and improve a service, by adding something to what is already being done, or by opening up new possibilities. As voluntary bodies are expected to take on more provision of services through contract funding, volunteers are now being asked to carry out work of an increasingly professional nature. The incentive to exploit volunteers is more prevalent than previously. There is some evidence to suggest that the withdrawal of the State from welfare provision is leading to volunteers being utilised in inappropriate ways, so as to substitute statutory services. It is easy for the unpaid work of women, as relatives, neighbours and friends, to be exploited. There is a growing body of evidence showing that female volunteers are carrying out essential and necessary functions which should be fulfilled by professional workers. For example, the study by Bagilhole[76] of a voluntary home visiting scheme, which offers support for families in difficulties, described how volunteers, with very limited training, were having to cope with extremely challenging situations.[77] This 'over-use' of volunteers may backfire, as individuals become more reluctant to volunteer if they feel that they are simply being used as a replacement for statutory services. The 1997 survey of volunteering found that there was an increase in criticism from volunteers about the amount of time that their volunteering takes up.[78] The view was also expressed by some that too much was expected of volunteers.

Volunteers and employee status

For many years, voluntary bodies have taken advantage of the services of their 'invisible' volunteers, generally without fear of such workers being able to claim any employment rights protection. However, there have been several developments which may suggest that changes are under way. For example,

---

75 The Commission on the Future of the Voluntary Sector, *Meeting the Challenge of Change: Voluntary Action into the 21st Century*, 1996, London: NCVO, p 76.

76 Bagilhole, B, 'Tea and sympathy or teetering on social work? An investigation of the blurring of the boundaries between voluntary and professional care' (1996) 30 Social Policy and Administration 189.

77 For example, volunteers described how lives of both mothers and children were sometimes at risk in the families that they visited.

78 *Op cit*, Davis Smith, fn 13.

in 1994, an industrial tribunal held in *Armitage v Relate*[79] that a Relate marriage guidance counsellor was in employment within the meaning of the Race Relations Act 1976.[80] She had volunteered on the understanding that Relate would provide her with training and supervision, in exchange for her working a minimum number of hours. There was also provision in the agreement for the recoupment of training expenses from counsellors who did not fulfil their obligations. In addition, the agreement foresaw that counsellors could effectively be 'dismissed'.[81]

Another case, which has caused some concern for voluntary sector organisations, is that brought in 1997 by Mrs Chaudri, who worked for the Migrant Advisory Service (MAS), and who sought to challenge her volunteer status.[82] She worked four days per week, from 10 am to 1 pm, undertaking general typing and office administration duties. She had done so since 1994. She was originally paid £25 (later increased to £40), which was stated to be weekly 'travel and subsistence expenses' by MAS. However, Mrs Chaudri lived near to the office where she worked and finished work by lunchtime each day and, therefore, incurred no travel or subsistence expenses. The payments were also made when Mrs Chaudri was off work, either on holiday or due to sickness. The termination of her arrangement with MAS followed her announcement that she was pregnant. She then commenced an application in the industrial tribunal claming unfair dismissal,[83] sex discrimination,[84] and breach of contract of employment.[85]

Unless she could show that she was an employee,[86] she would not be able to bring her claim in the industrial tribunal either for unfair dismissal or for breach of contract.[87] MAS argued that she was not an employee because: she did not receive a salary; she did not have a written contract of employment; there was no intention on the part of MAS to create a contract of employment; and she was not treated as an employee. The tribunal did not accept these arguments. Looking behind the 'label' placed upon the relationship, the tribunal was influenced by the fact that 'expense' payments were made to her at a flat rate, even though her expenses were negligible. In effect, the payment was merely a disguised payment of wages. Other influencing factors were

---

79 *De Lourdes Armitage v Relate and Others* IT Case Number: 43538/94, 11 October 1994.

80 Race Relations Act 1976, s 78(1).

81 Relate had the right to 'no longer support the Counsellor's continued work'.

82 *Chaudri v Migrant Advisory Service* IT Case Number: 2201678/96, 2 September 1997; upheld in the EAT: *Migrant Advisory Service v Chaudri*, EAT/1400/97, 28 July 1998.

83 Under Employment Rights Act 1996, s 94.

84 Under Sex Discrimination Act 1975.

85 Under Industrial Tribunals (Extension of Jurisdiction) Order 1994, SI 1994/1623, reg 3.

86 Defined, in Employment Rights Act 1996, s 230, as an individual who has entered into or works under a contract of employment.

87 'Employment' is defined more widely under the Sex Discrimination Act 1975.

that she worked regularly and for a substantial period of time. The result of this finding was that she was free to pursue all her claims.

A subsequent employment tribunal[88] found that a 'genuine' volunteer of St John Ambulance had no legal remedy against her employers when she complained of sexual harassment by a fellow volunteer and this decision was upheld by the Employment Appeal Tribunal.[89] In response to the suggestion that 'employment' in the Sex Discrimination Act 1975[90] should be construed widely, so as to include voluntary activity, Hicks J, in the Employment Appeal Tribunal, said:

> ... we see no detectable legislative purpose, at either the European or the national level, of including the voluntary members' activities of the members of a voluntary organisation. Quite the contrary.[91]

These decisions demonstrate that, unless apparent 'volunteers' can prove that they are in fact employed by a voluntary organisation, they are excluded from many employment protection provisions in the legislation. The Equal Opportunities Commission (EOC), in its recommendations in November 1998 to the government for a new sex equality law,[92] in which the EOC suggests that the Sex Discrimination Act 1975, the Equal Pay Act 1970 and other relevant laws should be replaced by a single Sex Equality Act, also recommends that protection from sex discrimination should be extended to volunteers.[93] The EOC considers that employers should have the same duties towards volunteers as they do towards anyone working under a formal contract of employment. The EOC, therefore, advocates that the new statute should define the circumstances in which it would be unlawful for an 'employer' of volunteers to discriminate.

These developments show that the tribunals are attempting to distinguish genuine volunteers, currently largely unprotected by employment law, from those whose real employment status is disguised and whose relationship with their employers will, in fact, be governed by employment law provisions. The cases provide evidence of some legal uncertainty, which employers can easily exploit to the detriment of those who undertake work on a voluntary basis. Unless and until the EOC's recommendations are adopted, employers can ensure that volunteers gain no legal protection from sexual harassment, for example, by ensuring that there is no obligation on their volunteers to attend

---

88 *Yu v St John Ambulance* IT Case Number: 2901522/97, 27 February 1998.

89 *Uttley v St John Ambulance* Appeal Number: EAT/635/98, 18 September 1998.

90 Sex Discrimination Act 1975, s 82, defines employment as 'employment under a contract of service or of apprenticeship or a contract personally to execute any work or labour ...'.

91 *Uttley v St John Ambulance* Appeal Number: EAT/635/98, 18 September 1998, p 14.

92 Equal Opportunities Commission, *Equality in the 21st Century: A New Sex Equality Law for Britain*, 1998, Manchester: EOC.

93 *Ibid*, p 10.

the workplace and that, if any payments are made, they cover genuine expenses only. On the other hand, cases such as *Chaudri* show that employers who fail properly to assess the working relationships that they have with their 'volunteers' may find that their workers are, in reality, employees. From the perspective of vulnerable female volunteers, this is one aspect of the formalisation of their role which is welcomed, as it gives them legal protection hitherto only afforded to employees.

Payment of volunteers

Paradoxically, the exploitative aspect of volunteering is leading to an increase in the practice of paying volunteers – 'volunteers are not prepared to wipe bottoms and empty catheters for free'.[94] However, when more than expenses but less than the market rate is paid, volunteers in effect become under-paid employees. A survey on the extent of paying volunteers in the 1990s[95] found evidence that voluntary organisations may be seen as cheap alternatives to the statutory sector through their potential use of paid volunteers in three ways: paying honoraria to co-ordinators; not payrolling volunteers for PAYE;[96] and arranging for volunteers to be paid directly by service users.

All volunteers should be able to claim back any money spent in the course of their voluntary work. No one should be out of pocket through volunteering or discouraged from undertaking voluntary work because they can not afford to do it. The 1997 survey of volunteering[97] found that, of all the volunteers who had incurred expenses, 54% had received no expenses payments at all. Non-payment of expenses is often stated as one of the barriers to volunteering by under-represented classes.[98] Expenses for which repayment is generally offered include travelling, postal and telephone expenses, occasionally secretarial expenses or protective clothing and, sometimes, even child care. The dividing line between payment of travelling and out of pocket expenses and payment for service is very fine, and great care must be exercised to ensure that reimbursement is made only of expenses which have actually been incurred. The problem of distinguishing between payment and expenses arises where a fixed flat rate sum is paid 'to cover expenses'.

Problems can arise if volunteers are paid any amounts other than actual out of pocket expenses. Sessional payments, pocket money, subsistence payments, honoraria or lump sums to cover possible expenses can all give rise

---

94 *Op cit*, Blacksell and Philips, fn 74, p 28.

95 *Op cit*, Blacksell and Philips, fn 74.

96 Pay As You Earn is the name given to the system of deduction of tax at source from employees' wages.

97 *Op cit*, Davis Smith, fn 13.

98 See, eg, *op cit*, Joseph Rowntree Foundation, fn 18, which presents evidence to this effect.

to legal consequences. In a survey on the extent of paying volunteers in the 1990s,[99] it was found that 19% of the managers interviewed expressed anxieties about the legal status of paid volunteers.[100]

It has been seen that voluntary organisations making payments to their volunteers may be creating a relationship of employer and employee, with the individuals concerned having all the normal statutory employment rights. Furthermore, payments to volunteers can cause problems in three additional areas: taxation; welfare benefits; and rates of pay under the minimum wage legislation.

Tax implications

A survey on the extent of paying volunteers in the 1990s[101] found that 81% of groups surveyed had not put their paid volunteers on the payroll for PAYE. However, volunteer expenses, paid without tax and national insurance deductions, which are later found to have been wages,[102] could mean that the voluntary body will have to pay the tax bill. The same survey reported that the Volunteer Centre UK had received several requests for assistance from local voluntary groups faced with large fines imposed for non-registration of employees for taxation purposes.[103]

Benefits implications

A study undertaken in 1995[104] by the Personal Social Services Research Unit at the University of Kent and The Volunteer Centre found that women are generally more likely than men to volunteer in community care work. The study also suggested that caution is needed in concluding that people from higher socio-economic groups are the most likely to volunteer. It was found that this is not true of informal volunteering in community care, such as visiting sick or elderly people, where people in lower income groups are just as likely to be involved. The study suggests that action needs to be taken to remove the barriers which may deter women on low incomes from getting involved in their local communities. This includes ensuring that regulations do not prevent women on unemployment or other State benefits from volunteering.

---

99 *Op cit*, Blacksell and Philips, fn 74.

100 There was also some evidence to this effect in *op cit*, Russell and Scott, fn 69.

101 *Op cit*, Blacksell and Philips, fn 74.

102 See, above, the discussion of *Chaudri v Migrant Advisory Service* IT Case Number: 2201678/96, 2 September 1997.

103 *Op cit*, Blacksell and Philips, fn 74, p 18.

104 Joseph Rowntree Foundation, *The Determinants of Volunteering*, Social Policy Research Findings 75, 1995, York: Joseph Rowntree Foundation.

The State benefits system should not be a deterrent to volunteering. Yet, the interpretation of welfare benefits legislation often means that those who are unemployed can find that their receipt of benefits is under threat if they take up voluntary work.[105] A 1997 study of voluntary work by unemployed people found evidence that Job Centre staff had dissuaded some individuals from pursuing voluntary activities.[106] The benefits regulations are complicated and the study found that knowledge of the impact of voluntary work on benefits was, generally, sparse. There was considerable confusion, by both claimants and staff, about the amount of time a person could spend on voluntary activities and the amount of notice that volunteers would be required to give to their 'voluntary employer' if they were offered a job. There was also a fear of being wrongly reported for undeclared paid work.

Volunteer claimants should not suffer due to the ignorance of Employment Service and Benefits Agency[107] staff or their misinterpretation of rules. However, volunteering may affect a person's entitlement to jobseeker's allowance (JSA) and incapacity benefit.[108] Environmental charities, whose projects often need full time volunteers based in remote areas away from home, may have particular difficulty retaining volunteers who are claimants. To get JSA, a person must be actively seeking work and must be available for work.[109] Undertaking voluntary work will not necessarily affect JSA, as long as a person remains available to take up paid employment and is actively seeking it.[110] This means that volunteers must: continue to look for employment as agreed with their employment adviser; be contactable while doing voluntary work if a job opportunity arises; be willing and able to start a job[111] or to attend a job interview, at 48 hours notice; and not get any payment apart from reimbursement of expenditure.[112] This last requirement, of no remuneration, can cause problems. For example, in July 1998, it was

---

105 See, eg, *op cit*, Joseph Rowntree Foundation, fn 18, which presents evidence to this effect.

106 *Op cit*, fn 17. See, also, *op cit*, Blacksell and Philips, fn 74, p 19, to the same effect.

107 Claimants receiving incapacity benefit may do voluntary work without it affecting their entitlement to benefit: the Social Security (Incapacity for Work) (General) Regulations 1995, SI 1995/311, reg 17. The 16 hour per week limit on voluntary work was abolished in October 1998.

108 See Leaflet FB26 – *Voluntary and Part Time Workers: Your Benefits, Pensions and National Insurance Contributions*, April 1998, UK: Benefits Agency.

109 Jobseekers Act 1995, s 1 and the Jobseeker's Allowance Regulations 1996, SI 1996/207.

110 The Jobseeker's Allowance Regulations 1996, SI 1996/207, regs 5 and 12. See, also, Leaflet JSAL7, *Voluntary Work When You're Unemployed*, Employment Service.

111 In general, a person must be available to take on a job for at least 40 hours per week.

112 Claimants who receive any payment other than reimbursement of out of pocket expenses will have their benefits reduced for any week in which they receive more than the allowed earnings disregard.

reported[113] that a full time National Trust volunteer warden who was working in an isolated location had been refused JSA on the basis that the free accommodation provided constituted remuneration. This is despite the fact that the volunteer's predecessor had received JSA following an appeal decision. This case clearly highlights the inconsistencies that can occur in this area.

Voluntary work is not considered to be a step taken to satisfy a jobseeker's duty actively to seek work. However, in considering whether the steps a volunteer has taken are reasonable, the Employment Service must consider all the circumstances of the individual case, including time spent in voluntary work and the extent to which it may improve prospects of finding employment. Employment Service internal guidelines now recognise the beneficial role voluntary work can play in getting people back into paid employment.[114] Nevertheless, staff have considerable discretion in applying regulations. While local interpretation can make the system more flexible, it may also lead to inconsistencies. The evidence from the 1995 study[115] suggests that these problems may particularly affect women, who are more likely to be involved in community care voluntary work and may well be on low incomes.

Minimum wage implications

The National Minimum Wage Act 1998 sets up a legislative framework for a national minimum wage, expressed as an hourly rate. The prospect of a national minimum wage for voluntary sector workers is both welcomed (by employees) and dreaded (by employers). Whereas 6.6% of manufacturing workers earn less than £4 per hour, as do 7.1% of those in the public sector, the proportion is as high as 20.6% in the voluntary sector.[116] More than 90,000 employees in the sector (almost 14%) earn less than £3.50 per hour. The NCVO estimates that, with a national minimum wage set at £3.60, staff costs for general charities will increase by £51 million, assuming that current staffing levels are maintained.[117] The greatest impact will be felt by smaller organisations and those employing part time workers.

Although volunteers are exempted in the Act,[118] the original definition used was narrow and required volunteers, in order to be exempt, to be

---

113 'Jobseeker's allowance withdrawn', *Third Sector*, 9 July 1998.

114 Employment Service internal guidelines, 1998, para 397.

115 Discussed above.

116 'Charities: cost of loving' (1998) *The Guardian*, 21 January.

117 *Op cit*, Hems and van Doorn, fn 9.

118 National Minimum Wage Act 1998, s 44.

working for a charity or voluntary organisation only, and to be receiving expenses only. After much intense lobbying by voluntary organisations, the original clause in the Bill was amended and the definition has been extended. The exempt category now also includes those volunteering in the State sector, so that those who volunteer in schools, hospitals and social services departments are not within the scheme. The definition of allowable expenses has also been widened to include an element of subsistence. It ensures that volunteers receiving 'benefits in kind', such as meals, travel expenses or, where the volunteering activity warrants it, accommodation, will continue to be classed as volunteers. One type of volunteering which would have caused problems under the original provisions is that of full time placements away from home for young people. These volunteers usually get their board and lodging, plus a small weekly allowance or 'pocket money' of around £25. Under the Act, it seems that, if a volunteer is working away from home, accommodation and food are reasonable expenses, together with an allowance for necessary extra clothing. Also, any training provided with the sole or main aim of enhancing a volunteer's ability to do their voluntary work is not to be considered as a benefit in kind.

Despite some clarification in the legislation, there are still many grey areas. For example, some people are referred to, and regard themselves, as 'volunteers' but they will not fall within the exemption. These include those who, in retirement, have offered their services to a voluntary organisation in exchange for a small payment which is comparable with that earned by regular workers for the same voluntary organisation. Also, some young 'legitimate' volunteers, many of whom have no paid employment, may receive a token payment in respect of the service which they give as members of voluntary organisations, which may mean that they, too, fall outside the exemption. The legislation provides the first attempt at a definition of a volunteer and this is to be welcomed, as it should make such relationships clearer. In time, the modern phenomenon of 'paid volunteering' should become a thing of the past: a worker is either one thing – employee – or another – volunteer.

Clearly, paid employees of voluntary organisations are covered by the legislation. Some charities are finding solutions to this problem – they are asking staff to give some of their work time voluntarily. An advert for a part time job with a salary of £2,495 for 12 hours paid and 4 voluntary hours per week means that the worker gets £4 per hour. The 'real' wage is £3 per hour. Will it fall foul of the minimum wage provisions? Some workers in voluntary organisations do, genuinely, have dual roles, part volunteer and part paid staff. Their voluntary effort should not be discouraged but, at the same time, their paid work should be properly rewarded.

THE NEW ERA OF VOLUNTEERING

Some of the developments considered in this chapter suggest that the 'gendered' nature of the voluntary sector may be changing. Prochaska commented: '... one might say that organized philanthropy had become "womanized" in the 19th century.'[119] By contrast, it is now increasingly displaying more masculine characteristics.

The less personal, more detached professional characterisation is exemplified through the new funding regime for voluntary organisations (the contract culture). Negotiating such contracts, which become fundamental to the survival of voluntary organisations, requires the skills of lawyers and accountants, not social skills. The use of business jargon, with its entrepreneurial culture and managerial emphasis, means that 'Lady Bountiful' would not stand a chance! Caring is now considered, and evaluated, by the 'cold' rules of commerce.

However, it should not be assumed that to formalise informal activity is totally undesirable. This formalisation does bring with it certain advantages. Immediately, the voluntary sector becomes visible. Earlier discussion has shown that, at present, volunteers remain unrecognised, and simply ignored, in most contracts. However, this may change in time. For example, the Charity Commission, in its official advice on costing of contracts,[120] points out that a charity might not always be able to rely on the availability of volunteers. It is, therefore, recommended[121] that a charity should consider costing the service as if it were staffed by paid workers or, at least, a clause should be included to the effect that performance of the contract at the agreed fee is subject to the charity's ability to recruit enough volunteers. If a price has to be put on it, then women's skills as carers may become more widely recognised and respected. Also, formalising the role of volunteers brings both certainty and some status to their position. For example, previously, the legal position of volunteers was often problematic. In the past, legislators did not usually consider the implications for volunteers. The discussion in Parliament of the consequences of the minimum wage legislation is a good example of the new era in practice. When this legislation is in force, the opportunity to take advantage of the goodwill of unskilled 'volunteers' in order to provide social services 'on the cheap' should be greatly diminished. Payment for caring affects the perception and status of caring as a job. Paid work is valuable work.

Voluntary organisations are beginning to acknowledge that they have responsibilities towards volunteers in areas such as health and safety, insurance and training, which closely resemble their duties towards paid staff.

---

119 *Op cit*, Prochaska, fn 20, p 223.
120 Charity Commission, *Charities and Contracts*, 1998, Leaflet CC37, London: HMSO.
121 *Ibid*, para 50.

There is a move towards interviewing volunteers, taking up references and defining the terms and conditions of volunteer work, in a similar way to that which applies to paid workers. The Equal Opportunities Commission even recommends giving volunteers equal status to employees for the purposes of certain aspects of equality legislation.

However, this enhanced status for volunteers does not come without a cost. For example, paying volunteers undermines the voluntary ethic of the voluntary sector, and this may be felt most acutely by the service user. One of the unique features of voluntary activity has always been its informality, flexibility and innovative nature. The very fact that volunteers are not part of 'the mainstream' is advantageous. Some users may feel less embarrassed if services are provided through voluntary, rather than statutory, bodies. For example, the friendly 'unofficialdom' of volunteers is often stressed as being a quality which enables them to forge easier relationships with service users and to be more readily accepted by them than paid workers.[122] A comment from an Age Concern project manager, on a home visiting scheme for the elderly, neatly encapsulates this particular advantage of voluntary activity:

> Many older people have this fear that social workers will parachute into their lives and start taking over. But, an Age Concern volunteer can come in as a friend, because they are not perceived as anything to do with 'the authorities'.[123]

Freedom, enthusiasm and the ability to spend more time on individuals are often mentioned as other advantages which volunteers offer. Also, since volunteers do not need to concern themselves with administrative distinctions, they can ignore any restricting functional and geographical boundaries and simply concentrate on providing flexible and spontaneous responses to human needs. Often, their passion, partiality and specialist concern single out volunteers from their statutory counterparts. The more this versatility and autonomy are stifled through the increased bureaucracy and professionalisation of national voluntary organisations, with hierarchical structures, the less unique and different voluntary activity becomes.

In what can now be seen as a prescient statement, Josephine Butler, in her introduction to the volume of essays *Woman's Work and Woman's Culture*, published in 1869, observed:

> We have had experience of what we may call the feminine form of philanthropy and independent individual ministering, of too mediaeval a type to suit the present day. It has failed. We are now about to try the masculine form of philanthropy, large and comprehensive measures, organizations and systems planned by men and sanctioned by Parliament.[124]

---

122 See, eg, the views of the mothers in the study described in *op cit*, Bagilhole, fn 76.
123 'Tea, talk and lots of TLC' (1998) *The Guardian*, 28 January.
124 *Op cit*, Butler, fn 2, p xxxvii.

She went on to predict that this masculine version of philanthropy would not succeed if, through its large and magnificently ordered institutions, it failed to embrace the philosophy of the feminine form, with its 'individual touch'. She suggested 'Why should we not try, at last, a union of principles?'. Her words ring as true today as they did in the 19th century, when 'Lady Bountiful' reigned.

CHAPTER 7

THE INTERSECTION BETWEEN GENDER AND 'RACE' IN THE LABOUR MARKET: LESSONS FOR ANTI-DISCRIMINATION LAW

Diamond Ashiagbor[*]

INTRODUCTION

Whilst it would be mistaken to assume that law alone can bring an end to inequalities in the labour market, nevertheless, within certain limits, law can deal with some of the more conspicuous manifestations of discrimination in employment on grounds of race and gender. However, anti-discrimination law and policies aimed at tackling labour market discrimination tend to be predicated on an understanding of the labour market, which views race and gender as mutually exclusive categories of experience and thus sees the two forms of discrimination which arise as singular and discrete examples of disadvantage which may, at most, be experienced cumulatively, rather than simultaneously, within employment.

In the context of analyses of the labour market, it would seem that the intersections between gender and 'race' have been under-theorised, in particular, with regard to how the law may identify and remedy the disadvantage encountered by those, namely black and Asian women, whose social identity cannot be analysed along a single axis. This chapter will focus on how, within the UK, black and Asian women's experience of paid work, the restructuring and segmentation of the labour market and anti-discrimination laws compares with that of white women and black men, and the implications this has for anti-discrimination law.

THE INTERSECTIONS BETWEEN GENDER AND 'RACE'

Universalising tendencies within feminist theory and politics, which attempt to describe the world from a woman's standpoint and to speak for all women, are based on the supposition of a unitary gender identity: namely, that there is an 'essential' woman's experience which can be described independently of factors such as race or class. Such 'standpoint' feminism can, as Martha

---

[*]   An earlier version of this chapter was presented at a seminar of the Feminist Legal Research Unit, University of Liverpool, in April 1997; I am grateful to participants for their comments. I am also particularly grateful to Lucy Anderson, Aileen McColgan and Stephen Tierney for their detailed comments on earlier drafts. The usual disclaimer applies.

Minow has argued, provide a useful political strategy: 'Cognitively, we need simplifying categories, and the unifying category of "woman" helps to organise experience, even at the cost of denying some of it.'[1] Furthermore, in the legal arena, women's claims to equality of treatment have sought legitimacy by appealing to a common experience of gender oppression: that disadvantages encountered by women are experienced *qua* women, thus justifying legal intervention on behalf of this disadvantaged group.[2] However, there is a danger in using the category of 'woman' as the foundation for feminist knowledge and politics, of succumbing to essentialism and failing to address the specific experiences of, for example, black and Asian women.[3] With respect to analyses of the UK labour market, ethnic differences in women's labour market participation and positioning, which are explored below, would seem to require a reassessment of anti-discrimination laws, which seek to disrupt the workings of the market, if the rationale for such laws is that gender can be isolated from other elements of identity, such as race, which impact upon how one is treated within the UK labour market.

Nancy Fraser and Linda Nicholson address the danger of the essentialism of 'standpoint' feminism by adopting an anti-foundationalist analysis, which recognises the need to:

> ... replace unitary notions of 'woman' and 'feminine gender identity' with plural and complexly constructed conceptions of social identity, treating gender as one relevant strand among others, attending, also, to class, race, ethnicity, age and sexual orientation.[4]

It is arguable that anti-discrimination theory is impoverished by its failure to recognise this plurality and by its tendency to treat race and gender as entirely separate categories of experience.[5] For example, within Anglo-American

---

1   Minow, M, 'Feminist reason: getting it and losing it' (1988) 38 JLE 47.

2   See Jackson, E, 'Contradictions and coherence in feminist responses to law' (1993) 20 JLS 398.

3   To engage in a meaningful discussion of black and Asian women's experiences of the labour market, it will be necessary to draw attention to some questions of terminology. As part of a political discourse calling for unity between the UK's Caribbean, African and Asian communities, the term 'black' has been used in the past to mean 'people affected by racism' in order to emphasise the common experience, especially of racial oppression, of non-white people in the UK: see Mama, A, 'Black women and the British State', in Braham, P *et al* (eds), *Racism and Anti-Racism: Inequalities, Opportunities and Policies*, 1992, London: Sage/Open University. However, for the purposes of this analysis of the labour market and discussion of ethnic differences within it, I shall be adopting the categorisations used in official statistics, namely White, Black Caribbean, Black African, Black Other, South Asian, Indian, Pakistani, Bangladeshi, Chinese and Other Asian.

4   Fraser, N and Nicholson, L, 'Social criticism without philosophy: an encounter between feminism and postmodernism' (1988) 5 Theory, Culture and Society 373.

5   As one commentator has written, 'In this society, it is only white people who have the luxury of "having no color"; only white people have been able to imagine that sexism and racism are separate experiences'. See Harris, AP, 'Race and essentialism in feminist legal theory' (1990) Stanford L Rev 581.

jurisprudence, anti-discrimination legislation designed to confront labour market disadvantage tackles either sex discrimination or racial oppression but does not envisage the two forms of disadvantage occurring simultaneously. When seeking strategies for legal intervention in the labour market, it would seem necessary to explore how race interacts with gender to shape the employment experiences of black and Asian women. To speak solely of 'blacks and women' in the context of anti-discrimination law, without specifying whether black women are included in 'blacks' or in 'women', suggests that black women are not being considered, since it would appear that the interests of black women are protected by law only to the extent that their experiences coincide with those of either white women or black men.[6]

In the UK, whilst there has been a great deal of feminist analysis of the complicated inter-relations between class and gender and class and race, particularly within the socialist/feminist tradition, as exemplified by the debate across the pages of *Feminist Review*,[7] there has been a tendency to centre the debate on whether gender and 'race' can be reducible to class, a tendency which may be located in the modernist tradition. For example, Michèle Barratt and Mary McIntosh have questioned whether the social divisions associated with ethnicity and racism should be seen as absolutely autonomous of social class, as reducible to social class, or as having different historical origins but articulating with class.[8]

More recently, critiques of 'totalising stories' (such as that of Fraser and Nicholson, above) have led to the abandonment or minimising of those social theories which employ general categories not just of class but also of gender and 'race' as being too reductive of social complexity. For example, with regard to class, whilst it is true that black men and women have a tendency to be clustered within the manual working class, there is great variation in class positioning both between different ethnic minorities and within them; it is, thus, inadequate to see racial groups and their position in the labour market solely as forming an underclass or a subordinate stratum within the working class.[9]

If one accepts that categories such as gender are internally differentiated, these universalising perspectives are, arguably, untenable. The extent to

---

6   Crenshaw, K, 'Demarginalizing the intersection of race and sex: a black feminist critique of anti-discrimination doctrine, feminist theory, and anti-racist politics' [1989] Chicago L Forum 139.

7   See, eg, Barratt, M and McIntosh, M, 'Ethnocentrism and socialist-feminist theory' (1985) 20 Feminist Review 23, pp 23–47; Ramazanoglu, C (1986) 22 Feminist Review 83, pp 83–86; Bhavnani, K and Coulson, M 'Transforming socialist-feminism: the challenge of racism' (1986) 23 Feminist Review 81, pp 81–92.

8   *Ibid*, Barratt and McIntosh.

9   Anthias, F and Yuval-Davis, N, *Racialised Boundaries: Race, Nation, Gender, Colour and Class and the Anti-Racist Struggle*, 1992, London: Routledge, Chap 3. See, also, Aziz, R, 'Feminism and the challenge of racism: deviance and difference', in Safia Mirza, H (ed), *Black British Feminism*, 1997, London: Routledge.

which such categories do have some continued utility in the context of anti-discrimination law lies in the recognition of the complexity of social identity. First, by focusing on the perspective of black and Asian women, one may reach an understanding of whether race and gender are merely cumulative forms of disadvantage, or whether they might, in fact, interact to create new challenges for anti-discrimination law. Secondly, by recognising that multiple forms of oppression may exist simultaneously, one may illuminate how the law might more effectively deal with multiple discrimination, where race and gender disadvantage are experienced concurrently.

BLACK WOMEN AND THE LABOUR MARKET

Notwithstanding 20 years of sex discrimination and equal pay legislation, gender inequalities persist in the workplace, and women in the UK continue to earn, on average, less than three-quarters of men's wages.[10] Empirical studies of women's involvement in the labour market have identified a number of factors to explain this continued disadvantage, in particular, the importance of gender segregation, namely, the overcrowding of women into sectors of the labour market to which lower value or status is attributed.[11] Such analyses of women's employment patterns have been useful in redressing the previously male centred theories of labour market participation. However, in view of the heterogeneity of the category of women workers, the accuracy of those analyses of paid work and gender which treat women as if they were a unitary category is also open to question. This heterogeneity has implications for the effectiveness of measures, including legislative measures, aimed at tackling women's labour market disadvantage, since it is arguable that, within the larger body of 'women's work', there exist ethnic niches wherein black and Asian women are, effectively, segregated.[12] If it is the case that black and Asian women are either segregated into particular sectors of the labour market, or even excluded altogether from participation in the formal economy, then a recognition of the cumulative effect of the dynamics of race and sex would seem necessary for anti-discrimination legislation to be truly effective. Strategies of legal intervention which are based on remedying the disadvantage encountered by white women will, arguably, be inadequate to

---

10 According to the 1994 New Earnings Survey, the percentage of women's average earnings relative to men's was 72%: Sefton, R, 'Patterns of pay: results from the 1994 new earnings survey' (1994) 102 Employment Gazette 453.

11 See, eg, Hakim, C, *Occupational Segregation: A Comparative Study of the Degree and Pattern of Differentiation Between Men's and Women's Work in Britain, the United States and Other Countries*, Department of Employment Research Paper No 91979, London: HMSO.

12 Phizacklea, A, 'Gender, racism and occupational segregation', in Walby, S (ed), *Gender Segregation at Work*, 1988, Milton Keynes: OU Press.

address the disadvantage of women who face different obstacles due to the interaction of race and gender.

The following section will examine the implications of assuming that the experience of white women within the labour market speaks for all women and addresses the diversity of experience of women of different ethnic minorities through an analysis of the ethnic variations in women's labour market positioning and the segregation of the labour market along lines of gender and race.

Ethnic differences in labour market participation

In a report to the European Commission's Equal Opportunities Unit on changing work patterns and the impact of gender divisions,[13] Jill Rubery and her colleagues identified how women's employment patterns in Britain differ from many other countries in Europe and North America. They identified three distinct typologies: the continuous pattern, where women remain in paid employment (exemplified by Denmark, France and the US); the interrupted pattern, found in Britain, The Netherlands and Germany; and the curtailed pattern, found in Ireland and Southern Europe. These differences may be attributed to factors such as differences in public policy regimes – for example, child care provision and employment legislation. However, research since the 1991 census has shown that the 'British' pattern of women's employment is, in fact, a white pattern and cannot be generalised to other ethnic groups within Britain.

In particular, in 1995, the economic activity rate[14] of white women within the UK labour market was 72.9%, that of black women (that is, Black African and Black Caribbean) 69%, that of women of Indian origin 61%, and that of Pakistani/Bangladeshi women 22%.[15] However, any analysis of the ethnic variation in women's employment patterns is problematic: first, although the Labour Force Survey has included a question on ethnic origin for some time, it was only with the incorporation of a question on ethnic origin in the 1991 UK Population Census that occupational distribution by gender and ethnic group could be properly analysed. Secondly, the figures must be treated with caution, as ethnic minorities constitute very small groups within the workforce and are, thus, subject to a relatively high number of sampling

---

13 Rubery, J, Fagan, C and Smith, M, *Changing Patterns of Work and Working Time in the European Union and the Impact of Gender Divisions*, 1995, Brussels: Report to the European Commission Equal Opportunities Unit.

14 Percentage of people of working age (16 to 64 for men; 16 to 59 for women) who are either employed or seeking employment, divided by the total number of people of working age.

15 Sly, F, 'Ethnic minority participation in the labour market: trends from the labour force survey 1984–95' (1996) 6 Labour Market Trends 266.

errors.[16] Thirdly, the Labour Force Survey has been shown to under-record the number of black and female headed households in the population[17] and is most likely to miss the poorer black and Asian households, thereby under-recording homeworking and family employment.

Within the UK, feminist analyses of the position of women in the labour market have, traditionally, placed great emphasis on gender divisions within the family and women's responsibility for domestic work as having necessary implications for women's labour market participation and positioning. For example, the tendency of married women or women with child care responsibilities to work part time is adduced in support of the conventional view that processes prior to entry into the labour market determine women's segregation into lower paying sectors.[18] The fact that the majority of part time workers in the UK are women with family responsibilities[19] has ramifications for the proper role of anti-discrimination law: both domestic courts and the European Court of Justice have recognised that unequal treatment of part time workers may amount to indirect sex discrimination, since any exclusion of part time workers is likely to have a disproportionate impact on women (compared to the impact on men).[20] Furthermore, there has been much empirical research to show that, in spite of equal pay legislation, occupation by occupation, part time workers earn less per hour than full time workers. Whilst the differential between men and women's hourly pay can be explained in part by differences in skill distribution, a persistent percentage of the differential remains attributable to women receiving unequal pay for jobs of similar skill levels.[21]

However, it is questionable whether sex discrimination alone can provide a satisfactory explanation for the labour market disadvantage experienced by black and Asian women. The prominence given to part time work and domestic responsibilities as determinants of the sexual division of labour and of differential rewards between men and women's paid work can be seen as ethnocentric. Whilst this analysis has proved useful to highlight inequalities as

---

16 According to the Labour Force Survey, in 1995, 2.2 million adults in the UK, 4.9% of the population, aged 16 and over, identified themselves as members of ethnic minorities: (1996) 6 Labour Market Trends 260.

17 Morris, P, 'The labour force survey: a study in differential response' (1987) Statistical News 79.

18 Beechey, V, *Unequal Work*, 1986, London: Pluto; see *op cit*, Walby, fn 12, for alternative explanations of labour market segregation, including the role of the gendered structuring of the market itself.

19 In spring 1996, 82% of all those who worked part time were women: 'Women in the labour market, results from the Spring 1996 Labour Force Survey' (1997) 3 Labour Market Trends 99; see, also, fn 25 and accompanying text.

20 *Jenkins v Kingsgate Clothing Productions Ltd* Case 96/80 [1980] ICR 592 (ECJ) and [1981] ICR 715 (EAT); *Bilka-Kaufhaus GmbH v Weber von Hartz* Case 170/84 [1986] IRLR 317.

21 Rubery, J *et al*, 'Part time work and gender inequality in the labour market', in MacEwen Scott, A (ed), *Gender Segregation and Social Change*, 1994, Oxford: OUP.

between white women and white men and has achieved legally significant gains for part time workers,[22] it also serves to hide the particular experience of black and Asian women within the labour market, since part time working is not, in fact, a major factor in keeping black and Asian women's pay and prospects so far below those of white men. While some 46% of white women employees worked part time in 1993, only 33% of non-white women did so.[23] For black women (namely, Black Caribbean, Black African and Black Other), the figures are starker, with less than 22% of black women working part time.[24]

Whilst responsibility for child care and home management *does* have a major influence on the participation of women in the labour market, this influence varies significantly between ethnic groups.[25] White women who work full time tend to be free of immediate child care responsibilities, while those with such responsibilities tend to work part time. However, this does not appear to apply to Black Caribbean women, who have a high rate of single parenthood relative to other groups but, also, have high rates of participation in the labour market and high rates of full time employment.[26] It would, thus, appear that factors other than domestic responsibilities (for example, economic necessity) determine black women's participation in the labour market. As the Greater London Council noted in 1986, black women are 'much more likely [than white women] to have to bring in a second wage and to work full time, partly because black men are also trapped in low status, low paid jobs'.[27] Further, Clare Holdsworth and Angela Dale, in their study of ethnic differences in women's employment published in the journal *Work, Employment and Society*,[28] reach the interesting conclusion that, historically, part time jobs were constructed for white women. They point to evidence from the Commission for Racial Equality[29] which suggests that employers have continued to make part time jobs preferentially available to white

---

22 In *R v Secretary of State for Employment ex p Equal Opportunities Commission* [1994] IRLR 176, the House of Lords struck down the hours qualifying thresholds which excluded certain part time workers from statutory employment protection rights, on the ground that they indirectly discriminated against women.

23 1994 Labour Force Survey (1995) 6 Employment Gazette 258; Bruegel, I, 'Sex and race in the labour market' (1989) 32 Feminist Review 49.

24 Owen, D, *Ethnic Minority Women and the Labour Market: Analysis of the 1991 Census*, 1994, Manchester: Equal Opportunities Commission, p 86.

25 *ibid*, pp 54 and 77: the rate of labour market participation tends to be lower for women where the mean number of dependent children per household is higher.

26 Rees, T, *Women and the Labour Market*, 1992, London: Routledge, p 19.

27 Greater London Council, *London Labour Plan*, 1986, London: GLC, p 144.

28 Holdsworth, C and Dale, A, 'Ethnic differences in women's employment' (1997) 11(3) Work, Employment and Society 435, pp 435–57.

29 Commission for Racial Equality, *Annual Report*, 1993, London: CRE.

women, so that full time employment may, sometimes, be the result of discrimination rather than choice.

Another factor explaining the full time and high economic activity rates of black, especially Black Caribbean, women is the nature of the relationship between paid work outside the home and work, whether paid or unpaid, within the home. Patricia Hill Collins has criticised traditional social science research into African-American women's experiences of family and work for using the normative yardstick developed from experiences of middle-class American and European nuclear families.[30] One criticism is that the contrast between a public economy and a private, non-economic domestic sphere creates a distinction between the paid labour of the public sphere and the unpaid labour of the domestic sphere, which does not, in reality, hold true for African-American women's experience of the labour market, since 'African-American families exhibit ... fluid public/private boundaries because racial oppression has impoverished disproportionate numbers of Black families'.[31]

Although household arrangements and family structures in the UK also differ enormously across race and culture, the type of intervention into the labour market envisaged by sex discrimination law – in particular, by the concept of indirect discrimination – seems predicated on a unitary view of the position of women in the family and their reasons for seeking paid work outside the home.

What, then, of the incidence of homeworking? The seemingly low economic activity rates of Asian women – in particular, Asian Muslim women – may, in part, be accounted for by the fact that they are more likely than white or black women to be involved in work, such as homeworking and family employment, which is less amenable to official statistical collation. For example, research conducted in the West Midlands clothing industry concluded that, for every factory worker in this industrial sector (that is, for every worker in the formal economy), there were at least two unregistered homeworkers;[32] a pilot study published in 1989 found that the Muslim women interviewed were employed largely as homeworkers or as unpaid workers in family businesses and, in a few cases, in paid work outside the home.[33]

For these 'atypical' workers, therefore, their concentration in the ethnic economy or exclusion from the formal economy must be examined before an appropriate legal response can be forthcoming. Many homeworkers are

---

30 Hill Collins, P, *Black Feminist Thought*, 1990, London: Routledge, p 46.

31 *Ibid.*

32 Rai, K and Sheikh, N, *Homeworking*, 1989, Birmingham: National Unit on Homeworking; Phizacklea, A and Wolkowitz, C, *Homeworking Women: Gender, Racism and Class at Work*, 1995, London: Sage.

33 Afshar, H, 'Gender roles and the "moral economy of kin" among Pakistani women in West Yorkshire' (1989) 15(2) New Community 211.

classed as being self-employed rather than employees, providing a partial explanation for the higher than average incidence of self-employment amongst Asian women (see below). Although self-employment is often seen as an indicator of entrepreneurship, clearly this is an inaccurate description of the position of many homeworkers or those working in the clothing industry.[34] The attribution of the status 'self-employed' to such workers, by an employer who is unwilling to accept the fiscal and legal consequences of treating homeworkers as employees, can result in these 'atypical' workers being denied the protection of employment legislation in a manner similar to the traditional exclusion of part time workers from the reach of employment protection legislation.[35] However, the extent to which present formulations of indirect discrimination law can be manipulated to provide redress for *all* 'atypical' workers, is limited. Reliance on sex discrimination law alone is insufficient to protect the interests of this particular group in the labour market, Asian homeworkers and 'self-employed' workers.

Segregation by race and sex

These ethnic differences in labour market positioning have ramifications for anti-discrimination law, in that the disadvantage faced by black and Asian women in the labour market may owe as much, if not more, to their race as to direct or indirect discrimination on grounds of gender.

For example, the Labour Force Survey reveals that qualification levels (above GCE A level or equivalent) attained by black and Asian 16 to 24 year olds, both male and female, were very similar to those of white young people,[36] yet, strikingly, for the most part, black women earn less, relative to their qualifications, than white women. The concentration of black women in certain sectors of the labour market and their relative exclusion from other sectors is, arguably, one factor in the under-utilisation of their skills and qualifications and, hence, to their lower pay.[37]

The industrial distribution of women's employment varies greatly between ethnic groups: 51% of black women are employed in the public sector, compared with 31% for all women, and 19% of women of South Asian origin are classed as self-employed, compared with an average of 7% for all women.[38] Whilst public sector employment is high among Black African and Black Caribbean women, they are under-represented (in comparison with

---

34 *Op cit*, Phizacklea and Wolkowitz, fn 32, p 62.

35 See Dickens, L, *Whose Flexibility? Discrimination and Equality Issues in Atypical Work*, 1992, London: Institute of Employment Rights.

36 1993 Labour Force Survey (1994) 102 Employment Gazette 155.

37 *Op cit*, Bruegel, fn 23, pp 59–60.

38 Sly, F, 'Ethnic groups and the labour market: analyses from the Spring 1994 Labour Force Survey' (1995) 6 Employment Gazette 256.

men and white women) as employers, managers or professional workers,[39] tending to be employed in particular sectors of the welfare state, such as nursing and hospital ancillary work, catering and cleaning. In contrast to the general concentration of black women in the service industries, women of South Asian origin are more usually found in manufacturing, including the clothing and textile industries, and in distribution.[40]

Such segregation would, also, seem to make black and Asian women more vulnerable to the effects of recession, as they are more likely to be concentrated in those sectors of the labour market susceptible to technological change and fluctuation (such as manufacturing) or to restructuring and privatisation (such as the welfare state). The Labour Force Survey shows that black and South Asian women tend to experience higher rates of unemployment than white women and are disproportionately represented amongst the unemployed: the unemployment rate in 1991 among white women of working age was 6.3%, compared with 16.6% for black women and 16.5% for South Asian women.[41]

Racialised segregation, coming in addition to the division of occupations in to 'men's' and 'women's' work, serves to locate black and Asian women at a point in the labour market which is particular to them as black female workers. It would, thus, appear that racism and sexism combine to confine black and Asian women to a uniquely subordinate position prior to their entry into the labour market and then to restrict them to gender specific and ethnically segregated work. A number of explanations for the continued racialised segregation within the labour market are given in two reports published by the Equal Opportunities Commission in 1994.[42] The EOC suggests, first, that ethnic minority women may have less access to informal organisational networks which may help them to gain entry to a wider range of jobs; secondly, that some ethnic minority groups are more likely to use word of mouth recruitment methods, which distance them from formal job search methods; and, finally, that employers may, in addition, be more likely to use discriminatory employment practices during a period of recession.

As far as anti-discrimination statutes are concerned, although the Race Relations Act 1976 (see below) formally addresses the issue of segregation, it would appear inadequate to address, or even to acknowledge as discrimination, such deep seated segregation within the labour market. Section 1(2) of the Race Relations Act, which applies in the employment

---

39   Abbott, P and Tyler, M, 'Ethnic variation in the female labour force: a research note' (1995) 46(2) British Journal of Sociology 339.

40   *Op cit*, Owen, fn 24, p 81.

41   The unemployment rates for certain ethnic minority groups are even higher: 34.5% for Bangladeshi women, 29.6% for Pakistani women and 24.7% for Black-African women: *op cit*, Owen, fn 24, p 136.

42   *Op cit*, Owen, fn 24, and Bhavnani, R, *Black Women in the Labour Market: Research Review*, 1994, Manchester: Equal Opportunities Commission.

sphere, provides that segregating a person from others on racial grounds amounts to less favourable treatment, namely direct discrimination. This provision presents a potentially powerful challenge to the operation of the labour market, to prevent black and Asian workers being consigned to lower paid, lower status areas of work. However, the Act would appear to prohibit discrimination by segregation only if the segregation is 'deliberate'; the mere fact of segregation is not sufficient.

For example, in the joined cases *Furniture, Timber and Allied Trades Union v Modgill* and *PEL v Modgill*,[43] 16 African Asian men complained that they had been treated less favourably on grounds of their race, as only Asians were employed in the employers' paint shop, where the work was dirty and the shifts longer than those in the rest of the workplace. The Employment Appeal Tribunal was of the view that, if there had been a deliberate company policy to segregate, this would have amounted to discrimination. However, since the all-Asian shift had arisen through word of mouth recruitment, by recommendations from existing employees, then the failure of the employers to intervene and to insist on white or non-Asian workers going into the paint shop did not constitute an act of segregation within the meaning of the Act. The failure of the company to have a more positive employment policy which would have removed any element of factual segregation, or suspicion of it, arising in the paint shop could not be held to be capable of constituting segregation on racial grounds.[44]

The Commission for Racial Equality subsequently issued a Code of Practice, which warns against the use of such word of mouth recruitment, 'where the workforce concerned is wholly or predominantly white or black and the labour market is multi-racial',[45] especially as this might lead to a self-perpetuating racial group, as in *Modgill*. However, there is no equivalent to s 1(2) within the Sex Discrimination Act 1975 and, thus, no overt statutory prohibition on segregation of male and female workers. There is, therefore, no explicit prohibition against the 'ghettoising' of black women into certain sectors of employment.

BLACK WOMEN'S EXPERIENCE OF ANTI-DISCRIMINATION LAWS

This section will examine the operation of anti-discrimination laws with a view to determining the extent to which existing formulations reflect the

---

43 [1980] IRLR 142 (EAT).

44 *Ibid*, para 35.

45 Commission for Racial Equality, *Code of Practice for the Elimination of Racial Discrimination and the Promotion of Equality of Opportunity in Employment*, 1983, London: CRE, para 1.10.

reality of inequality within the labour market. Two questions will be addressed, in particular: first, are the conceptions of equality underlying current anti-discrimination provisions sufficiently flexible to encompass the particular ways in which black and Asian women may experience discrimination, in light of the aforementioned ethnic variations in women's participation in an ethnically segregated labour market; secondly, can anti-discrimination law respond to the interaction of race with gender discrimination to prohibit what might be termed 'multiple discrimination'?

Competing conceptions of equality

At its simplest, anti-discrimination law is based on the premise that law is capable of promoting equal treatment and protecting the most vulnerable against arbitrary discriminatory practice.[46] However, there exists a tension at the root of anti-discrimination law, arising from competing views as to the nature of equality which law can, or should, achieve. Whilst numerous theories of equality and egalitarianism abound,[47] it is possible to identify four types of equality which may claim to inform legal definitions and the legal process: first, ontological equality or the fundamental equality of individuals, wherein all human beings are considered equal; secondly, equality of opportunity, namely meritocratic access to opportunities such as employment, which leaves initial starting points untouched; thirdly, equality of condition, where there is an attempt to make conditions of life equal for relevant social groups; and, fourthly, equality of outcome or of result, which would require some form of legislative or other intervention to compensate for inequality in starting points.[48] Such definitions might best be understood as forming a spectrum ranging between, on the one hand, a more restrictive notion of equality which treats equality as a process, wherein the primary objective of anti-discrimination law is to prohibit future discriminatory practices; and, on the other hand, a more expansive conception of equality which emphasises equality as the net product of the process and which may involve the use of the law to redress present manifestations of past injustice.[49] Such 'equality of results' presupposes a model of group justice, as opposed to a model of individual justice: any anti-discrimination law designed to achieve equality of outcomes would necessarily concern itself with rectifying historical disadvantage by, for example, compensating disadvantaged groups.

---

46 MacEwen, M, *Tackling Racism in Europe: An Examination of Anti-Discrimination Law in Practice*, 1995, Oxford: Berg, p 17.

47 See Pojman, LP and Westmoreland, R (eds), *Equality: Selected Readings*, 1997, Oxford: OUP.

48 Turner, BS, *Equality*, 1986, Chichester: Ellis Horwood, Chap 2.

49 Crenshaw, K, 'Race, reform, and retrenchment: transformation and legitimation in anti-discrimination law' (1988) 101 Harv L Rev 7, pp 1331, 1341–42.

A common criticism levelled at the concept of equality employed in UK anti-discrimination law is that it is confined to the achievement of formal 'equality of opportunity',[50] recognising only the more restrictive notions of equality outlined above, rather than making possible forms of substantive equality which would result in something akin to distributive justice. Statutory formulations of the principle of equality, therefore, appear to give limited scope to the sort of group justice envisaged by the more expansive notion of equality outlined above.

The present law recognises two forms of discrimination: first, it is prohibited to treat someone less favourably on grounds of their sex[51] or on racial grounds;[52] that is, on the grounds of colour, race, nationality, or ethnic or national origins. This is commonly known as direct discrimination, and the burden of proof is on the complainant throughout, to show not only that there has been less favourable treatment but, also, that this treatment was on grounds of race or gender. The other form of discrimination prohibited by law, indirect discrimination, appears to offer the potential to challenge the effects of long standing practices: it is unlawful for an employer to impose a requirement or condition on all workers with which a smaller proportion of the complainant's sex or race can comply, and which is not justified.[53] This is a more precise and detailed formulation than the prohibition on indirect discrimination contained in the US Civil Rights Act 1964, which made it unlawful for an employer to use a practice or procedure that disproportionately affected black workers, unless this was a matter of 'business necessity'.

In order to be truly effective in remedying gender or racial disadvantage in the labour market, the legal definitions of direct and indirect discrimination would require a recognition of collective racial or gender disadvantage. The concept of 'disparate impact' contained in the statutory definition of indirect discrimination, dealing with employment practices which whilst superficially neutral between men and women or different ethnic groups, significantly disadvantage members of one group, provides the potential to challenge social or institutional practices which perpetuate group disadvantage. Since indirect discrimination turns upon the adverse impact of practices upon groups, this requires courts and tribunals to determine and evaluate social facts in order to provide an effective challenge to discriminatory practices or structural discrimination. However, unlawful discrimination on grounds of race or gender is categorised as a statutory tort, and, as such, there seems little

---

50 See, eg, Lacey, N, 'Legislation against sex discrimination: questions from a feminist perspective' (1987) 14 JLS 411.
51 SDA 1975, s 1(1)(a).
52 RRA 1976, s 1(1)(a).
53 SDA 1975, s 1(1)(b); Race Relations Act 1976, s 1(1)(b).

scope for the courts to investigate social facts underlying discrimination, such as the operation of the labour market and the socio-economic condition of ethnic groups.

Some assistance may, however, be sought from recent developments within European Union law on the burden of proof in sex discrimination cases.[54] The new Burden of Proof Directive does not go so far as to require an employer to prove a non-discriminatory reason for an employment decision or pay practice; it does, however, draw upon and consolidate the case law of the European Court of Justice (ECJ), which has done much to ease the burden on those claiming discrimination. In *Enderby*,[55] for example, the ECJ held that, as far as equal pay claims under Art 119 and the Equal Pay Directive were concerned, national courts must apply a broader notion of indirect discrimination than that contained in s 1(1)(b) of the Sex Discrimination Act. According to *Enderby*, there is no need to show some deliberate employment practice or condition which disbars women from the higher paid jobs; a *prima facie* case of sex discrimination arises under Art 119, where statistics reveal an appreciable difference in pay between two jobs of equal value, one of which is carried out almost exclusively by women and the other predominantly by men. The burden of proof is then shifted onto the employer to show an objective justification for the difference in pay. The new Directive follows the reasoning of the ECJ in *Enderby*, by shifting the burden of proof to the employer in certain circumstances: it provides that Member States should take measures to ensure that the burden of proof shifts onto the employer where the complainant establishes 'facts from which it may be presumed that there has been direct or indirect discrimination.' It will then be for the employer to 'prove that there has been no breach of the principle of equal treatment.' As seen in the aftermath of the *Marshall (No 2)*[56] case, case law and legislation in the area of gender discrimination has inevitable repercussions on the law, practice and procedure in race discrimination cases.[57]

In general, however, with regard to the effectiveness of anti-discrimination law in tackling the labour market discrimination encountered by black women, it would appear from the data on labour market participation and

---

54 In December 1997, the EC Council of Ministers finally adopted a draft directive on the burden of proof, which will apply to cases brought under Art 119 of the Treaty of Rome (on equal pay between men and women) and the Equal Pay Directive, as well as cases under the Equal Treatment Directive, the Pregnant Workers Directive and the new Parental Leave Directive.

55 *Enderby v Frenchay Health Authority* [1993] IRLR 591.

56 *Marshall v Southampton and South West Hampshire Area Health Authority* Case C-271 [1993] IRLR 445.

57 The Sex Discrimination and Equal Pay (Remedies) Regulations 1993 were passed to implement the finding of the ECJ in *Marshall* that the upper limit on compensation for sex discrimination was contrary to the Equal Treatment Directive; the Race Relations (Remedies) Act 1994 followed, bringing compensation for race discrimination claims into line with those for sex discrimination.

segregation discussed above that present formulations of the law are inadequate to address the complexities of the intersection between gender and 'race' in the labour market, precisely because they are premised on an approach to equality which is located at the restrictive end of the definitional spectrum. By focusing on individual rights to equality, anti-discrimination law as it is currently constituted is not sufficiently flexible to allow the collective enforcement of rights to equality and thereby fails to expand a meaningful rights discourse to groups defined by their common experience of disadvantage mediated along lines of race, gender, or both.

Individualised nature of enforcement

Not only are the concepts of equality which inform anti-discrimination law seemingly hostile to the idea of group rights and the recognition of black women as a discrete group within anti-discrimination discourse but the nature of enforcement further reinforces the individualised form of equality which the law sets out to achieve. Twenty years after the Race Relations Act 1976, there is a large body of evidence of the continuing discrimination against black and Asian workers in access to employment, promotion and training. Forbes and Mead's comparative analysis of measures to combat racial discrimination in European Union Member States[58] recognises that, in spite of Great Britain's extensive legislation on race discrimination in employment, the small number of cases and the lack of successful outcomes shows that potential claimants are discouraged by every step of the process. In 1995–96, the last full year for which statistics are available, from a total of 1,737 race discrimination cases registered with industrial tribunals, only 109 (6.3%) were successful at the tribunal hearing, compared with a success rate of 11.2% for unfair dismissal cases.[59] To this must be added the equally unsatisfactory record of the sex discrimination legislation in combating gender inequalities within the workplace, as discussed above. The rate of success for sex discrimination cases fluctuates but, for 1995–96, was lower than that for race discrimination claims, at 5.9%.

The statistics are compiled in such a way as to make it impossible to uncover the outcome of those claims in which both race and sex discrimination was alleged. This is unsurprising, since legislation prohibits direct or indirect discrimination on grounds of sex or on racial grounds, not

---

58 Forbes, I and Mead, G, *Measure for Measure: A Comparative Analysis of Measures to Combat Racial Discrimination in the Member Countries of the European Community*, 1992, Sheffield: Department of Employment.

59 *Labour Market Trends*, April 1997, p 151. It is important to note that as many as 60–70% of cases are settled (often under the auspices of the Advisory, Conciliation and Arbitration Service) or withdrawn by the applicant prior to an industrial tribunal hearing.

on grounds of the cumulative interaction of race *and* sex. For example: it may well be indirectly discriminatory to apply a two year qualifying period for bringing an unfair dismissal complaint if this requirement has a disparate adverse impact on women, who are, statistically, less likely to have the required period of continuous employment.[60] However, this prohibition on indirect discrimination cannot be extended to protect those who find themselves similarly disadvantaged in the labour market due to a combination of their gender and race – for example, those excluded from the reach of the employment protection legislation on account of their concentration in 'atypical' work, such as homeworking. Thus, for example, the qualifying conditions to bring an unfair dismissal complaint arguably have a disproportionate adverse impact on Asian women, who, by virtue of their race and gender, are over-represented in homeworking and other 'atypical' forms of employment.

The emphasis on individual enforcement of the anti-discrimination legislation and the lack of formal provision for class actions is an omission from the legislation which seriously restricts the reach of the law, limiting it to the enforcement of individual rights rather than the redress of collective wrongs. As MacEwen notes, the Race Relations Act is 'essentially protective and results in the individuation (or individualising) of actions and remedies, which renders it ineffective in reducing racial discrimination in a systematic manner'.[61] The risks and costs of litigation are borne by the individual and any successful outcome is rarely permitted to benefit others similarly disadvantaged by virtue of being members of the same oppressed group.

There are, thus, a number of practical advantages which the availability of class actions could bring to litigants: first, by spreading the cost of litigation, class actions could ease the financial burden which currently has to be borne by individuals, due to the lack of legal aid for industrial tribunal claims; secondly, as existing protection against victimisation for bringing a discrimination claim has been shown to be less than effective it is in protecting individual litigants and those who assist them,[62] the weight of numbers in a class action may minimise the likelihood of repercussions; thirdly, class actions would enable the bringing of 'test cases' to ensure a wider application of any successful outcome. On a more theoretical level, the absence of the right to bring a class or group action on behalf of a group disadvantaged by systematic discrimination inhibits the ability of the courts to investigate

---

60 In *R v Secretary of State for Employment ex p Seymour-Smith and Perez* [1995] IRLR 464, the Court of Appeal found a *prima facie* case of discrimination contrary to the EC Equal Treatment Directive; the House of Lords, however, referred the case to the European Court of Justice for a preliminary ruling on whether the qualifying threshold does, in fact, breach Art 119 of the EC Treaty or the Equal Treatment Directive: [1997] IRLR 315.

61 *Op cit*, MacEwen, fn 46, p 195.

62 SDA 1975, s 4; RRA 1976, s 2; *Aziz v Trinity Street Taxis Ltd* [1988] ICR 534.

structural discrimination, since discrimination is portrayed as a matter of isolated acts against individuals. As Lustgarten and Edwards argue:

> By definition, discrimination is the antithesis of individualised decision. A person is ill treated, or shares some social circumstances, because of his involuntary membership of a group. There is, therefore, a collective dimension to every discrimination case, which it is difficult to fit within the traditional processes of law.[63]

In addition, since the paradigm legal subject is represented as an abstract individual, there will be limitations inherent in a notion of equality based on comparison with, and equalisation to, a male norm or a white norm.

The anti-discrimination law does contain some provision for more strategic enforcement, which might go some way to combat structural discrimination, but which is limited. Both the Commission for Racial Equality (CRE) and the Equal Opportunities Commission (EOC) are empowered to work toward the elimination of discrimination, to promote equality of opportunity and to monitor the operation of the legislation, including providing legal assistance to individual complainants.[64] The powers of the CRE and the EOC to institute formal investigations into discriminatory practices and to undertake strategic litigation on behalf of specific groups offers some way out of the cul-de-sac of individualised enforcement.

However, there remain serious obstacles to the realisation of group rights through the route of litigation – even strategic litigation taken by the CRE and EOC. First, the procedural limitations imposed by the anti-discrimination statutes and by case law on the use by the CRE and the EOC of their enforcement powers mean that this form of strategic enforcement falls far short of the type of class action which might enable the legislation to achieve some form of group justice. For example, each Commission must draw up terms of reference prior to launching a formal investigation into alleged discriminatory practices, which act as self-imposed restrictions on the scope of the investigation.[65] Further, judicial interpretation of the law has prevented the Commissions from initiating wide ranging formal investigations into named respondents, unless they first have sufficient evidence to found a belief that unlawful acts may have occurred.[66]

Secondly, the existence of two separate equality Commissions, with differing agendas and litigation strategies, creates a conceptual and institutional hurdle before those, such as black women, whose experience of

---

63 Lustgarten, L and Edwards, J, 'Racial inequality and the limits of law', in *op cit*, Braham *et al*, fn 3.

64 SDA 1975, s 53; RRA 1976, s 43.

65 SDA 1975, ss 57–61; RRA 1976, ss 48–52.

66 *R v Hillingdon London Borough Council ex p CRE* [1982] QB 276 and *Re Prestige Group plc* [1984] IRLR 166, in which the court interpreted restrictively the CRE's powers.

discrimination straddles the boundaries of the regulatory agencies. The EOC's litigation strategy, for example, has, in recent years, placed emphasis on using European Community equal treatment and equal pay law, both in domestic courts and by making references to the European Court of Justice, especially in the area of pensions equality.[67] There is little room within such a strategy for challenging discrimination experienced by women due to their structural location as black or Asian workers. Whilst there is some joint work with the CRE – for example, in the area of education[68] – it remains the case that, on a practical level, complainants alleging race and sex discrimination cannot appeal to a one stop agency which can adopt a 'holistic' approach to multiple discrimination.[69]

The continued utility of a rights based discourse

The failures of a system of enforcement based primarily on individual complaints, particularly its failure to accommodate the multiple discrimination experienced by black and Asian women, beg the question whether a more strategic approach to tackling discrimination, focusing on the attainment of group rights through flexible forms of class action, can ever be truly effective, since the problem of inequality goes beyond law and cannot be remedied by legislation and litigation alone.

There is an understandable scepticism over the use of the legal process to advance meaningful change with respect to gender and race oppression. Certain recent critiques of traditional liberal legalism, which present law as a series of ideological constructs operating to support existing social arrangements, contend that legal reform cannot serve as a means for fundamentally restructuring society: law, the legal process and the use of rights discourse are, it is argued, radically indeterminate.[70] According to Tushnet,[71] rights discourse results in abstraction rather than the realisation of substantive social change. This criticism, that 'new social movements' lose

---

67 See Barnard, C, 'A European litigation strategy: the case of the Equal Opportunities Commission', in Shaw, J and More, G (eds), *New Legal Dynamics of the European Union*, 1995, Oxford: Clarendon.

68 Commission for Racial Equality/Equal Opportunities Commission, *Further Education and Equality: A Manager's Manual*, 1995.

69 See Justice/The Runnymede Trust, *Improving Equality Law: The Options*, 1997, London: Justice, p 12, for proposals for reform of the existing anti-discrimination legislation on this point; and the Institute for Public Policy Research's report on a proposed Human Rights Commission (forthcoming).

70 For examples of scholarship within the loose grouping of 'critical legal studies', see critical legal studies symposium (1984) 36 Stanford L Rev 1–674; Kelman, M, *A Guide to Critical Legal Studies*, 1987, Cambridge, Mass: Harvard UP; Fitzpatrick, P and Hunt, A (eds), *Critical Legal Studies*, 1987, Oxford: Basil Blackwell; and Kairys, D (ed), *The Politics of Law*, rev edn, 1990, New York: Pantheon.

71 Tushnet, M, 'An essay on rights' (1984) 62 Texas L Rev 1363.

whatever transformative potential they have by virtue of an over-reliance on the notion of rights, is a familiar one within the critical evaluation of rights strategies[72] and is particularly pertinent to this discussion of the limits of litigation, since it is, further, arguable that identification with the politics of rights may lead to a preoccupation with litigation, on the assumption that rights only have meaning when articulated within the legal process.

At least in pragmatic terms, a rights discourse does have some merit and should not be jettisoned in its entirety. American critical race theorists, whilst agreeing with the perspective that rights discourse is indeterminate, nevertheless argue that such discourse holds a 'social and transformative value in the context of racial subordination that transcend[s] the narrower question of whether reliance on rights [can] alone bring about any determinate results'.[73] However, use of legal rights is not without difficulties: a preoccupation with litigation, to the detriment of other strategies, may serve to atomise social struggles, a particular danger for black and Asian women who combine two collective claims. A broader approach to tackling labour market discrimination would, for example, also need to include programmes of action (by public authorities, employers and trade unions) involving the adoption of such measures as positive monitoring of the workforce by employers, contract compliance and the 'mainstreaming' of equal opportunities through the inclusion of an assessment of the impact of legislative and other government proposals on women and ethnic minorities.[74] In particular, it has been suggested that the introduction of a statutory minimum wage would play a significant part in improving the earnings of women and ethnic minority workers (both male and female) who are over-represented in the ranks of the low paid.[75]

Nevertheless, the focus of this chapter has been on law as a mechanism for change rather than on broader regulatory or public policy approaches, for two reasons. First, although law may well be a 'secondary force' in social and economic life, it is not without some influence as a means of achieving policy goals through intervention in the workings of the labour market; and, secondly, there remains much to explore in assessing the extent to which existing formulations of anti-discrimination law can recognise, or be

---

72 See Fudge, J and Glasbeek, H, 'The politics of rights: a politics with little class' (1992) 1 Social and Legal Studies 45; and Herman's rejoinder: Herman, D, 'Beyond the rights debate' (1993) 2 Social and Legal Studies 25.

73 Crenshaw, K et al (eds), *Critical Race Theory: The Key Writings that Formed the Movement*, 1995, New York: The New Press, p xxiii.

74 *Op cit*, Justice/The Runnymede Trust, fn 69. See, also, European Commission, *Third Medium Term Community Action Programme on Equal Opportunities for Women and Men*, COM (90) 449 Final and European Commission Communication on Mainstreaming, 21 February 1996 (COM(96)67). See, also, Nott, Chapter 10, this volume.

75 'Minimum wage benefits women and ethnic minorities', Analysis of the 1996 Labour Force Survey, 73 EOR 1997.

interpreted to deal with, instances where race and gender discrimination exist simultaneously. This latter point will be the focus of the next section.

CONCLUSIONS: BLACK WOMEN AS A DISCRETE GROUP WITHIN ANTI-DISCRIMINATION LAW?

In view of the above discussion, the main question which remains unanswered is whether law is *capable* of conceptualising the right to equal treatment and equality with sufficient complexity to enable black and Asian women, as distinct from white women, to seek redress for disadvantage experienced within the labour market. Nicola Lacey has examined one of the ways in which the legal process might try to respond to the scepticism outlined above, namely a shift of emphasis from the exclusive reliance on individual enforcement to include a focus on the 'rights, interests and claims of groups'.[76] She envisages group rights as remedial rights, centring on socio-economic disadvantage and redistribution. These rights would apply to groups which were suffering disadvantage as a result either of present oppression or the present effects of past oppression.

Taking the notion of group rights further, attempts have been made within United States case law to explore the idea of black women as a discrete group in relation to both white women and black men, although not without some judicial resistance.[77]

As with the anti-discrimination law of Great Britain, black women have had to choose whether to base their discrimination claims on the sex or race equality legislation. This can be as problematic as asking someone to decide, for example, whether it is her race, class or gender which most oppresses her within the labour market. In one of these cases, *DeGraffenreid v General Motors*,[78] five black women alleged that their employer's redundancy policy of 'last in, first out' and its reliance on a seniority system perpetuated the effects of past discrimination against black women, as there had been a refusal to hire black women in the past. The court rejected the plaintiffs' attempt to bring a claim, not on behalf of blacks or women, but specifically on behalf of black women, arguing that black women should not be treated any differently from white women or black men: 'They must choose to bring either a race

---

76 Lacey, N, 'From individual to group?', in Hepple, B and Szyszczak, EM (eds), *Discrimination: The Limits of the Law*, 1992, London: Mansell.

77 *DeGraffenreid v General Motors*, 413 F Supp 142 (ED Miss 1976); *Moore v Hughes Helicopters Inc*, 708 F2d 475; and *Payne v Tavenol*, 416 F Supp 248 (ND Miss 1976); see *op cit*, Crenshaw, fn 6.

78 413 F Supp 142 (ED Miss 1976).

action or a sex action in order to avoid the creation of an unauthorised class which would give black women greater standing and relief.'[79]

As Kimberlé Crenshaw argues:

For white women, claiming sex discrimination is simply a statement that, but for gender, they would not have been disadvantaged. For them, there is no need to specify discrimination as *white* females because their race does not contribute to the disadvantage for which they seek redress ... Because the scope of anti-discrimination law is so limited, sex and race discrimination have come to be defined in terms of the experiences of those who are privileged *but for* their racial or sexual characteristics. Put differently, the paradigm of sex discrimination tends to be based on the experiences of white women: the model of race discrimination tends to be based on the experiences of the most privileged blacks.[80]

Subsequent cases, such as *Jeffries v Harris Community Action Association*,[81] rejected the approach that a black woman must choose between her race and sex claims, substituting the 'sex plus' concept, where it is alleged that a person discriminates against another on the basis of sex, plus an additional characteristic or factor related to sex. However, although this decision recognised the possibility of a claim based on both race and sex discrimination, it required the race claim to be subordinated to the sex discrimination issue. 'The "sex plus" methodology forces black women to choose gender as their principal identification, thereby perpetuating a fundamental misunderstanding of the nature of the discrimination experienced by black women, most of whom do not consider their race to be secondary to their sex.'[82]

However, the claims brought by black women in America, under Title VII of the Civil Rights Act 1964,[83] are useful for illustrating the positive potential contained in what is essentially a rights based approach to tackling disadvantage through law, to uncover a number of issues, such as the intersectionality of black women's experience, traditionally ignored by discrimination law.[84]

Returning to the question of the segregation of black and Asian women into particular sectors of the labour market within the UK, whilst appeal may be made to the concept of indirect discrimination on grounds of gender to attack unequal treatment of part time workers who are predominantly

---

79 Scarborough, C, 'Conceptualizing black women's employment experiences' (1989) 98 Yale LJ 1457.

80 *Ibid.*

81 615 F 2d 1025 (5th Cir 1980).

82 *Ibid*, Scarborough, p 1471.

83 42 USC & 2000e, *et seq*, as amended (1982).

84 Fredman, S and Szyszczak, EM, 'The interaction of race and gender', in *op cit*, Hepple and Szyszczak, fn 76.

women, the same cannot be said for unequal treatment of atypical workers who are disadvantaged in the labour market due to a combination of their race and gender. If it is the case that black or Asian women are subject to detrimental treatment in circumstances where white women are not, the concepts of direct or indirect discrimination do not appear to lend themselves to the argument that these women have been subject to less favourable treatment or suffered a disparate impact *as women*. Similarly, it may also be impossible to show less favourable treatment on grounds of race if black men are not subject to the same detrimental treatment as black women.

In response to this impasse, the Institute of Employment Rights has proposed the adoption of an approach which acknowledges that black women may be subject to both race and sex discrimination and should, thus, be recognised as a distinct legal group deserving of legal protection.[85] Multiple discrimination would, therefore, be unlawful, where it can be demonstrated that a group of people sharing certain characteristics is a group 'which warrants protection in its own right, because it carries an inordinately large burden of disadvantage'. Thus, it would be unlawful to discriminate against black women, who suffer a synthesis of gender and race discrimination.

Whilst adopting a legislation and rights based approach to redress social inequalities may be problematic, nevertheless, instrumental benefits can be gained from the pursuit of collective rights aimed at remedying social disadvantage. Emphasising group rights to equality, however, requires careful consideration of the criteria by which a group is to be defined, recognising race and gender as simultaneous rather than merely cumulative forms of experience.

With regard to redressing labour market disadvantage and, in particular, in view of ethnic differences in women's labour market participation, the realisation that individual workers may occupy multiple social junctures is vital to a progressive anti-discrimination theory; a theory which acknowledges that race and gender interact to shape experiences of workers, that these experiences are unique to them as black or Asian women workers, whose interests cannot be addressed by traditional formulations of anti-discrimination law. Through developing the concept of multiple discrimination, together with a more expansive conception of equality, based on group justice, rights discourse can be applied to provide a useful starting point for the effective legal redress of composite forms of disadvantage in an increasingly fragmented labour market.

---

85 Ewing, K (ed), *Working Life: A New Perspective on Labour Law*, 1996, London: Lawrence & Wishart/Institute of Employment Rights, pp 162–63.

CHAPTER 8

'FEMINISING' THE WORKPLACE?
LAW, THE 'GOOD PARENT' AND
THE 'PROBLEM OF MEN'

Richard Collier

INTRODUCTION

This chapter presents a critical analysis and overview of attempts presently taking place in Britain to use law to shift cultural attitudes and practices in relation to what has been widely perceived to be the growing need to achieve a more desirable 'balance' between the demands of employment and the 'quality' of 'family life'. What follows is an exploration, more generally, of the relationship between the shifting contours of family structures, the changing experience of employment and the possibilities of, and limits to, legal intervention as a means of changing the practices and attitudes of both employers and employees to both paid work and child care. At the present moment in Britain, the promotion of 'equality' in the workplace is widely seen, at the level of rhetoric at least, as being a desirable goal of both government and employers alike.[1] This chapter seeks to question the ways in which present debates about work and family life are dealing in certain ideas of both the 'gendered' (feminine, masculine) *and* 'gender neutral' subject (whether conceived of as parent or as worker). It seeks, in particular, to question the pervasive and multi-faceted notion of the 'feminisation' of work via a surfacing of something of the complexity of men's subjective experiences as both 'workers' and, I shall suggest, 'family men'.[2] It does so by addressing, first and foremost, the way in which ideas of sexual difference become, in particular instances, socially, politically and ethically significant. What follows does not seek to reproduce current understandings of 'gender' at 'work'. The

---

1   By this, I mean that there are few employers who would not claim to be equal opportunity employees. See, further, below.

2   Just as the diversity of paid employment makes it impossible to address 'work' as a unitary experience, in talking of a relationship between 'men' and 'work', it is necessary, at the outset, to note that these categories need to be treated cautiously. It is not possible to extrapolate from a particular study of, say, middle-class men and their employment to the category 'men' in general. Socio-economic background, 'race' and ethnicity, age, geographic location (urban, rural areas), educational credentials, employment history, physical ability, sexuality and so forth are factors which mediate the 'lived experience' of both work and 'masculine' gender. On the limits of the concept of 'masculinity' in this regard, see, further, Hearn, J, 'Is masculinity dead? A critique of the concept of masculinity', in Mac an Ghaill, M (ed), *Understanding Masculinities*, 1996, Buckingham: Open University.

aim, rather, is to contribute to a more general project of 'opening [out] the present to different ways of being a woman or a man, along with different ways of negotiating that [sexual] difference'.[3]

FEMINISING THE WORKPLACE? WOMEN, MEN AND THE CHANGING NATURE OF WORK

Of all the areas of law in which the development of 'feminist perspectives' has taken place during the past 20 years or so, the field of 'employment law' can be seen to have had a particular pertinence to contemporary debates about the nature of shifting gender relations between women and men. At the end of the 20th century, interlinked concerns about the changing nature of men's and women's 'gender roles', in both the family and waged work, constitute two of the most pressing, and contentious, political issues of the day. Whilst hitherto traditional gender formations are seen as fragmenting, becoming fluid, unstable and (for some) threatening, not least in relation to the contours of the changing family,[4] in relation to employment, confusion and ambiguities about the meaning, nature and purpose of work in our lives is widespread.[5] In Britain, like other advanced post-industrial nations, the last two decades have been marked by a series of changes in the nature and location of waged work which have done away, irrevocably it would seem, with what had once appeared to be the certainties and securities of the post-war world, a period in which full time, waged employment – for *men* – was the norm.[6] By the end of the 1990s, the nature and structure of waged work, its organisation and rewards, the tasks which are undertaken in its name, as well as the people who do them and the places in which they labour, have each changed fundamentally in the face of a widespread restructuring of, and casualisation and polarisation within, the workforce. And, central to this process, has been a perceived (re)gendering of the relationship between men, women and work, in which the idea of the 'feminisation' of employment has assumed an increasingly central significance.

---

3 Gatens, M, *Imaginary Bodies: Ethics, Power and Corporeality*, 1996, London: Routledge, p 148.

4 On the responses of the 'new men's movement', see, further, Collier, R, '"Coming together?": post-heterosexuality, masculine crisis and the new men's movement' (1996) 4(1) Feminist Legal Studies 3, pp 3–48.

5 Pahl, R, *On Work*, 1988, Oxford: Blackwells, p 1.

6 Pahl, R, *After Success*, 1995, Oxford: Blackwells; and Pahl, R, *Divisions of Labour*, 1984, Oxford: Blackwells.

The 'feminisation' of work thesis

The future's bright. The future's female. As the next millennium dawns, we are looking at the feminisation of society.[7]

Within a diverse set of literatures during the 1980s and 1990s, a range of questions about the changing organisation and distribution of waged work have been conceptualised in terms of the 'feminisation of work' thesis; that is, an evident, apparently empirically demonstrable, '... trend towards the "feminisation" of work in contemporary Britain'.[8] The attrition of men's employment during the past 20 years has, unquestionably, been considerable. The vast majority of the jobs which have been lost as a result of manufacturing decline since the mid to late 1960s have been in jobs held by men. At the same time, a substantial proportion of the increase in jobs in private sector services has been in women's employment.[9] As a result, by the beginning of the 1990s, there were 3.5 million fewer men in waged employment than at the beginning of the 1960s and almost 3 million more women in employment, while more than half of all women, and almost 60% of married women, were considered economically active, compared to just over a third of all women, and a fifth of married women, in 1951.[10]

Such statistics have been widely interpreted as reflecting no less than a transformation in the labour market behaviour of women in Britain in the post war era.[11] The 'feminisation' thesis itself, however, has been taken to indicate much more than just this well documented numerical increase in the numbers of women entering waged employment. It has, also, come to encompass – indeed, it has become a byword for – a broader societal shift from predominantly manufacturing to service sector based employment, in which the personal and organisational attributes seen as desirable to a growing number of jobs and occupations at the turn of the century are based not on traditionally 'masculine' qualities (such as appeals to authority, order and hierarchy) but on the 'feminine' attributes of serving, empathy and caring. Both organisational theorists and management consultants have, thus, identified a clear trend towards the 'feminisation of management structures' marked by an emphasis on less hierarchical, more empathetic and co-operative styles of management. In turn, further evidence of the feminisation

7   'Successful females herald the dawn of a fairer future' (1996) *The Independent*, 21 June.

8   McDowell, L, *Capital Culture: Gender at Work in the City*, 1997, Oxford: Blackwells, p 11.

9   Dex, S, *Women's Occupational Mobility: A Lifetime Perspective*, 1987, London: Macmillan; and *ibid*, McDowell.

10 Source: Department of Employment, 'Results of the (1991) Labour Force Survey' (1992) 99 Employment Gazette 153, pp 153–72.

11 This issue has become a recurring theme during the 1990s within British media reporting of more general changes in gender relations between men and women as 'the big question of sex and society' ((1998) *The Observer*, 4 November): see, eg, 'Do men need jobs more than women?' (1997) *Independent on Sunday*, 16 November.

thesis has been found in the rising numbers of men complaining of sex discrimination at work.[12] The growing *economic* power of women has, in short, been accompanied, it has been argued, by an increasing *cultural* privileging of 'the feminine' in contemporary British society, with the result that, across a range of contexts and debates, it is boys and men who are now seen as 'losing out' to women and girls;[13] '... if these literatures are to be believed, if sheer numbers of women in the labour market are emphasised ... it might seem that women are entering a new period of success and empowerment in the late 20th century world of work.'[14]

There are, however, as a number of commentators have noted, several problems with the 'feminisation' thesis. Whilst it is the case that many of the jobs created during the 1980s and 1990s have, indeed, demanded well qualified employees, an increasing proportion of whom are 'credentialised' women,[15] the greatest expansion of employment during this period has been in poorly paid, casual and temporary work at the 'bottom end' of the service sector.[16] Seen in a context in which pay differentials have continued to widen between the well paid and the poorest paid in British society, it remains women who constitute the bulk of those in this bottom decile of income distribution. 'Women's work', in short, continues to be more likely to be part time, insecure and casualised.[17] This is not to underestimate the economic and cultural significance of the shifts in men and women's employment which have taken place; nor is it to deny the extent to which a range of issues related to the theme of 'women and work' have become central features of policy debates, not least in relation to concerns about the family, marriage and divorce, crime disorder and the meaning of community.[18] It is important,

---

12 In 1995, amongst much publicity, it was reported that the Equal Opportunities Commission (EOC) had received more complaints about sexism in job recruitment from males than from females for the first time in its 20 year history. There were 820 complaints of sex discrimination to the EOC by men in 1995, an increase of 10% over 1994, compared with 803 from women. There is some evidence, however, that some men are making 'ludicrous' job applications and then 'crying foul' when they are unsuccessful ((1996)*The Times*, 6 May).

13 Cf Collier, R, *Masculinities, Crime and Criminology*, 1998, London: Sage.

14 *Op cit*, McDowell, fn 8, p 12.

15 See, further, Crompton, R *et al*, *Changing Forms of Employment: Organisations, Skills and Gender*, 1996, London: Routledge; and McDowell, L, 'Life without father and Ford: the new gender order of post-Fordism' (1991) 16 Transactions 400, pp 400–19.

16 Castells, M, *The Informational City*, 1989, Oxford: Blackwells; Handy, C, *The Empty Raincoat: Making Sense of the Future*, 1994, London: Hutchinson; Lawless, P, Martin, M and Hardy, S, *Unemployment and Social Exclusion: Landscapes of Labour Inequality*, 1996, London: Jessica Kingsley.

17 *Op cit*, McDowell, fn 8; Walby, S (ed), *Gender Segregation at Work*, 1988, Milton Keynes: OU Press.

18 The legal profession itself is, arguably, one of the highest profile areas in which these debates about women and work are taking place: see, further, McGlynn, C, *The Woman Lawyer: Making the Difference*, 1998, London: Butterworths; and Gibb, F, 'An end to the sex war?' (1998) *The Times*, 3 February; also, 'My learned friends want to be more flexible' (1998) *The Times*, 14 April.

however, to read such statistics with caution. As well as being 'feminised' employment, the 'world of work' of the new millennium can be seen as being marked by discontinuity, interruption and uncertainty;[19] that is, by features of employment which have long been familiar to women. An alternative interpretation of recent events would thus be to see conditions of labour marked by insecurity, historically well known to groups such as women and migrant workers, as now being extended to (hitherto relatively privileged) middle class men.[20] Whilst it is the case that a minority of well educated women are able to enter, and hold on to, full time work in professional occupations, the majority of women in waged work continue to be employed in part time jobs at the bottom end of the labour market.

There are a number of other, related, problems with the 'feminisation' thesis. It is clear that men continue to dominate the upper echelons of the professions, public and private organisations (as well as government itself, notwithstanding the election of 'Blair's Babes' in May 1997). Despite the growing presence of women in higher level jobs, few women make it to the 'top' of occupational hierarchies. Moreover, at least part of women's improved position in certain areas of the workforce has been the consequence of an overall expansion of opportunities in these areas during the 1980s and 1990s, rather than a matter of women 'taking jobs' which had been previously held by men. Men continue to score more highly on evaluation and assessment schemes and to be promoted more quickly (see, further, on assertiveness training schemes, Belcher, Chapter 3, this volume), whilst women continue to be ascribed a range of feminine roles deemed appropriate to 'humanising' the culture of many organisations. At the same time, and across workplace cultures, considerable evidence attests to the continued prevalence of sex discrimination, harassment and other behaviour which is (at the very least) inimical to women's career success.

There remains another important problem with the feminisation thesis, however, which relates directly to the political question of what it means to conceptualise changes in employment relationships through such a *gendered* discourse. There is some agreement that the British economy is now dominated by occupations and jobs in which:

> ... the ability to conform to a particular embodied workplace performance is crucial ... the possession of a certain set of personal characteristics and skills ... is crucial, not only in recruitment and selection programmes but, also, in the reproduction of *an acceptable workplace performance*.[21]

---

19   Rifkin, J, *The End of Work*, 1996, New York: Tarcher Putnam.
20   For an analysis of the broader political and economic context of these developments, see Hutton, W, *The State We're In*, 1995, London: Jonathon Cape.
21   *Op cit*, McDowell, fn 8, p 206, my emphasis.

It cannot be assumed, however, that the 'performance' of this new 'feminised' worker is necessarily confined to women. Arguments supportive of the feminisation of management cultures have tended to assume that gendered identities and behaviour are fixed, with women expressing 'feminine' and men expressing 'masculine' attributes. Yet, as recent studies of gender and organisation have shown (see below), gendered identities and interactions are themselves, within bounds, fluid and negotiable. For example, the fact that the 'disembodied ideal' of the male bureaucrat has become, in some contexts at least, an increasingly unattractive and undesirable feature of workplace culture does not, by itself, mean that men are being *dis*advantaged and women *ad*vantaged by a cultural shift towards 'feminisation'. The ability to construct a feminine gendered identity is not something confined to, although it may be associated with, women. The parameters of compulsory heterosexuality might severely restrict the range of acceptable 'gender performances' for both men and women in the workplace.[22] However, the diversification of 'straight' male gender identities in the 1980s and 1990s, promoted by the increasing cultural commodification of masculinity,[23] has itself opened up new possibilities for 'straight' male appropriations of a range of characteristics traditionally associated with femininity. And, in so doing, the 'taking on' of attributes conventionally assumed to be feminine has become, for some men at least, a possible advantage in the present climate. When such a development is located in the context of the workplace cultures of an expanding urban 'service class',[24] in which questions of lifestyle, consumption and the ownership and possession of 'positional goods' has already served to mark out their owners as a distinct class faction, this new 'feminised' male worker might, himself, be seen as a significant feature of employment in late modern capitalist societies.[25] If it is the case that workplace performances are changing through being 'feminised', therefore, then, in order to retain their power and the monopoly of key positions, it is arguably in men's interests to co-opt such femininity, or at least a version of it: Feminine characteristics in a masculinised body may offer the best of all worlds. As McDowell has argued, 'after all, if femininity is a masquerade, men can be women just as well as, if not better than, women'.[26]

---

22 See, further, Bell, D and Valentine, G, 'The sexed self: strategies of performance, sites of resistance', in Pile, S and Thrift, N (eds), *Mapping the Subject*, 1995, London: Routledge, pp 145–49.

23 Mort, F, *Cultures of Consumption: Masculinties and Social Space in late Twentieth Century Britain*, 1996, London: Routledge.

24 Du Gay, P, *Consumption and Identity at Work*, 1996, London: Sage.

25 Featherstone, M, *Consumer Culture and Postmodernism*, 1991, London: Sage.

26 *Op cit*, McDowell, fn 8, p 208. See, also, Williams, CL, 'The glass escalator: hidden advantages for men in "female" professions' (1992) 39(3) Social Problems 253, pp 253–68: Williams, CL, *Gender Differences at Work: Women and Men in Non-Traditional Occupations*, 1989, Berkeley, California: California UP.

'New Labour' and the 'balance' of work and home: (or) 'the problem of men'

Notwithstanding these problems with the feminisation thesis, it is interesting – and, I now wish to suggest, troubling – to consider just how pervasive the idea has been. In particular, when it is allied to a series of policy interventions explicitly designed to *regender* (that is, to shift the gender practices) of women and men in relation to both the workplace and the family, it becomes important to question not just the ways in which issues around employment and family life are presently being 'gendered' but also, crucially, how the conceptualisation of social change as taking place *through* the language of changes in gender might itself be serving to efface questions of sex difference, power and inequality.

The 'New' Labour Government in Britain, elected in May 1997, has embraced a range of initiatives in the fields of both employment law and family policy which, in many ways, reflect this 'new mood' or attitude towards work in the 21st century. It is a mood, moreover, in which the idea of the 'feminised workplace' has become a growing theme.[27] This is not to understate the continuities of the Labour Government with the previous Conservative administration, not least in the desire to 'keep business happy' in terms of broader economic and employment policies.[28] It is, however, to detect in the package of employment policies of the new government, whether in the form of pre-existing manifesto commitments or of policies announced subsequent to election, evidence of this *new language*, through which the relationship between work and home is being understood. It is a language marked by two clear and interlinked strands or themes: first, a gendered discourse, outlined above, through which the workplace is depicted as being *feminised* by the promotion of a 'better', 'healthier' balance between 'work and family life'; and, secondly, by an overt identification – itself rare at the level of government policy in Britain – that the 'problem' in bringing about such change lies largely, if not exclusively, in changing the behaviour of *men*. In bringing the 'feminisation' thesis to bear on specific policy initiatives in the fields of both employment law and family law,[29] the government has embarked on what is no less than an attempt at socially engineering a 'new', 'improved' 'balance' between work and family life; and, in so doing, what has emerged as the key issue to be addressed is a particular – and, I wish to suggest, problematic – conceptualisation of what it means to talk of 'the

---

27 *Op cit*, Pahl, fn 6.

28 Hobsbawm, E, 'The death of neo-liberalism', 1998, *Marxism Today*, Nov/Dec 4, pp 4–9; and Hall, S, 'The great moving nowhere show', 1998, *Marxism Today*, Nov/Dec 9, pp 9–15.

29 The general 'pro-family' moral orientation of this policy is particularly clear in the Green Paper *Supporting Families: A Consultation Document*, 1998, London: HMSO.

problem of men' in relation to understanding tensions between 'work' and 'family' life.

Central to the policies of the New Labour Government in relation to employment law is a belief that the tension between the demands of work and parenthood can cause conflicting pressures. Accordingly, two of the main priorities in this field have been to tackle the excessive working hours of employees and to give parents in work the opportunity to experience greater 'flexibility' in balancing the demands of work and family life. In seeking to achieve this aim, the government has announced a series of measures which, together, have been depicted by Ministers as constituting a 'comprehensive package' of 'policies for working families'. These policies seek to promote new 'flexible ways of organising work and time' in a manner better suited to the changing needs of society. These measures include the implementation of the EU Parental Leave Directive (No 96/34), Working Time and Part Time Work Directives,[30] the implementation of the national minimum wage, the Out of School Childcare Initiative, consultation papers on early education and day care and the establishment of the 'National Childcare Strategy', launched in May 1998.[31] The executive summary of the latter document captures, in a particularly clear way, the reasoning informing government initiatives in this area. In seeking to highlight the key points of why a 'National Childcare Strategy' is needed, David Blunkett, Secretary of State for Education and Employment, and Harriet Harman, the then Secretary of State for Social Security and Minister for Women, declared their belief in:

> ... supporting families and children ... so, it is essential to support child care ... Society is changing, as more women go out to work ... and fewer people live in large families ... Child care is good for children ... it is good for their parents and others who look after them ... and it is good for the economy.[32]

Child care, the increasing employment of women, the wellbeing of parents and the needs of the economy are each entwined although, in this instance, there is no *explicit* reference to changing the behaviour of men. This, however, is in marked contrast to two other measures, which I wish to focus on here as illustrating the general direction of government policy in this area. These are, first, the Parental Leave Directive and, secondly, the White Paper *Fairness at Work*, published in May 1998, containing initial proposals and issues for

---

30 The Working Time Directive specifies minimum daily and weekly rest periods; rest breaks; annual paid holidays; a limit of 48 hours a week on the average time which employees can be required to work (except by voluntary agreement); and restrictions on hours worked at night.

31 See, also, the consultation paper *Supporting Families, op cit*, fn 29, especially Chap 4, 'Strengthening Marriage'.

32 Summary, 'Meeting the Childcare Challenge', 1998, para 1. These themes are taken up in *Supporting Families, op cit*, fn 29.

consultation on the implementation of the Parental Leave Directive, along with a range of other measures.

Parental Leave Directive

The Parental Leave Directive, originally adopted by the Member States of the EU (with the exception of the UK) in June 1996, provides employees with a right to a minimum of three months' unpaid leave on the birth or adoption of a child to enable them to take care of that child. It, also, provides for employees to take time off work for urgent family reasons. Such a directive on parental leave had first been proposed by the Commission in 1983, when it had been rejected on the grounds of a lack of unanimous approval. The proposal, later revised, gained a broad consensus and was subsequently added as part of the Social Chapter. The lack of previous implementation in the UK, it is widely accepted, had been a consequence largely of the previous Conservative Government's belief that there was 'little to gain and much to lose' from applying social rules and regulations across the European Union, alongside a concern with the potential expense of introducing a statutory right to parental leave which, it was believed, would meet with a low take-up. Flexible working time for *men* would be better achieved, it was argued, by local initiatives and negotiations rather than by government intervention. Thus, Michael Portillo, as Conservative Employment Secretary, described the provision of three months' unpaid leave for men as an 'immensely disruptive and destructive' intervention in the field of employment law.[33] Notwithstanding the disfavour of the Conservatives towards the idea of parental leave proposals, the Labour Government has agreed to support the Directive, noting not only the well publicised fact that men in Britain work much longer hours than their counterparts on the continent but that they, also, live in one of the few countries within the European Union which does *not* have some form of statutory parental leave.[34] Central to the reasons given in support of implementation of the Directive has been the explicit aim of helping '... people to balance the demands of work and family life. The government wants to encourage employers to make improvements in the workplace, generally, [and], in particular, in the provision of flexible and family friendly working arrangements'.[35] The implementation of the Parental Leave Directive has, also, been seen as contributing to broader 'Community objectives of improving working and living conditions and the reconciliation

---

33 (1997) *The Financial Times,* 23 January. Advocates of the Directive maintained, in contrast, any such lack of demand for the parental leave scheme was not due to lack of interest but, rather, a fear of being penalised if the leave was given or even asked for: 'unless leave is paid, the take-up is always going to be low' (1997) *The Observer,* 18 May

34 (1997) *The Times,* 9 June.

35 Select Committee on European Legislation Sixth Report, 1997, para 7.9.

of work and family life',[36] whilst meeting the economic imperative of 'getting more people into work'.[37]

The Fairness at Work White Paper

The White Paper *Fairness at Work* was described on the day of its publication by the Secretary of State for Trade and Industry, Margaret Beckett, as a 'further landmark in our drive to create both a more prosperous and a fairer Britain'.[38] The proposals in the paper fall, broadly, into three areas: rights for the individual, collective rights and, my specific concern here, the development of policies that are 'family friendly'. With regard to the latter, and echoing the arguments made in relation to parental leave, Beckett stated the government's clear intention to:

> ... recognise the *special responsibilities of parents*. We place great demands on them. Most need to work, to give their children a secure life, but children need their parents' time, too, *if family life and society are to be cohesive*. The White Paper sets out policies that will enhance family life, while making it easier for *both men and women* who work to avoid conflicts between their responsibilities at home and at work.[39]

Let us be clear: the key objective of each of these measures is, alongside the other, related initiatives noted above, not only the desire to 'balance' work and family life but an intention to promote *equality* between women and men.[40] The Preamble to the Parental Leave Directive expressly states that the Directive is to act 'as an important means of promoting equal opportunities and treatment between men and women' by enabling men and women 'to reconcile their occupational and family obligations'. And, crucially for my present concerns, the way in which such 'equal opportunities' are to be promoted is by *encouraging men* to assume an equal share of family responsibilities.[41]

---

36 Select Committee on European Legislation Sixth Report, 1997, para 7.10.

37 Para 7.13 continues: 'The government believes that providing an entitlement to time off for pressing family reasons and to parental leave will produce widespread benefits. The Minister believes that families as well as the employees themselves will benefit and that all workers will feel more secure and a barrier to employment will be lifted for people who fear that they may need to take days off. *This will serve the government's aim of encouraging more people into work*' (my emphasis).

38 *Hansard*, 21 May 1998, Col 1101.

39 *Ibid*, Col 1103, my emphasis.

40 In November 1998, the Equal Opportunities Commission presented to the government plans for a radical overhaul of sexual equality laws, involving a new equality 'super law' designed to tackle pervasive discrimination ('Workplace revolution for women' (1998) *The Guardian*, 5 November). At the time of writing, indications are that the government remains committed to the implementation of major reform of the sex equality legislation.

41 Note, eg, the Consultation Paper addressing the law on *Parental Responsibility for Unmarried Fathers*, March 1998, London: Lord Chancellor's Department.

On one level, it might be presumed that these proposals will be welcomed by large numbers of men. Research suggests that many men do experience real difficulties in combining paid work with child care and other commitments and would seek, *as a priority*, more 'balance' between the competing demands – and pleasures – of their work and family lives.[42] The importance of the subject to men can be seen, particularly when allied to concerns about workplace stress, as being reflected in the increasingly high profile of these issues. Yet, at the same time, there is a general recognition of a considerable reluctance on the part of men to change, a reluctance which cannot be reduced solely to the lack of specific provisions for parental leave. It is, at this point, that 'what men do' in both the *workplace* and the *home* can be seen to be interlinked. In the former, it is men who discriminate, harass or otherwise act in ways out of step with the ethical, cultural and economic imperatives of contemporary society (for example, the desire that women be fully integrated into the workforce as equals). In the *home*, it is men who appear unwilling (or, for some at least, unable) to take on a greater share of domestic labour, to become more involved in routine child care tasks or to 'reassess' the balance of their individual commitments to 'work' and 'home' in ways whereby the former will not always be given priority over the latter.[43] Before addressing *why* this might be the case, I wish to turn, first, to a body of scholarship which sheds a rather different light on the 'feminisation' thesis and, in particular, on the relationship between sex, gender and employment as it is presently being conceptualised within these government proposals.

'GENDERING' EMPLOYMENT: THEORISING ORGANISATION, SEXUALITY AND THE 'EMBODIED' SUBJECT

During the 1980s and 1990s, there has been a explosion of feminist influenced literature concerned with such issues as the 'gender' of organisations, the institutional structures of sex based occupational segregation and the gendered patterns of employment, recruitment and 'career'. This work has been marked by an investigation of the interpersonal dynamics of power, sexuality and the social construction of femininity and, more recently, masculinity 'at work'.[44] The scholarship, much of which has drawn on post-structuralist theorisations of the relationship between gender, work, identity

---

42 Oerton, S, *Beyond Hierarchy*, 1996, London: Taylor and Francis, p 178. See, also, eg, 'The great work/life debate' (1998) *The Times*, 1 June; and *Balanced Lives: Changing Work Patterns for Men*, 1995, London: New Ways to Work.

43 Social Focus on Men and Women, *Social Focus on Men and Women: Report*, 1998, London: HMSO.

44 For an excellent overview of this literature, see, further, *op cit*, McDowell, fn 8, pp 11–43.

and the 'sexed' organisation,[45] has addressed the nature of gendered and sexualised power relations within the workplace. It has explored, in particular, the complex ways in which inequalities and hierarchical power structures are set up and maintained and the ways in which women and men employ what are seen as distinctly 'gendered' strategies to overcome workplace relations which constrain (and empower) in differing ways.[46] There have been a number of recurring themes within this scholarship which have a direct bearing on how the 'gendered' subject of employment law is to be understood.

First, this work has questioned the idea that the gender categories of 'masculinity' and 'femininity' are, in any way, fixed or pre-given; that, for example, there exists a unitary 'masculinity' which can be said to constitute a 'problem' which needs to be addressed.[47] Notwithstanding a recognition of the existence of dominant or 'hegemonic'[48] versions – a point which is not to be underestimated in considering the deep rooted nature of discriminatory practices, as we shall see – both masculinity and femininity take multiple forms, which are defined, constructed and maintained not only by the institutional structures of capitalist economies but, also, through 'everyday' talk and behaviour in workplace locations. Research from diverse fields confirms the ways in which occupational sex stereotyping and the institutional and 'everyday' structuring of workplace interactions both maintain and reproduce gendered patterns of inequality. What has been termed the 'embeddedness' of patterns of domination and subordination within institutional and organisations structures, as well as the routine 'doing' of gender and gender relations, can thus be seen as part of a more general cultural understanding of women as different, as 'other' in relation to dominant constructions of gender hierarchies.

Secondly, and following on from the above, a recurring theme in this scholarship has been the identification of work and workplaces not as sites in or to which men and women 'come' in their daily lives as fixed and finished

---

45   Eg: Acker, J, 'Gendering organizational theory', in Mills, AJ and Tancred, P (eds), *Gendering Organizational Analysis*, 1992, Newbury Park, CA: Sage; Acker, J, 'Gendered institutions: from sex roles to gendered institutions' (1992) 21(5) Contemporary Sociology 565, pp 565–69; Acker, J, 'Hierarchies, jobs, bodies: a theory of gendered organizations' (1990) 4(2) Gender and Society 139, pp 139–58: Game, A and Pringle, R, *Gender at Work*, 1984, London: Pluto; Gubrium, JF and Holstein, JA, 'Family discourse, organizational embeddedness, and local enactment' (1993) 14(1) Journal of Family Issues 66, pp 66–81; Savage, M and Witz, A (eds), *Gender and Bureaucracy*, 1992, London: Basil Blackwell.

46   Collinson, D and Hearn, J, 'Naming men as men: implications for work, organization and management' (1994) 1(1) Gender, Work and Organization 2, pp 2–22; Kerfoot, D and Knights, D, 'Management, masculinity and manipulation: from paternalism to corporate strategy in financial services in Britain' (1993) 30(4) Journal of Management Studies 659, pp 659–77.

47   See, further, on the conceptual limitations of 'masculinity', *op cit*, Hearn, fn 2.

48   Connell, RW, *Gender and Power*, 1987, Sydney: Allen & Unwin.

gender subjects but, rather, as *active forces* in the social construction of workers themselves as gendered beings. Research has sought to unpack the diverse ways in which workplace and organisation play a key role in the constitution of specific gendered subjects, via such processes as the (gendered) encoding of cultural, social and economic capital in the field of work, in constructing work itself as an 'emotional' labour and in 'embodying' the ideal of the 'good' (gendered) worker in particular ways. This literature has proved particularly compatible with, and has drawn on, broader developments in social theory (not least around queer theory), in which gender itself has been widely seen as a 'performance' or a 'performative project',[49] with the body being seen as a site of the inscription and 'embedding' of gender. This, in turn, has been seen as raising a number of questions about the perpetuation of discriminatory practices in the workplace. What cultural, economic and *psychological* investments have men had in forms of working practices which are now being challenged by women's increased entry into work?[50] How does this relate to the differential sexualisation of the bodies of women and men in specific workplace contexts? And what do the forms of men's resistance to these changes say about the ostensibly 'natural' boundaries between work and family life? What does this tell us about the way in which gender and sexuality are 'interrelated with the production and reproduction of material and discursive relations of power and control in both hierarchical and less or non-hierarchical organisations, albeit in ways which are deeply embedded, complex and contradictory'.[51]

Conceptualising 'gender' at 'work' in such a way has several implications for understanding the relationship between sex, gender and employment law. On one level, it reinforces a central tenet of feminist legal theory, whereby the purportedly unmarked, disembodied and universal individual of the western intellectual tradition is revealed as having been a *gendered* subject all along; the 'man of law',[52] a 'male subject' embodying a particular 'masculine vantage point'. However, this work also surfaces, by engaging with the way in which diverse structural and discursive practices constitute and give meaning to *sexual difference* in the first place, those processes whereby, for women, 'doing gender' has been seen to involve the 'impossibility of being a man'. In so doing, the sexed (as different) experiences of both women's and men's

---

49   Butler, J, *Bodies That Matter: On the Discursive Limits of Sex*, 1993, London: Routledge; and Butler, J, *Gender Trouble: Feminism and the Subversion of Identity*, 1990, London: Routledge.

50   Cockburn, C, *Brothers: Male Dominance and Technological Change*, 1983, London: Pluto; and Nicolson, P, *Gender, Work and Organizations: A Psychological Perspective*, 1996, London: Routledge.

51   *Op cit*, Oerton, fn 42.

52   Naffine, N, *Law and the Sexes*, Sydney: Allen & Unwin.

'gendered lives',[53] whether in relation to the family or work, have become central to developing understandings of how women are consistently positioned as 'inappropriate' or 'vile' bodies in contrast to a masculine (desexed) 'norm' or benchmark across a range of workplace cultures. This integration of a 'politics of difference',[54] not least around questions of corporeality, reproduction and the 'sexuatedness' of discourse,[55] has important implications for attempts, whether by government or individual organisation, to promote 'social justice' via claims to be advocates of 'equal opportunity'. It, also, has important implications for understanding the attempts of the present government to construct a 'gender neutral' or 'ungendered' worker, a worker who might then, on leaving work, return to their 'gender neutral' practices as a 'good parent'. This point requires clarification.

The limits of law: the 'good parent', the 'good worker' and the myth of gender neutrality

Debates around work, family and gender have historically been framed, largely, as issues around 'women and ...' employment, 'women and ...' child care, 'women and ...' family policy, and so forth. This has resulted in the emergence of a policy agenda which has tended to take as axiomatic certain features of the relationship between men's work, parenthood and gendered identity: for example, the assumption that a man's primary commitment and identification should be with paid employment rather than full time child care, and that progression in a man's career will necessarily involve a temporal and spatial trade off between the domains of 'work' and 'family'. Yet, at the present moment, the association within government policy of 'work/family' policy as, primarily, a 'women's' issue' has been disturbed – to a degree at least, we have seen – by an emerging discourse which is positioning the behaviour of *men* as a 'problem' to be addressed in a number of ways.

There is, of course, a broader context to this 'man problem'. A number of social and economic changes have, notably from around the early-1980s through to the present day, been widely seen as necessitating a rethinking of men's 'role' in relation to both family and work. Economic, social, political

---

53 Fineman, M, 'Feminist legal scholarship and women's gendered lives', in Cain, M and Harrington, C (eds), *Lawyers in a Postmodern World*, 1994, Buckingham: Open University.

54 Young, IM, *Justice and the Politics of Difference*, 1990, Ewing, New Jersey: Princeton UP; Young, IM, 'The ideal of community and the politics of difference', in Nicholson, L (ed), *Feminism/Postmodernism*, 1990, London: Routledge; Young, IM, 'Together in difference: transforming the logic of group political conflict', in Squires, J (ed), *Principled Positions: Postmodernism and the Rediscovery of Value*, 1993, London: Lawrence & Wishart.

55 Leng, KW, 'New Australian feminism: towards a discursive politics of Australian feminist thought' (1995) 7(1) Antithesis 47, pp 47–63.

and cultural changes, not the least of which has been the impact of feminism on understandings of what constitutes desirable and 'acceptable' workplace practices, have surfaced some complex and difficult ontological questions about the meaning of men's 'success',[56] their emotionality and the nature of their commitments, not just to the children, women and other men with whom they share their lives but, also, to what had, for so long, been seen as the 'anchor' of masculine identity – the stable, unchanging core of men's (breadwinner) masculinity: their paid employment. It is tempting, in such a context, to interpret recent attempts to reconfigure the work/family relationship as somehow seeking to promote, and as being premised on, the presumed existence of a 'new' kind of male parenthood, a model of the 'father as active parent', more in tune with contemporary demographic changes, cultural shifts and changing gender ideologies (a purported shift in 'what men do' which was perhaps epitomised in the idea of the 'new man' during the 1980s and early 1990s).[57]

The point may be made more strongly. Implicit in the reforms outlined above is an assumption that men are to be 'responsible' not just (or not only) in relation to the demands of their employment commitments but also as 'good parents'; that is, as fathers who will read to and play with their children for something more than five minutes a day, as men who will 'pull their weight' domestically, as fathers who are *active parents* and, importantly, who will be considered by the law to be such active parents after divorce and/or separation.[58] It is a simultaneous (re)construction of men as 'good workers' and 'good parents' which underscores the model of the 'healthier', more 'balanced', working life ideal. Central to its promotion is a presumed shift in men's familial 'responsibility'. And, yet, it is an ideal which, in a number of important respects, clashes with what research suggests would appear to be the continuing disjuncture between the *rhetoric surrounding* and the *realities of* contemporary parenting practices. In particular, the assumption of the 'gender neutral' parent and worker runs counter to what has been widely identified within sociological scholarship to be the pervasive *dissociation* of men, in a number of respects, from the domain of the familial. By 'dissociation', I do not mean simply that the demands of paid employment have historically functioned to physically 'separate out' men from a familial sphere in which they had already been, in many ways, constituted as an 'absent' partner (be it

---

56 *Op cit*, Pahl, fn 6.

57 Although, according to the 1995 *Social Trends* analysis of lifestyle and expenditure, traditional divisions of domestic labour remain deeply rooted: see 'New Man fails to survive into the nineties' (1996) *The Independent*, 25 January; also, *op cit*, Social Focus on Men and Women, fn 43.

58 See, further, on the family policy dimensions of this notion, Smart, C, 'Wishful thinking and harmful tinkering? Sociological reflections on family policy' (1997) 26(3) Journal of Social Policy 301, pp 301–21; Smart, C and Neale, B, 'Good enough morality? Divorce and postmodernity' (1997) 17(4) Critical Social Policy 3, pp 3–27.

physically, because of the demands of work and the cultural pull of the homosocial or else absent in an emotional sense).[59] Men can be seen as having been dissociated from the familial because of the very ways in which the 'gender' construct of heterosexual masculinity has *itself* been historically institutionalised in dominant understandings of family and working life.[60]

Approaching parenthood as a material, embodied practice in terms of sex difference, as above, involves surfacing how these gendered experiences of parenting are themselves discursively produced.[61] To integrate questions of sexual difference is *not* to argue that women are somehow inherently or biologically more 'connected' or 'relational' than men. It is, however, to question the complex, contingent and contested nature of the overarching frame of heterosexual relating, in which men and women have already been positioned differentially within the material, cultural and emotional discourses which surround ideas of 'family life' (ideas of marriage, parenthood and divorce for example). Problematising the sociality of the 'heterosexuality' of parenthood, as it were, surfaces the ways in which a particular normative model of men's parenting practices has been constituted in the first place via reference to the making of certain assumptions about such issues as paternal presence/absence, about heterosexual marriage, economic status, emotionality and the nature of sexual difference/ontology.

What does this mean for the present 'family values' policy, as outlined above? The parenting ideal underlying the 'good parent', 'good worker' model envisages a sense of reciprocal obligation, duty and familial responsibility made manifest in the commitment to 'family life' (in effect, legal marriage) and, it is assumed, shared parenting. In terms of the discursive structuring of parenting as a gendered/sexed (as different) experience, however, this is a commitment which sits uneasily with the gendered nature of heterosexual relationships which, empirical studies of both fatherhood and family life suggest, tends to entail distinct and differential experiences for women and men.[62] What has been identified within a range of research on both 'gender and family life' and 'gender and work' is the existence of a male subject which tends to be configured as unified, solitary and autonomous, a man who subscribes to 'traditional' notions of gender relations, both in and outside marriage relationships, a man who is marked not so much by a connection *to* the familial but by a dissociation *from* it – and, not simply from the expression of individual feelings of vulnerability and powerlessness but

---

59 Morgan, D, 'The "family man": a contradiction in terms?', Fifth Jacqueline Burgoyne Memorial Lecture, February 1994, Sheffield: Sheffield Hallam University.

60 *Op cit*, Collier, fn 13.

61 For an example of this approach in relation to fatherhood, see Lupton, D and Barclay, L, *Constructing Fatherhood: Discourses and Experiences*, 1997, London: Sage.

62 On responses to divorce, eg, see Arendell, T, *Fathers and Divorce*, 1995, London: Sage; and *op cit*, Smart and Neale, fn 58.

also, importantly, a range of material practices associated with the 'everyday living out' of those 'dependencies' which, in Fineman's[63] terms, inevitably mark the familial sphere. It appears to be, above all, in relation to a differential relationship to/with children that these, sexed *as different* negotiations of heterosexual relationships are experienced. This suggests a distinct (though by no means clear cut) contrast between men's and women's gendered lives with it being – importantly – precisely the material and emotional dependencies surrounding child care (and, increasingly, elder care) which tend to mediate women's negotiations of moments of conflict between the work/family commitment. In short, and although the law may at present be seeking to 'reconstitute' the relationship between men and children in a number of ways, other economic, cultural, social and legal discourses continue to position men as social agents who are, if not effectively free, then at least dissociated in a number of important respects from a range of familial, emotional and material encumbrances in relation to children.

At the very least, this pervasive dissociation from the dependencies of the familial calls into question the material realities underlying the rhetoric of the 'new balance' between work and family life. Current policy envisages and seeks a relationship between men and children based on a model of shared parenting. However, the rhetoric and realities of paternal responsibility are by no means the same thing. Without underestimating the economic imperatives of advanced capitalist societies, as mediated in specific national and governmental contexts, a case can be made that men's reluctance to 'change' cannot *just* be reduced to questions of public provision of childcare (however significant such provision may be). Experience across jurisdictions suggests that it is by no means clear that men do assume a greater share of child care responsibilities even when specific public provision is established (for example, in the form of parental leave). In the UK context, where such structural support has historically been lacking, considerable evidence attests to the pervasive and deep rooted nature of attitudes and behaviour which, notwithstanding the very real changes which have undoubtedly taken place in many women's and men's familial roles, continue to reproduce quite traditional sexual divisions of labour.[64] The broader 'dissociation' of vast numbers of men from the 'everyday' dependencies of the familial is central to – *though it is frequently unspoken of in* – the present debates about the balance of work and family life. Current employment and family law policy envisages, and is seeking, a 'better' relationship between men and children based on a model of shared parenting and a subjective shift in men's attitudes and behaviour. However, it would be misleading to assume that changes in men's

---

63 Fineman, M, *The Neutered Mother, The Sexual Family and Other 20th Century Tragedies*, 1995, New York: Routledge.

64 See, further, as a strikingly clear example of this, *op cit*, Social Focus on Men and Women, fn 43.

behaviour which *do* take place in specific instances necessarily arise as a result of any rational, calculated choice on the part of the individual man to somehow 'renegotiate' family and work commitments in the way the law is promoting. Far from consciously seeking to 'forge new paths' or 'make creative choices' in the face of changing social conditions, research suggests that many men's embrace of domestic roles may be, at best, a reluctant response to circumstances beyond their control (not least the demands of their partners).[65] Moreover, it would also appear that, whilst both men and women might share the benefits associated with the more 'family friendly' workplace, sexual differences continue to appear in the ways in which men and women construct their 'ideal balance' between hierarchical environments, flexibility and tolerance. Whilst male workers may challenge dominant discourses of men's work by 'career abandonment' and presenting themselves as the 'good (harassed) father' in order to secure 'time off', research suggests that it is women who continue to bear the new burdens of managing both work and home, whilst facing the 'everyday' and routine struggles against discrimination, harassment and prejudice because of their sex, 'dealing with gender' not as part of a broader project of self-actualisation but, rather, as part of an everyday survival strategy in the workplace.[66]

CONCLUDING REMARKS

In this chapter, I have examined recent developments at the interface of both employment and family law policy, with a view to bridging contemporary policy debates in each of these areas. I have done so via a theoretical engagement with sex/gender and the way in which ideas of sexual difference are themselves accorded social, political and ethical significances across a range of discourses. I have sought to reconceptualise the shifting experience of (re)negotiating 'work' and 'family' relations at a time of heightened economic and ontological uncertainty, for both women and men, around ideas of 'success' and 'happiness' in relation to both work and 'family life'. What does it mean to be 'successful'? What does one gain – and what does one lose – by dedicating oneself to 'work' at the expense of 'family life'?[67] In exploring both the possibilities and limitations of recent attempts to integrate a range of 'family friendly' policies in the workplace, it is imperative that critical studies of employment law develop and integrate a more sophisticated understanding of work/family dynamics than those which have been premised on an unproblematic use of the gender categories of 'masculinity'

---

65 Gerson, K, *No Man's Land: Men's Changing Commitment to Family and Work*, 1993, New York: Basic Books.

66 *Op cit*, Oerton, fn 42.

67 See, further, *op cit*, Pahl, fn 6.

and 'femininity'. The need for such understanding is demonstrated, I have argued, in the widespread recognition – central to recent government policy – that there is a need to secure a more 'balanced' relationship between work and family life. In order to understand the persistence of gendered inequalities in the workplace, it is necessary, I have argued, to link together analysis of the material structures of power with those processes whereby particular 'gendered' subjects are constituted in the first place.[68] The law does not, as it were, 'speak to', regulate or otherwise 'operate on' ungendered or gender neutral subjects.[69] Whilst legal interventions – whether parental leave provisions or the encouragement of 'family friendly' working practices – may seek to socially engineer perceptions of both the 'good parent' and the 'good worker', the kinds of materialist and semiotic analyses of the workplace which are being produced within the field of gender and organisation scholarship suggest that the 'gendered performances' (of both men and women) may be deep rooted. Not only does an appreciation of this psychological complexity help to explain the persistence of gender divisions, it also casts a depressing light on the viability of law *alone* to promote change in this area.

To conclude and summarise the main points of my argument: first, in exploring the changing relationships between work and family commitment, I have argued that the notion of gendered (or the gendering of) 'responsibility' must be central. Men's and women's experiences of both paid employment and 'family life' have been constituted and ascribed meaning in ways underscored by particular conceptualisations of sexual difference. These ideas are themselves mediated by socio-economic background, 'race' and ethnicity, physical ability, sexuality and so on. Disturbing and fragmenting the hierarchical binary divisions through which understandings of the legal regulation of the employment/family relation have historically been made (for example, the binaries of public/private, work/family, sex/gender) involves surfacing the contingent nature of the encoding of the (sexed) subjects of employment law (and, indeed, family law) more generally. In seeking to move beyond socio-structural theorisations of gender, sexuality and work, the importance of human agency can be seen to have moved centre stage in recent feminist and post-structuralist accounts. The possibilities of gender performance may not be limitless. Indeed, they may be constrained in all kinds of ways. Yet, the 'creative tensions within the discourses of gender, sexuality and familial power relations may provide women and men workers ... with choices [which] should not be overlooked'.[70]

Secondly, and following on from this engagement with sexual difference, the analysis of the 'heterosexuality' of the family/work nexus presented in

---

68 See, also, the approach of McDowell, *op cit*, fn 8.

69 *Op cit*, Fineman, fn 63.

70 *Op cit*, Oerton, fn 42, p 13.

this chapter reveals a male subject encoded *as familial;* produced and sustained by interwoven discourses of sexuality and gender which are themselves rooted in the dualistic configurations pervading liberal legal thought. The (implicit) reconstruction of the 'good father', 'good worker' continues to embody normative presumptions about 'family', marriage and sexuality which only make sense in terms of the hierarchic binaries which have constituted (hetero)sexual difference in the first place. Importantly, the 'good worker', 'good parent' ideal actively participates in the construction of 'men' as a category, involving a 'way of seeing' that is constructed hegemonically through the mobilisation and consolidation of various practices and the exclusion of others. This chapter has explored how, in the context of employment law, legal struggles over meanings about gender can be reproduced, legitimised and refashioned in specific instances.

Thirdly, there remains a clear class bias to present debates about the 'family friendly' workplace. In the context of certain professions, for example, the balance between work and family life has been placed on the agenda of employers and employees alike (albeit, perhaps, some way down that agenda).[71] Yet, it is open to question whether the specific legislative reforms, and the broader cultural shifts of which they are part, are not *themselves* manifestations of an increasing polarisation in the workforce, in which certain changes are seen as desirable primarily for a section of the workforce (those in secure jobs with relatively high incomes) and are being accorded a greater cultural priority than others as a result of the political power of this group. For many people in contemporary Britain, it is creating jobs in the first place which is, arguably, the most pressing concern. Debates about the 'quality of work and family', 'cultural downsizing' and the advantages of a 'less pressurised lifestyle' for an urban elite may seem far removed to those men and women whose everyday struggle is to find ways of living with dignity and purpose and to earn decent incomes. These concerns, of course, ill fit the economic and cultural agendas of those who may seek to emphasise the 'aestheticisation' of work and 'lifestyle choices' whilst, at the same time, confining large sections of the population to unemployment as the 'price worth paying' for the economic prosperity of others.

Fourthly, and finally, what appears unthinkable in the present political climate is any engagement with the conceptual basis of the idea of the 'private' family itself.[72] In order for the law to contribute to developing a more 'inclusive' workplace (the official policy of the present government), as well as an improved sense of wellbeing amongst both women and men, it is essential to critically address the conceptual framework which presently informs the implementation of policy questions in this area. Whilst the

---

71 Again, the legal profession is a case in point: see, *op cit*, McGlynn, fn 18.
72 *Op cit*, Fineman, fn 63.

difficulties of implementing change cannot be underestimated, it is imperative that ideas of 'progress' be facilitated by the introduction of a more appropriate conceptual framework. In particular, without a critical engagement with the structural and individual psychical processes whereby the commitments of both men and women to 'work' and 'family life' are constituted, it is likely that recent interventions, however welcome, will fail to significantly shift cultural practices around the balance between 'work' and 'family' life.

CHAPTER 9

WORKERS FIRST, WOMEN SECOND? TRADE UNIONS AND THE EQUALITY AGENDA

Anne Morris

INTRODUCTION

The emergence of 'employment law' (as opposed to 'labour law') is a comparatively recent phenomenon. Labels may not be conclusive,[1] but this one reflects the increasing focus on the individual rather than the collective. There has been a marked shift from the idea of the law supporting the orderly conduct of collective bargaining towards employment rights for the individual worker. The legislation of the 1980s and 1990s was explicitly intended to redress the perceived imbalance of power acquired by trade unions under the laws granting them immunities in respect of industrial action and those allowing them control over membership and expulsion but statute also granted specific rights to members within the unions for the sole purpose of controlling the conduct of the union.[2]

Legislation was not the only source of attack on trade unions. While the 1980s witnessed decline in manufacturing industries, rising (male) unemployment and an increase in 'atypical' workers,[3] including part timers and temporary workers, the government fostered and directed the move towards privatisation, not only by the sell-off of previously public owned utilities but, also, by the introduction of compulsory competitive tendering. At the same time, it encouraged the move towards decentralised collective bargaining, derecognition of unions, the introduction of personal contracts, performance related pay and profit sharing schemes. The effect on unions was dramatic. Membership fell drastically – amongst all unions, it fell by 4 million members between 1979 and 1992.[4] There was a sharp decline in union recognition and a concomitant decline in collective bargaining.[5]

---

1 See Ross, Chapter 5, this volume; *Carmichael v National Power plc* [1998] IRLR 301.

2 See, now, Trade Union and Labour Relations (Consolidation) Act 1992.

3 'Worker' is used here in a general sense to cover those in paid employment.

4 McIlroy, J, *Trade Unions in Britain Today*, 1995, Manchester: Manchester UP, p 386. The rate of union membership in the UK fell by nearly 30% between 1985 and 1995: *World Labour Report 1997–98, Industrial Relations, Democracy and Social Stability*, London: ILO.

5 Millward, N *et al*, *Workplace Industrial Relations in Transition*, 1992, Aldershot: Dartmouth.

Although the contraction of the trade union movement, together with its traditionally masculinist culture, may raise questions as to the utility of trade unions in improving the condition of working women, scepticism should be tempered by a consideration of what unions are for and what they can achieve. A good deal of attention has been paid to the involvement – or otherwise – of women in trade union government and in collective bargaining. Certainly, the composition of unions, both in terms of membership and in organisational structures, can affect bargaining priorities.[6] The presence of women can encourage the pursuit of 'women's issues' – for example, workplace nurseries, maternity leave, flexible hours and job sharing. Adequate representation of women at all levels of trade union organisation is, however, only part of the story – particularly since some unions, reflecting the industries in which their members work, have very few women members. If trade unions are to achieve better working conditions they must not only involve women in the organisation but must also be alerted to the 'relatively restricted agendas of [their] bargaining platforms'[7] and must adopt a wider understanding of equal opportunities. The question which this chapter will consider is whether, and to what extent, the interests of women are served by focusing on them as women. Is it time, given the limited gains made under the anti-discrimination laws, to de-gender issues? Trade union members, asked in 1996 what their unions should be doing, overwhelmingly answered: protecting jobs, improving working conditions and improving pay (76%) – only 2% mentioned working for equal opportunities for women.[8] What, then, should be the bargaining agenda for working women in the 21st century?

WOMEN IN PAID EMPLOYMENT IN THE UK

The participation of women in the labour market has reached an all time high[9] and the shift from the traditionally male dominated areas of manufacturing to the service sector, deregulation and 'flexibility' have all had a significant impact on women. Women's employment continues, however, to have features making it different from that of the traditional male worker. Most strikingly, in the United Kingdom, almost a quarter of all workers are part timers, of whom over 80% are women. About 44% of women employees work

---

6   Heery, E and Kelly, J, 'Do female representatives make a difference? Women full time officials and trade union work' (1988) 2(4) Work, Employment and Society 487.

7   Bercusson, B, 'EC equality law in context: collective bargaining', in Hervey, T and O'Keefe, D (eds), *Sex Equality Law in the European Union,* 1996, Chichester: Wiley, p 183.

8   (1998) 28 Social Trends 73, Table 4.23.

9   Spring 1997: 11.4 million women were 'in employment' (14.5 million men); see Sly, F *et al,* 'Women in the labour market: results from the Labour Force Survey' (1998) 3 Labour Market Trends 97.

part time (8% of men). Official figures[10] suggest that the vast majority of women working part time *choose* to do so – only a small percentage say it is because they cannot find a full time job. However, nearly one third of those 'choosing' to work part time say that the reason for not wanting a full time job is 'domestic commitments'. Without adequate or affordable child (or elder) care, it is quite possible that women would say they do not want a full time job. How many women would work full time given the necessary support to do so? A TUC survey found that 61% of mothers with children under 12 would like to work, but 67% of those said that lack of suitable child care is the reason they do not.[11] Further, some of those who do not want full time work say it is because they want more time with their family. This raises wider questions about the relationship between work and family life which are not restricted to women – men are, increasingly, complaining about the pressures that work is putting on their personal relationships.

Women are also found in significant numbers in the ranks of temporary workers: fixed term contracts, 'temping' or casual work. Traditional forms of temporary work – casual or seasonal – have long been associated with poor pay and conditions but temporary jobs are, increasingly, dominated by fixed term contracts. The greatest concentrations of temporary employees are now found in professional occupations, where one in seven are on temporary contracts, and in public administration, education and health industry sectors, where one in 10 employees are temporary.[12] Employment protection is, crucially, affected by temporary employment: in 1997, 29% of full time employees and 41% of part timers had no employment protection, due to lack of tenure in their current job.[13]

There is nothing inherently wrong with part time or temporary work where that is a genuine choice – the problem is the low pay and poor conditions which attach to work historically seen as dominated by women. The real advances made in the legal protection available to part timers can, thus, be seen as a positive step for women workers. However, campaigning for improvements for part timers and temporary workers is not specifically or necessarily gendered. Benefits gained – even those within the framework of the equality legislation – are available to all; male and female. Indeed, the typical male part timer – a student or semi-retired worker – will find

---

10   1997: 24.4% of all employed and self-employed respondents were in part time work (respondent's own assessment). 79% of women 'did not want' a full time job: (1998) 4 Labour Market Trends LFS 20.

11   (1996) 85(8) Labour Research 4.

12   Sly, F and Stillwell, D, *Temporary workers in Great Britain* (1997) 9 Labour Market Trends 347.

13   (1998) 2 Labour Market Trends LFS 11. See, also, (1997) 73 EOR 43.

particular benefit from the lowering of thresholds for employment protection. The Part Time Workers Directive[14] will focus attention on this sector of the workforce and should give impetus to trade union efforts to improve conditions. In turn, improvements may serve to encourage more people – including men – to consider it as an option.[15] Employers tend to regard part timers as less valuable and more easily expendable – a notion coloured by the view that such workers have different priorities *because* they are women. If men were to see part time work as a feasible option (as a result of better pay and conditions), this would challenge that notion, and is one argument for ceasing to see part time work as a gender issue. It seems certain that part time employment will continue to grow, with the inevitable result that more men will work part time thus making *all* part timers an important constituency for trade unions.

Women in the unions

The history of women in the trade union movement[16] demonstrates that women have struggled not only on behalf of the movement but also within it. The formation (in 1874) of the Women's Protective and Provident League (later the Women's Trade Union League) was a response in part to women's exclusion from existing unions. However, women had not been entirely absent from the early trade unions. They were particularly noticeable in the textile industry, where it is also clear that they were discriminated against in relation to pay rates and access to skilled jobs. This is early evidence of the pattern of disadvantage faced by women in paid employment where discrimination by employers was condoned, even encouraged, by male co-workers. Female labour was a problem for male trade unionists, who feared that men would be forced out of the market by women who were prepared to work for lower wages, even in so called 'men's' jobs. The trade unions could have fought for equal pay but the general reaction was rather that women should be kept out of work designated as men's work and, moreover, should organise separately.

Separate organisation did not mean that women were unheard. In 1875, the League won the right to send delegates to the Trades Union Congress

---

14 Adopted December 1997. Text reproduced (1997) 74 EOR 37. Note: discrimination may be justified and casual workers may be excluded. Access to particular conditions may be made subject to period of service, time worked or earnings qualification.

15 Significantly, although the proportion of men working part time remains small, it is increasing.

16 Boston, S, *Women Workers and the Trade Unions*, 1980, London: Davis Poynter; Drake, B, *Women in Trade Unions*, 1920, repr 1984, London: Virago; Soldon, NC, *Women in British Trade Unions 1874–1976*, 1978, Dublin: Gill and Macmillan.

(TUC), founded in 1868; and, in 1888, the TUC adopted a campaign for equal pay as a part of its official policy (although it was not always actively pursued). After 1918, women trade unionists were, increasingly, brought into the mainstream of the movement, though they were far from adequately represented at any level and the social conditions of the inter-war years hampered their progress. High unemployment, for example, meant that female labour was again seen as a threat by men. In response, women began to organise themselves into Women's Committees within and outside the TUC. After 1945, women became more important to trade unions, as their employment rate and their membership increased, although this was not matched by any commitment to a changed agenda by the male dominated union hierarchy. Equality, however, gradually found its way onto the agenda. Trade unionists were influenced by the resurgence of feminism in the women's movement. 'Women's issues' within trade unions were widened from equality of pay, access and conditions of employment to include matters involving child care, maternity rights and equality in health care and access to finances.[17]

Perhaps the most notable development in union membership in the last decade has been its inexorable decline.[18] However, *female* membership has not been as adversely affected and is even increasing in certain unions. Figures for the end of 1996 show that two out of five members of the 75 TUC affiliated trade unions were women, an increase of 1% between 1995 and 1996, as compared to a decrease of 1% for male membership. TUC affiliated unions have 6.75 million members, of whom 2.6 million are women. The presence of women does not mean, however, that they are adequately or proportionately represented within the unions. This is a failing which has been recognised by the movement and some unions have taken steps to remedy matters, though few have achieved proportionality, particularly at senior levels including paid officials. UNISON, with a membership of 1.3 million, has women as 78% of that total but only 38% of national full time officers are women and only 24% of regional full time officers. Other unions lag way behind: the NUT has a membership of 75% women but only 14% of national full time officers and only 11% of regional full time officers are women. On the other hand, these figures represent an improvement, indicating the base from which most unions started.[19]

---

17 The 1979 TUC *Charter for Equality for Women Within Trade Unions* was concerned, princi-pally, with achieving equality for women within the movement, including special women's committees and reserved seats, rather than with general issues of equality.

18 *Op cit*, McIlroy, fn 4; and (1998) 87(8) Labour Research 15.

19 (1998) 87(3) Labour Research 13.

Although this chapter is not specifically concerned with the representation of women within unions,[20] that is inextricably bound up with the pursuit of rights for working women, since it is imperative that women have a voice within unions and that they are able to influence the content and direction of union negotiations. It would seem axiomatic that women would be particularly interested in – or at least sensitive to – women's issues. Boston notes that the early attitude of unions to women workers was less a conscious denial of rights of women and more a result of the dominant Victorian ideology, which saw women as second class in every sense: '... by accepting the social and economic position of women, trade unionists created a trap for themselves, from which they were only to emerge when they could see women as workers and not as a separate group – women.'[21]

It is far from clear, however, when judged in the context of what trade unions do and say, that trade unionists – male or female – have abandoned, or *should* abandon, the idea of women as a separate constituency with separate and 'special' concerns. There are two questions: how should we define *women's* issues and are women likely to benefit if changes at work are not seen as *workers'* rights?

Equal treatment or employment rights?

Women certainly cannot afford to rely exclusively on what might be termed Britain's equality laws, contained in the Equal Pay Act 1970 and the Sex Discrimination Act 1975. These statutes, along with the Race Relations Act 1976,[22] were specifically and expressly concerned to prohibit less favourable treatment of individuals on grounds of their sex or race. At the same time, however, the Labour Government of the day was passing other measures designed to ensure fairer conditions at work for all employees. The Employment Protection Act 1975 continued earlier protection against unfair dismissal (with a mere 26 week qualifying period) and introduced a number of new rights for workers, including the right to paid time off for trade union duties and, for women workers, the first package of maternity rights.

While the equality legislation aims to prohibit discrimination on grounds of sex, race and, latterly, disability, the employment protection legislation has been described as providing a minimum set of rights for all workers. The former approach presupposes a group, or subdivision of a greater whole,

---

20 Nor with the important questions raised by separate organisation: see, eg, Cunnison, S and Stageman, J, *Feminizing the Unions*, 1993, Aldershot: Avebury; Colgan, F and Ledwith, S, 'Sisters organising – women and their trade unions', in Ledwith, S and Colgan, F (eds), *Women in Organisations – Challenging Gender Politics*, 1996, Basingstoke: Macmillan.

21 *Op cit*, Boston, fn 16, p 16.

22 See now, also, Disability Discrimination Act 1995.

which is at a disadvantage: for example, *women* workers amongst workers in general (although it should be noted that the law is equally available to men). In contrast, the goal of establishing a statutory floor of minimum rights for all workers is, in theory, universal – applying regardless of gender or race. Of course, this is a fiction, as was most clearly illustrated by the express restriction of many rights to long serving full time employees – but, superficially, it is inclusive. To pursue better terms and conditions for all avoids the allegation that a particular class (women, ethnic minorities, disabled) are being 'unfairly' advantaged or that the class in question is unable to compete without special help, or that they do not belong there in the first place. It also avoids the criticism directed at the Sex Discrimination Act – that it treats women as a homogeneous group – even though it is clear that certain sections of workers may be multiply disadvantaged.[23] Importantly, it may be easier to address the need to change the traditional structures of working life if measures are presented as not being gender specific. Such an approach would, also, avoid some of the problems created by the very notion of equality.[24] The Sex Discrimination 1975 and Equal Pay Act 1970 require equal treatment, meaning that men and women are to be treated identically,[25] an idea which caused untold (if unnecessary) difficulties for judges in the pregnancy discrimination cases,[26] when they were faced with the legislative instruction to compare 'like with like'. These cases graphically underline the fact that working women who wish to be treated 'equally' must act like men (even when they cannot). The norm against which they are to be judged is male in all respects and a woman wanting equality must conform to the traditional image of the male worker. This is not only *not* what many women want, it is patently impossible for many of them, given the reality of their lives outside the workplace. It is women's role as primary carer (as opposed, traditionally, to principal breadwinner) that has shaped the needs of working women and given rise to the particular agenda which comprises women's issues. It is, in other words, women's social – not simply biological – role which dictates that agenda. Women 'need' part time employment, child care and flexible hours because of their domestic responsibilities. This perpetuates a division of labour (at work and at home) which does not lend itself to equality of opportunities or responsibilities, either for women or men. To achieve that equality, it is necessary to challenge prevailing orthodoxies and to break down traditional barriers. Employment rights which give all workers

---

23 See Ashiagbor, Chapter 7, this volume.

24 See Conaghan, Chapter 2, this volume.

25 The concept of indirect discrimination does allow a woman to argue that an apparently gender neutral requirement disproportionately disadvantages women: Discrimination Act 1975, s 1(1)(b).

26 *Turley v Allders Department Stores* [1980] IRLR 4 (EAT); *Hayes v Malleable Working Men's Club and Institute* [1985] IRLR 367; *Webb v Emo Air Cargo (UK) Ltd* [1990] IRLR 124; [1992] IRLR 116 (CA); [1993] IRLR 27 (HL).

access to flexible ways of working, or paid leave for family reasons, might do more in the long term to achieve real equality. The difficulties currently faced by women permeate their private and public existences – and trade unions are not exempt.

A trade union is a collection of workers organised in response to the power of the employer. In Kahn-Freund's view, the essence of the employment relationship is subordination: '... there can be no employment relationship without a power to command and a duty to obey ...'[27] He also wrote, 'typically the worker, as an individual, has to accept the conditions which the employer offers. On the labour side, power is collective power'.[28] Despite the common law fiction that contracts are bilateral agreements freely entered by parties of equal bargaining power, the employment relationship is not an equal one and this is true for all workers, irrespective of gender. Trade unions are a means of counteracting this subordination, by protecting workers from the excesses of the market. Historically, unions fought for better wages, lower hours and better conditions at work. The legislation defines unions as organisations which consist wholly or mainly of workers[29] and, since all workers are vulnerable to exploitation by the employer, it might be assumed that – at least at this level of abstraction – gender is not a issue. Unions are set up to fight for the rights of all members, regardless of gender or, come to that, ethnicity, sexuality or disability. They seek to ensure justice for the worker – a fair reward for labour by hand or brain. There is, however, a problem with the simplistic idea that all workers are 'united against the might of capitalism'. A trade union would, in most circumstances, regard itself as being there to defend the rights of its particular members (although even its own members may not all be equal). It may be driven to oppose – for example – the opening up of previously skilled trades to unskilled (cheaper) workers. It may resent the organising activities of other unions in what it considers to be its sphere of influence. Historically, trade unions have not been sympathetic to ideas of equality which were perceived to threaten the advantages enjoyed by their (white, male) members. This has had obvious repercussions for women and those from ethnic minorities (and especially for black women). If women's subordination is systemic, the trade union movement is, or has been, part of that system. The worker may be subordinated to the employer, but women are subordinated to men in all spheres, including that of the workplace – both in respect of employer and fellow workers.

The equality legislation which was intended to redress this is almost entirely focused on the individual worker, although equality within the

---

27 Kahn-Freund, O, *Labour and the Law*, 2nd edn, 1977, London: Stevens, p 7.
28 *Ibid*, Kahn-Freund, p 6. See, also, Hyman, R, *Industrial Relations: A Marxist Introduction*, 1975, Basingstoke: Macmillan, p 23.
29 TULRCA 1992, s 1.

workplace is rarely an issue confined to one person. The Equal Pay Act 1970 operates by inserting an equality clause into each *individual* contract of employment. Group actions are not possible: there must be one worker willing to claim equal pay in an industrial tribunal – and fund the case – even though the outcome of the case may affect many co-workers. A sex discrimination case must also be brought by a named individual, though it may be representative of a significant number of workers. Of course, resort to law is not the only way to achieve reform – collective bargaining is an alternative route. Trade unionists have traditionally shared with some feminists a distrust of the law although naturally this has derived from rather different experiences. Given the nature of collectivism and a suspicion of the legal system, it is unsurprising that trade unions would prefer, by and large, to achieve reform through 'voluntary' means and one of the undoubted advantages of collective bargaining is that – where successful – it achieves benefits for a class, as opposed to an individual. It also removes from the individual the responsibility for and stress of direct conflict with the employer. Relatively few workers use the law directly: most are beneficiaries not because they have appeared in court but because of collective bargaining in which the law plays an indirect part. Unfortunately, collective bargaining is itself not immune from bias –inequality may be evident in differential rates of pay or, less obviously, present in the priority placed on different bargaining issues.[30]

Perhaps, therefore, we could look to the law to help eliminate those inequalities. Unfortunately, there are further problems faced by an employment lawyer in advancing law as an instrument of social change, since it addresses the problem of inequalities in the workplace without challenging the social condition and conditioning of women. There has been no attempt to redefine the role of the *worker*, as opposed to a move towards accommodating the *female* worker within the workplace. Women have two jobs and it seems the aim has been to enable them to combine both more easily. Within and outside legislative schemes, matters are designated as 'women's issues' based on assumptions about women's (domestic) roles. There are practical consequences, since the very act of categorising something as being for working women can mean that the issue is marginalised. Even the superficially neutral term *'family-friendly'* policy may be interpreted as the kind of arrangement which assists *women* in their efforts to combine work and family. This is a gender issue, in so far as it reinforces stereotypical assumptions about male/female roles. Parental leave,[31] for example, is welcome but may, in practice, mean *mothers* taking time off work. Flexible working hours may be seen as a means of allowing *mothers* to accommodate

---

30 Colling, T and Dickens, L, *Equality Bargaining: Why Not?*, 1988, London, HMSO.
31 See below, p 194.

child care. If women workers are constructed as domesticated, family policies are seen as benefits for women. Moreover, while these benefits are seen as 'concessions' rather than rights, there is an expectation that they have to be earned. So, for example, a woman must work for two years in order to qualify for extended maternity leave, and parental leave may be subject to up to one year's service qualification.[32]

WORK AND FAMILY

One in four responding to a survey did not think it possible to have a good family life and advance at work.[33] As attention focuses on the problems inherent in balancing work with family, so called 'family friendly policies' are emerging. It is intriguing, however, that these policies are frequently identified with *women* workers. It is true that there is a lot of law on maternity rights – and, effectively, none on paternity rights or elder care – but the idea of the principal carer being female is particularly resistant to change. The Transport and General Workers Union, for example, produced a 'Family Pack' aimed principally at working mothers. The Communications Workers Union concluded an agreement with British Telecom which included up to two weeks paid special leave per application to care for a sick or elderly relative. When BT proposed to make this a non-core issue which would allow for divisional variations, the CWU commented that this was a matter for serious concern because the policy could be worsened in the areas employing the largest number of *women* members.

Pregnancy and maternity

There is one area of life where it is futile to attempt to be gender blind – only women get pregnant. The package of employment rights for pregnant workers is renowned more for its horrendous complexity than its generosity, which means in practice that the average employee (or employer) has little chance of fully understanding and taking advantage of them. The rights are found in the employment legislation[34] and do not call for equal treatment of men and women, since this law recognises that women are, in this respect,

---

32 The White Paper *Fairness at Work* Cm 3968, May 1998, contained a proposal to reduce the unfair dismissal qualifying period from two years to one year (para 3.9).

33 'Work and personal life', WFD Inc 1997, see (1997) 75 EOR 7. See, also, 'The quality of working life: 1998 survey of managers' changing experiences', 1998, Institute of Management, reported (1998) 82 EOR 7.

34 Employment Rights Act 1996, including changes introduced to comply with EC Directive on the Protection of Pregnant Women at Work, 92/85/EC. Some maternity rights are subject to qualifying periods of employment or minimum earnings.

different. It was, however, this very difference which was used against women who sought to use the anti-discrimination legislation because they did not qualify for protection under the employment laws. When asked if it was sex discrimination to dismiss a woman because she was pregnant,[35] it was held that she could not bring a complaint under the Sex Discrimination Act because that requires like to be compared with like and there is no such thing as a pregnant man. It took the European Court of Justice to establish that, in this context, comparisons are unnecessary and that a woman refused a job because she is pregnant suffers direct sex discrimination because only a woman can receive that treatment.[36] This is a welcome[37] and necessary protection but it is, significantly, temporary – once a woman has returned from maternity leave she is judged once again by the male norm.[38] She is expected to rejoin the workplace as though nothing had happened to change her circumstances. The argument is encapsulated in the words of the Advocate General: 'If, as a result of giving birth at any time in their lives, women could claim what amounted to a sort of insurance against dismissal for the rest of their working life ... that would amount to a privilege contrary to the principle of equal treatment.'[39]

Whilst there is force in this argument, given the way that the law is structured, it is a fact that a woman does not return on the same basis as before. Leaving aside 'physiological' consequences of pregnancy, a woman may find that she cannot return to her full time job because of problems with child care or because the double burden of full time work and child care proves too much. Where then does she turn? At this point, her difference ceases to work to her advantage – the sex discrimination laws may not protect her if she is refused the opportunity to job share, work flexible hours or if she is ill.[40] But, this would not be such an issue were it not for the social (not biological) fact that men do not take – for whatever reason – the principal burden of child care.

Pregnancy and maternity – the one clear 'gender' issue – is, thus, an intriguing example of a 'women's issue'. True, only women give birth, but the arrival of a child is the start of a new phase of work/family compromises and

---

35 [1980] IRLR 4 (EAT). Cf [1985] IRLR 367.

36 *Dekker v VJV Centrum* [1991] IRLR 27; *Webb v Emo Air Cargo (UK) Ltd* [1994] IRLR 482 (ECJ); *Brown v Rentokil Ltd* C-394/96 [1998] IRLR 445.

37 Though the fact that pregnancy is not to be likened to illness has been used to defeat a discrimination claim in a case where sickness and disability payments were more generous than maternity pay. A sick man would be better treated than a pregnant woman but this was not *sex* discrimination: *Todd v Eastern Health and Social Services Board and DHSS* [1997] IRLR 410.

38 *Hertz v Aldi Marked K/S* [1991] IRLR 31

39 In his Opinion in *Brown v Rentokil* reported in (1997) 78 EOR 2 and 56.

40 This often turns on the issue of whether the employer can justify indirect discrimination. See *British Telecommunications plc v Roberts* [1996] IRLR 601 and, also, Cox, S, 'Flexible working after maternity leave' (1997) 78 EOR 10.

these are not, biologically, confined to mothers. Pregnancy lasts nine months, and means the woman must take some time off work, but the birth of a child changes lives besides that of the woman who gave birth. There are obvious reasons for special provision for women in relation to pregnancy and childbirth but it is not clear that 'peripheral' rights (for example, extended leave) should be limited to mothers. Certainly, there are many reasons for allowing *paternity* leave. Unlike some other EU members, the UK has no provision for paternity leave, although it is estimated that about one third of companies permit fathers to take very limited leave – usually, however, only a few days. The Policy Studies Institute found that family-friendly arrangements around childbirth (additional to legislation) were provided to parents by 27% of establishments surveyed. Paternity leave was provided by 24%, 9% gave additional maternity leave and 6% additional maternity pay. 'Most' fathers entitled to paternity leave took 'some' of their entitlement.[41] Why should fathers not have – and be encouraged to take – more generous 'birth' rights? Interestingly, there is an example of gender neutral provision in this area: *parental* leave is granted in the majority of EU countries. The EU Commission has been pushing for a directive on parental leave since 1983 and the Parental Leave Directive[42] was adopted in 1996. The Directive provides for a minimum of three months' unpaid leave at any time until the child's eighth birthday. One survey[43] suggests that only a fifth of working people under 40 would be likely to take unpaid parental leave and, bearing in mind the pay gap between men and women (below), it is more likely that women would take leave. If fathers are to have the chance to participate more actively in bringing up their children, it is clear that paid leave is vital. Without that, non-gendered parental leave is, effectively, additional maternity leave – the result of gender influences elsewhere.

The same is true for the other, unpaid, right found in the Directive, 'family leave', which is available in family emergencies, such as ill health or hospital appointments. The idea of family leave emphasises the fact that caring for children is not the only kind of domestic responsibility which affects the ability or desire to work a traditional full time week. Reports from Help the Aged in 1994 and 1996 showed that around 15% of employees have specific elder care responsibilities.[44] The Institute of Employment Studies stated in 1997 that there are more women looking after elderly relatives than looking

---

41 Forth, J *et al*, 'Family-friendly working arrangements in Britain' (1997) 10 Labour Market Trends 387. Compare Cully, M *et al*, *The 1998 Workplace Employee Relations Survey – First Findings*, DTI: over two-thirds of workplaces surveyed had formal equal opportunities policies but 46% of employees had no access to 'family-friendly' policies.

42 Parental Leave Directive 96/34/EC.

43 Time Out: The Costs and Benefits of Paid Parental Leave, Demos 1997.

44 See (1997) 73 EOR 23.

after pre-school children.[45] Unions have begun to see this as an issue for negotiation, though there is a risk that this, too, will be categorised as a women's issue, with the implication not only that women put family first (and, thus, are problematic employees) but also that real men do not take time off work to look after their dependants – even though this is patently not so. It does, however, make it more difficult for men to voice their concerns and needs and does nothing to break down stereotypes. It has been suggested that: 'Perhaps nowhere in late 20th century society is the gendered division of domestic labor more obdurately institutionalized than in the provision of care by families to their frail elderly relatives'.[46] It is also suggested that the very idea of a carer is translated as an unpaid female relative. Indeed, until very recently, this sexual stereotyping was apparent in the UK tax system: only in the 1998 Budget was it announced that the tax allowance which had previously been available to men with children whose wives were incapacitated would now be extended to mothers with dependent children and sick or disabled husbands.

Women with caring responsibilities need their unions to bargain on their behalf to make it possible for them to earn a wage and care for their dependants. However, the very fact that more women are working means that elder care is ceasing to be an exclusively female preserve (if it ever was) and it is thus not simply a gender issue.[47] Although it is still the case that most carers are women, Help the Aged found in 1996 that 30% of carers for the elderly were men. It is clear that, as people live longer, as more women work outside the home and as cutbacks in state provision continue, the need to balance work with the care of elderly or other dependent relatives will become a central issue and one which unions must address on behalf of all their members. It is not something which is, or should be seen as being, restricted to women. There are currently few men, relatively speaking, who work part time or job share[48] and yet these ways of working are of obvious benefit to those who have responsibilities at home. It must be as acceptable for men to seek flexibility in their working patterns as it is for women. What must change is the assumption that those who do not wish to work a 'traditional' working week are somehow less committed or that they are exploitable and expendable. This is about changing the culture of the workplace as much it is about sex equality – although women will inevitably benefit.

---

45   *Ibid*. The lack of time off for elder care is prevalent throughout the European Union: see Bettio *et al*, *Care in Europe*, 1998, Brussels: European Commission.

46   Applegate, JS and Kaye, LW, 'Male elder care givers', in Williams, CL (ed), *Doing 'Women's Work': Men in Non-traditional Occupations*, 1993, Newbury Park: Sage. See, also, Hunt, A, 'The effects of caring for the elderly and infirm on women's employment', in *Women and Paid Work: Issues of Equality*, 1988, Basingstoke: Macmillan.

47   See, also, Morris, Chapter 6, this volume.

48   In 1997, 18,000 men were in job shares, compared to 158,000 women: (1998) 5 Labour Market Trends 213.

PAY: EQUALITY OR FAIRNESS?

Eradicating pay inequalities may seem, superficially, to be a more straightforward task. It certainly represents for trade unions not only an easily identifiable goal but, also, more traditional bargaining priorities and methods than the more problematic aspects of the integration of work and family.[49] Despite successes, however, women still earn less than men. Before the Equal Pay Act came into force (in 1975), women's average gross hourly earnings were 64% of men's. In 1975, the figure improved to 72%. Over 20 years later, women receive 80 pence for each pound earned by men[50] and are clustered at the lower end of pay scales. Part timers are worse off: only four in 10 part timers receive the same rates of pay and fringe benefits (including sick pay, paid leave, pensions, maternity leave) as full timers doing the same jobs.[51] Forty five per cent of part timers earn less than £4.50 an hour, as compared with 13% of full timers. This is not, however, a problem confined to women: 25% of male part timers earn less than £3.00 an hour (13% of female part timers). Many of the lowest paid also have very low hours of work, and earn less than the Lower Earnings Level (below which National Insurance contributions are not payable). In 1996, 2.7 million employees earned less than the LEL, of whom 78% were women and 94% were part timers (male and female). Such workers are unable to build a National Insurance contribution record and are excluded from maternity allowance, job seekers allowance, incapacity benefit, widow's pension and, crucially, retirement pensions. On the other hand, those earning at, or just above, the LEL have found themselves liable to contribute on the whole of their earnings, thus depleting further the level of take home pay. Although the proposal to abolish, from 1999,[52] the contribution on the first £64 earned is of benefit to those earning at least that, it does not address the problems of those entirely excluded.[53]

Basic pay is important but only part of the picture, since for many workers overtime, productivity bonuses, shift premiums, and so on, are a significant part of wages. Where women predominate, the pay structure is less likely to incorporate additional payments and even where women are eligible, they do not receive as much as men. Part timers are especially unlikely to receive additional payments, such as overtime and shift premiums, though there is,

---

49 Hyman, R, 'Changing trade union identities and strategies', in Hyman, R and Ferner, A (eds), *New Frontiers in European Industrial Relations*, 1994, Oxford: Blackwells.

50 Average hourly earnings: 1998 New Earnings Survey, Part A, ONS.

51 Policy Studies Institute, *Value for Money*, 1996, London: PSI.

52 See *First Report of the Low Pay Commission*, 1998, Cmnd 3976, p 200.

53 At the Trades Union Congress 1997, a motion called for legislation to provide for all workers to qualify for benefits currently linked to the lower earnings limit: Congress Report, p 29.

theoretically, no reason why they should not, having worked their agreed hours.[54] The proportion of a manual worker's pay made up by overtime, incentive pay and shift premiums is 23% for men, while for women it is just 14%.[55] Not surprisingly, given the demands on women's time, more men than women do shift work but the type of shift work done is itself gendered: more women than men work weekend shifts and evening or 'twilight shifts'.[56] It cannot be coincidence that such shifts are (slightly) easier to fit in with child care and other responsibilities. What is shocking is what follows from this insidious gendering. First, a report in 1994 found that workers on twilight or part time evening shifts are unlikely to receive shift premiums.[57] Some employers argued that these were not really 'shifts' in the traditional sense of 'unsocial hours' but were examples of workers choosing the hours for their own convenience. The fallacy of the latter argument is contradicted by a separate finding that twice as many women shiftworkers have to pay for child care as do working women in general.[58] Inequalities are not confined to shift workers: newer pay systems include merit pay and performance pay but here, too, there are gender differences. Jobs where women predominated had lower average merit rises than those where men predominated.[59] It has, also, been suggested that pay systems based on skills and competencies may perpetuate gender differences.[60]

Given the continuing disparities in pay, it is particularly unfortunate that the law on equal pay is both substantively and procedurally complex. The complexities are exacerbated by European law, although Art 119 of the Treaty,[61] which requires each Member State to ensure and maintain the principle that men and women should receive equal pay for equal work has been crucial in many of the advances which have been made. Significantly, Art 119 has been held to have both an economic and social function – the latter being the improvement of living and working conditions of EC citizens.[62] Complexity apart, however, one of the most obvious drawbacks of the legislation is that it is a measure aimed at sex discrimination and not at fair

---

54 Cf *Stadt Lengerich v Angelika Helmig* [1995] IRLR 216.
55 Nichol, C, 'Patterns of pay: results from the 1997 New Earnings Survey' (1997) 11 Labour Market Trends 469. In 1997, 35% of men received overtime pay, compared to 19% of women.
56 (1997) 11 Labour Market Trends LFS 60.
57 Labour Research Department, *Bargaining Report 143*, 1994, London: LRD.
58 Daycare Trust, *Not Just Nine to Five*, 1994, DT.
59 *Pay and Gender in Britain: A Research Report for the EOC from the Industrial Relations Services*, 1991 IRS.
60 Strebler, M *et al*, *Skills, competencies and gender: issues for pay and training* (1997) IES Report 333.
61 See, also, Directives 75/117, 76/207, 79/7, 86/378, 86/613: equal pay, equal treatment, and equal treatment in social security, occupational pension schemes and self-employment.
62 *Defrenne v Sabena (No 2)* Case 43/75 [1976] ECR 455, p 472.

wages. The provision which requires equal pay for 'like work' is irrelevant where there are no men doing the same job, even though, on any view, the women are being paid poorly, underlining the fact that women's work is undervalued. It is possible now to bring a claim based on equal value[63] but the procedure is complex and protracted. Moreover, even though the work may be 'equal', an industrial tribunal may reject a claim if it is shown that the difference in pay is genuinely due to a material factor which is not the difference of sex.[64] Although 'market forces' (men's refusal to work for women's wages) have been allowed as a defence,[65] it has, at least, been held (in Enderby[66]) that the mere fact that men and women are covered by different collective agreements is not necessarily a sufficient objective justification for a difference in pay. It was acknowledged that women tend to be concentrated in traditionally lower paid work and that separate bargaining structures are simply evidence of the inherent discrimination. As Gregory has commented, when discussing this 'enlightened decision' of the ECJ: 'It is a pity that it required 10 years of litigation to reach an understanding of the potentially discriminatory impact of collective bargaining.'[67]

The number of equal pay cases which make it to a tribunal is relatively small and fewer still are successful.[68] Generally, pay and conditions of workers are determined by collective bargaining by trade unions and employers or their organisations. Although trade unions initially viewed equal pay as an issue for collective bargaining[69] and were suspicious of State intervention in wage regulation, union backing for equal value cases in tribunals has increased significantly.[70] Also, tribunal applications (or the threat of them) are used as a bargaining tactic in negotiations for revised pay structures or regrading schemes. Equal pay has, however, been a troublesome area for unions. Male trade unionists have, historically, wanted to protect their privileged position in the labour market. There have been fears about the upsetting of clearly defined pay differentials and traditional segregation of the labour market which leave men in superior positions regarding pay and other conditions. To assess attitudes to the EC's policy of equal pay and the impact of the equal value amendment, Pillinger conducted a survey of 20 unions at

---

63 Equal Pay (Amendment) Regulations 1983 SI 1983/1794 following *EC Commission v UK* [1982] IRLR 333.

64 Equal Pay Act 1970, s 1(3).

65 There are limitations: *Rainey v Greater Glasgow Health Board* [1987] ICR 129.

66 *Enderby v Frenchay Health Authority* [1993] IRLR 591.

67 Gregory, J, 'Dynamite or damp squib? An assessment of equal value law' [1996] IJDL 313, p 322. See, also, *Danfoss* [1989] IRLR 532.

68 Only 82 cases reached a tribunal in 1995–96 and only 36 were successful: (1997) 74 EOR 36.

69 See the results of Pillinger's survey, below.

70 See, eg, 'Equal value update' (1996) 70 EOR 13, pp 13–27, showing that trade unions play a key role in pursuing equal pay for work of equal value for members.

the national level in 1983 and 1984.[71] The response prior to the 1983 amendment showed an awareness of the limitations and complexities of the UK legislation (including the need for a male comparator and the lack of collective claims). The issue of women's pay was seen as particularly important but the steps taken by unions to inform women of developments that would affect their rights varied. Few unions had made use of (or were aware of) the direct effect of Art 119 and, if they did take equal pay cases to tribunals, relied principally on the Equal Pay Act. The response to the follow up questionnaires, following the amendment, revealed greater knowledge of the law but criticism of its complexities continued. Most unions still thought that claims would be sought initially through collective bargaining, with industrial tribunals as a last resort. Collective bargaining was seen as far more effective in achieving better pay for larger numbers of women workers, although the legal right to equal pay for work of equal value was seen as a bargaining strategy. The route to equal pay through collective bargaining is not without problems: given the nature of the legislation, which requires comparison within the workplace or with an associated employer, the effect could be to increase the disparities between unionised and non-unionised workplaces – and many women do work in smaller and unorganised workplaces. On the other hand, it would appear that unionisation does have a positive effect on the levels of women's pay[72] and, therefore, that both women and the union movement could benefit from the increased recruitment and representation of women by all trade unions.

Collective bargaining is, undoubtedly, one way of achieving equal pay and successful recourse to law provides additional support for that bargaining. Nevertheless, even the amended equal pay legislation has been less than successful, in that it has failed to alter significantly women's earnings and, more importantly, to tackle low pay and job segregation. Pillinger's survey elicited the response from some unions that flat rate increases for women and a national minimum wage were of greater benefit to women's earnings than equal pay legislation. Although a minimum wage is, on its face, gender neutral, it is very much a women's (and race) issue. As women and ethnic minority groups are particularly vulnerable to low pay, they will benefit significantly from a minimum wage. In a survey of Labour Force Survey data, the *Equal Opportunities Review* found[73] that over 3 million female employees and 1.6 million male employees earn less than £4.00 an hour (the figures for those earning under £3.50 are 2.1 million and 1.1 million,

---

71 Pillinger, J and Campling, J, *Feminising the Market: Women's Pay and Employment in the European Community*, 1992, Basingstoke: Macmillan, p 114 *et seq*.

72 See Sloane, P, 'The gender-wage differential', in Scott, A (ed), *Gender Segregation and Social Change: Men and Women in Changing Labour Markets*, 1994, Oxford: OUP.

73 'Minimum wage benefits women and ethnic minorities' (1997) 73 EOR 13.

respectively). Women are the majority of those earning less than £3.50 an hour in seven out of 11 industries, with particularly high profiles in education and health.[74] In other words, a campaign to eradicate low pay – irrespective of gender – will, in fact, benefit women. It may have considerably more impact on the most vulnerable workers than the Equal Pay Act and, for this reason, the Equal Opportunities Commission supports a minimum wage. There are particular groups of workers who will benefit from the minimum wage, not least low paid manual workers. Between 1977 and 1997, weekly earnings for female non-manual workers in the lowest 10% of earners rose from 65% to 78% of men's wages.[75] Amongst a similar section of manual workers, earnings rose from 62% to only 67% of men's earnings. For the many low paid women who are currently unable to use the Equal Pay Act because they are employed in small businesses working only with other women, the minimum wage could bring real progress.[76]

Together with reforms announced in the 1998 Budget, the minimum wage will also have an impact on the complex relationship between paid employment and social security benefits. A particular problem for the lowest paid workers has been the poverty trap – the withdrawal of in work benefits at excessive marginal tax rates as wages rise. In the context of this chapter, one of the more interesting of the Budget reforms is the scrapping of Family Credit and the introduction of the Working Families Tax Credit, aimed at families (with children) earning below a certain threshold.[77] This further exemplifies dangers in apparently gender neutral measures. Family credit was paid to the *mother*, while, from April 2000, the tax credit will appear in the wage packet. In so far as the main earner is male, this allows for (though it does not compel) a switch of resources to the other partner – a criticism which was levelled at the tax credit formerly available in respect of children and which was replaced by child benefit payable to the mother. True, many families currently receiving Family Credit, and who will continue to receive Working Families Tax Credit, are headed by a lone parent (usually the mother) but the change shows how astute campaigners and legislators must be to the potentially differential impact of their policies.[78] Women have always known that money channelled through a wage packet may never reach its intended destination.[79]

---

74 *Op cit*, fn 73.

75 'A minimum boost to equality' (1998) 87(3) Labour Research 17, pp 17–18.

76 *Ibid*.

77 For a straightforward explanation, see *First Report of the Low Pay Commission*, 1998, Cmnd 3976, p 200.

78 For a clear example of the importance of gender impact assessment, see Nott, Chapter 10, this volume.

79 See 'Whose money is it anyway?' (1998) 2 The New Review 4. The majority of couples regarded family credit as 'her' money since it was paid directly to the wife.

CONCLUSION

Sadly, neither the laws on sex equality nor the laws on employment protection have succeeded in redressing the disadvantages faced by women. While 'family' policies and 'women's' issues are now part of the vocabulary of government and other agencies and appear on many agendas, including those of trade unions,[80] this, too, is insufficient. If trade unions are to work for women, they must place 'traditional' bargaining priorities alongside those which address the problems of integrating work and domestic responsibilities and members must accept that, if such integration is to be achieved, women *and* men must be included. Women must deny the notion that the provision of child care, for example, is of interest only to women. They must challenge traditional ideas of their roles and the value of their work – wherever it is done and whether paid or unpaid. The great struggle now facing women in the unions is not 'simply' one of achieving equality of access, so that they can fit into the male shaped space offered by the average employer, it is to create a workplace which provides rights and protections for all employees, regardless of gender, race, sexuality or disability. It would seem that de-gendering the agenda will not serve the cause of women if designating them 'workers' rather than 'women workers' disguises the additional disadvantages they suffer precisely because they are women within a male society. On the other hand, it will not help women if changes merely allow them to juggle competing responsibilities with marginally more ease without redistributing the burden. There must be a recognition and acceptance of the need for wider social changes in the way in which we all structure our lives – in work and out of it. The issues which have been identified with women are capable of bringing far reaching changes in the way all working lives are structured. To that extent, at least, it is not a gender issue but one of improving the conditions of all workers. Women have fought their way into the world of work and have been – by and large – poorly rewarded for their efforts while continuing to shoulder the bulk of unpaid work. What is needed for the 21st century is a new way of ordering working life. Trade unions must expand their bargaining agendas beyond the confines of the workplace to address the wider social implications of work and of lack of work. It is not yet time to abandon 'women's issues' but it should be a part of the campaign for equality to show that making the working environment more 'woman' friendly is, ultimately, to the benefit of all – men, women and their families.

---

80   What matters is not the rhetoric but the deed: *op cit*, Heery and Kelly, fn 6.

CHAPTER 10

MAINSTREAMING EQUAL OPPORTUNITIES: SUCCEEDING WHEN ALL ELSE HAS FAILED?

Susan Nott

INTRODUCTION

One of this century's constant themes has been women's struggle for equality. Much of the effort to eliminate discrimination and promote equality between the sexes has been focused on the workplace. Anti-discrimination measures, such as the Equal Pay Act 1970, and social policy initiatives, such as the provision of maternity leave for pregnant workers,[1] are familiar features of employment law. These initiatives have, however, produced limited gains. Whilst there are women who pursue well paid and rewarding careers, the statistics show that, generally speaking, women in the United Kingdom and, indeed, elsewhere in Europe, earn less than men, occupy the lower grades in the occupational hierarchy, experience higher rates of unemployment and are more likely to be low paid than men whilst in work, and poor once they have retired.[2]

The purpose of this chapter is to consider why, despite a century of effort, inequality between the sexes persists and to analyse a new strategy – mainstreaming – for promoting equality. Mainstreaming aims to integrate gender equality into the policy making process by inquiring whether all proposed laws and policies will have an equal impact on men and women. Forcing policy makers to ask this question obliges them to take into account the different roles that men and women play in society. The issue that this chapter will address is whether mainstreaming can succeed in making laws and policies more responsive to women's and men's needs. Using examples from the United Kingdom, it will explore mainstreaming's potential to help

---

1   Directive 92/85, on the introduction of measures to encourage improvements in the health and safety at work of pregnant workers and workers who have recently given birth or are breast feeding. This Directive was implemented by the UK in the Trade Union Reform and Employment Rights Act 1993. See, now, Employment Rights Act 1996.

2   Equal Opportunities Commission, *Facts about Women and Men in Great Britain*, 1997, Manchester: EOC. This shows, eg, that, in 1996, the average weekly earnings of women were 72% of those of men. 'Women in the labour market' (1998) 79 EOR 30, pp 30–31; European Commission, *Equal Opportunities for Women and Men in the European Union, Annual Report 1996*, 1997, Brussels: European Commission, Chap 2; European Commission, *Equal Opportunities for Women and Men in the European Union, Annual Report 1997*, 1998, Brussels: European Commission, section 2.

women break free from a depressing cycle of low pay, occupational segregation and well meaning, but often ineffective, equal opportunities initiatives.

Before embarking on this analysis, some explanation is needed of mainstreaming's relevance in a book which offers feminist perspectives on employment law. Mainstreaming equality is a strategy that affects *all* laws and policies, not simply employment law. It is, however, this very feature that gives mainstreaming its potential to engineer significant changes. Existing equal opportunities initiatives have been frustrated not only by their emphasis on the public sphere of the workplace – whilst the private sphere of the family and home remains untouched – but, also, by the existence of, apparently gender neutral, laws that undermine their achievements. To secure employment laws that are responsive to men *and women's* needs, equal opportunities must be a concept that applies at all levels. Feminist perspectives on employment law can, and do, draw attention to aspects of the law that work against women's interests. The difficulty is that making discrete areas of employment law more women friendly will achieve very little if laws in general are oriented toward male values and male life styles.

PROMOTING EQUAL OPPORTUNITIES: THE CAUSES OF FAILURE

A variety of reasons, some of which are discussed in detail elsewhere in this book, have been put forward to explain why women have not made the progress in the workplace, in terms of wages or breaking through the 'glass ceiling', that one might expect. Part of the explanation is, clearly, related to the differences in men and women's experience of life and work. These differences manifest themselves in the pressures on women to combine work and family life, which may force them to take career breaks or part time employment.[3] This may, in turn, jeopardise their chances of promotion or raise doubts about their commitment to their job. Occupational segregation is another well established feature of the labour market. Certain work is regarded as women's work[4] and is, as a consequence, poorly paid. The

---

3 A report compiled by Labour Market Trends, March 1998, and summarised in (1998) 79 EOR 30 indicates that the economic activity rate of women with dependent children is continuing to rise. The proportion of women who are economically inactive because they are looking after a home/family has dropped from 60% in 1987 to 49% in spring 1997. In spring 1997, three-fifths (61%) of employed women with dependent children worked part time, compared with one-third (32%) of women without dependent children.

4 Perhaps because it can be performed by part time workers or reflects the tasks, such as caring, that women perform, unpaid, in the home. On this point, see the comments of the court in *Ratcliffe v North Yorkshire District Council* [1995] ICR 837.

initiatives that have been taken by the European Union and at national level to tackle these disparities have failed to secure equality between the sexes, because there are flaws associated with the strategies they employ.

A range of criticisms has been levelled at the legislation designed to tackle sex discrimination. Anti-discrimination measures, such as the Equal Pay Act 1970 and the Sex Discrimination Act 1975, have been condemned for their complexity, their restricted application and their ineffective enforcement machinery.[5] In addition, the fact that policies designed to tackle sex discrimination originate at national and European level further complicates matters and leads to mismatches and ill-considered amending legislation.[6] Commentators have concluded that the faith placed in anti-discrimination legislation to remove barriers to equality is largely misplaced.[7] This is not to say that the legislation is worthless but, rather, that the concept of equality it employs, which requires a woman to compare her treatment with that of a man, is limited in what it can realistically achieve.[8] Feminist theorists have been at pains to point out that treating women and men in the same fashion is no guarantee of equality, since there is such a difference between the reality of men's and women's lives.[9] Asking whether a woman has been less favourably treated than a man makes male behaviour patterns the paradigm to which law and legal systems respond. If equality means no more than treating women in exactly the same fashion as men, then many women have little to gain, since their work patterns and their life styles are very different from those of men.

Even the alternative approach to equality – equality of opportunity – which demands positive measures to rectify past and present discrimination has had a limited impact. Such measures stand little prospect of success as long as they are isolated acts, resorted to only when governments feel the

---

5   See, eg, Morris, A and Nott, SM, *All My Worldly Goods*, 1995, Aldershot: Dartmouth, pp 65–82. The Equal Opportunities Commission has put forward a set of proposals to reform the anti-discrimination legislation.

6   There has been considerable litigation regarding the relationship between the Equal Pay Directive, Art 119 and the Equal Pay Act 1970. In *Commission of EC v UK* 61/81 [1982] ICR 578, the UK was found to be in breach of Art 119 and the Equal Pay Directive. The tortuously drafted amendment of the 1970 Act which resulted was the subject of litigation in *Pickstone v Freemans plc* [1988] ICR 697. See, also, Ellis, E, 'Equal pay for work of equal value: the United Kingdom's legislation viewed in the light of Community law', in Hervey, T and O'Keeffe, D (eds), *Sex Equality Law in the European Union*, 1996, Chichester: Wiley.

7   See, eg, Fredman, S, *Women and the Law*, 1997, Oxford: Clarendon; Townshend Smith, R, *Discrimination Law*, 1998, London: Cavendish Publishing.

8   In order to prove direct discrimination, a woman has to demonstrate that, because of her sex, she has been treated less favourably than a man. Indirect discrimination is a more complex notion. It occurs when a requirement or condition is applied equally to men and women but a considerably smaller proportion of women as compared with men can comply with it. If, irrespective of sex, there is no justification for imposing that condition, then, providing a woman cannot, to her detriment, comply with it, she has suffered indirect discrimination: Sex Discrimination Act 1975, s 1.

9   See, eg, Lacey, N, 'Legislation against sex discrimination: questions from a feminist perspective' (1986) 14 JLS 411.

need to address a particular problem. For example, encouraging women into occupations that were previously the preserve of men will not succeed if the ethos of that particular occupation is a male ethos.[10]

Apart from the shortcomings of the strategies to promote equality, the situation is made worse by the fact that these strategies are part of a legal system which is condemned as producing what, at first sight, appear to be gender neutral laws which, in reality, work against women. One example was the way in which equal opportunities issues were totally neglected, in favour of the perceived economic benefits of compulsory competitive tendering (CCT). Studies undertaken in Great Britain and Northern Ireland[11] demonstrated the adverse effect that CCT had on equal opportunities by pushing women's wages downwards and cutting their working hours in order to achieve 'efficiency savings'.

Many of the measures adopted in the United Kingdom to combat sex discrimination have originated with the European Union (EU), which is often seen as being well disposed towards the promotion of equal opportunities. Yet, even in the EU, measures to promote equal opportunities have been in constant danger of being marginalised by economic considerations. When the Community first came into being, social policy figured little in the Treaty of Rome.[12] The Community's focus was economic and, although steps were taken to redress this balance, the Community's ability to promote equality was restricted by its competence, as stipulated in the Treaties. Apart from a brief period in the 1970s, when some very positive measures were instituted to combat sex discrimination,[13] there has been opposition from some Member States, particularly the United Kingdom, to all but the most conservative of initiatives,[14] because of the economic or administrative burdens they were

---

10 In terms of hours that are expected to be worked or time that has to spent away from home.

11 Equal Opportunities Commission (GB), *The Gender Impact of Compulsory Competitive Tendering in Local Government*, 1995, Manchester: EOC; Equal Opportunities Commission (NI), *Report on the Formal Investigation into Competitive Tendering in the Health and Education Services in Northern Ireland*, 1996, Belfast: EOC(NI).

12 The Treaty of Rome did contain a Title on Social Policy but there were few Articles in it. The most important of those Articles was, of course, Art 119. As Catherine Barnard points out in 'The economic objectives of Art 119', in *op cit*, Hervey, and O'Keeffe, fn 6: '… Arts 117 and 118, on the need to improve working conditions and co-operation between States, even if textually broad, are legally shallow – at least, when considered in isolation from Art 100. Articles 119 and 120, by contrast, are specific provisions designed to protect French industry': Chap 20, p 325, footnotes omitted.

13 Eg, the Equal Treatment Directive, 76/207, the Equal Pay Directive, 75/117 and the Social Security Directive, 79/7. These measures were, apparently, agreed in order to give the EC a more 'human' face and increase its popularity.

14 Directive 92/85, which contains measures designed to protect pregnant workers or those who have recently given birth started life with a much more radical content than was eventually agreed by the Member States. See Beveridge, F and Nott, SM, 'A hard look at soft law', in Craig, P and Harlow, C (eds), *Lawmaking in the European Union*, 1998, London: Kluwer, p 287.

perceived to impose. As a consequence, other strategies have been employed, such as soft law initiatives and Community programmes, to promote equal opportunities – but, with limited degrees of success.[15]

More recently, however, Member States have agreed to insert a commitment to equality in the Treaties themselves. Provisions in the Treaty of Amsterdam[16] place an obligation on the Community to promote equality between men and women. National law and Community law that conflicts with this duty can be challenged in the European Court of Justice as being in breach of the Treaty. In addition, the Treaty of Amsterdam has sanctioned positive action programmes[17] and given the Council the power to 'adopt measures to ensure the application of the principle of equal opportunities and equal treatment of men and women in matters of employment and occupation, including the principle of equal pay for work of equal value'.[18]

Only time will tell whether this revision of the Treaties will put equal opportunities at the heart of the EU's law and policy making process. Even if it does, the EU's focus on the workplace may mean that women's role in the private sphere of the unreconstructed family will still prevent them from participating fully in the public sphere of the workplace.

GENDER MAINSTREAMING:
RESPONDING TO WOMEN'S EXPERIENCE?

For those seeking some way of breaking free of this failure to make progress, there is a new strategy to consider – that of mainstreaming gender. Mainstreaming gender is not seen as an alternative to the anti-discrimination legislation or positive action but as building upon what such measures have achieved. There are a variety of definitions of what, exactly, mainstreaming entails. The European Commission has characterised it as a process of:

> ... not restricting efforts to promote equality, to the implementation of specific measures to help women, but *mobilising all general policies and measures specifically for the purpose of achieving equality* by actively and openly taking into account at the planning stage their possible effects on the respective situations of men and women (*gender perspective*). This means systematically examining measures and policies and taking into account such possible effects when defining and implementing them: thus, development policies, the organisation

---

15 *Op cit,* Beveridge and Nott, fn 14.
16 TOA, Arts 2, 3, 13, 137 and 141. These are the numbers of the Articles as they will appear in the Treaty after its ratification.
17 *Ibid,* Art 141(4).
18 *Ibid,* Art 141(3).

of work, choices relating to transport or the fixing of school hours, etc. may have significant differential impacts on the situation of women and men which must, therefore, be duly taken into consideration in order to further promote equality between women and men.[19]

The Equal Opportunities Commission (EOC), which is a supporter of mainstreaming,[20] has offered this explanation of how the process works: 'Mainstreaming is about the integration of a gender dimension into policy development, implementation and appraisal. It is, literally, the process of integrating equality into the mainstream of policy work and service delivery.'[21]

Mainstreaming is not a new equality strategy and there are numerous examples of its use on a national and international level. In 1990, for example, the United Nations High Commission for Refugees (UNHCR) produced a policy document on refugee women which acknowledged that women's experiences of being refugees were different from those of men and sought to 'integrate the resources and needs of refugee women in all aspects of programme planning and implementation'.[22] The Global Platform for Action, agreed at Beijing in 1995, refers to the need to integrate gender perspectives into legislation, public policies, programmes and projects.[23] The EU is, also, firmly committed to mainstreaming, as are EU Member States such as Sweden and The Netherlands. Elsewhere in the world, countries such as Canada and New Zealand are exploring this strategy.[24]

Before examining examples of mainstreaming in action, some preliminary thought needs to be given to its advantages and disadvantages, as well as to how exactly it might work in practice. If mainstreaming is about 'the integration of a gender dimension into policy development, implementation and appraisal', then this would have the effect of putting equality at the centre of the decision and policy making process. As matters currently stand, the anti-discrimination legislation and other social policy measures designed to complement it are 'bolt on' strategies, existing at the periphery of policy and decision making. In contrast, mainstreaming demands that those responsible for formulating and implementing policies ask themselves whether what they

---

19 Communication on incorporating equal opportunities for men and women into all Community policies and activities. COM(96)67, 21/02/96, p 5.

20 The EOC has been involved in a research study into mainstreaming in local government: Equal Opportunities Commission, *Mainstreaming Gender Equality in Local Government: A Framework*, 1997, Manchester: EOC.

21 Frank Spencer, Head of Operations and Policy, Equal Opportunities Commission, *Briefing on Mainstreaming*, Manchester: EOC, p 1.

22 United Nations High Commission for Refugees, *Policy on Refugee Women*, 1990, New York: UNHCR, 111, 5.

23 Strategic Objective H2.

24 For a discussion of gender mainstreaming and details of a variety of schemes visit web site: http://www.dhdirhr.coe.fr/equality/Eng/mainstreaming.html

plan to do will adversely affect the respective situations of men and women. This would seem to address directly the maleness of the legal system and society as a whole, as well as those laws and policies masquerading as gender neutral. In addition, it would replace the technical test for discrimination with the much broader question of whether women or men would be disadvantaged by a particular law or policy.

On first impression, therefore, mainstreaming would seem to have the potential to make far reaching changes in society, by ensuring women's interests are taken into account. A note of caution should, however, be sounded over what mainstreaming can be expected to achieve. Doubts have been expressed over the feasibility of predicting what effect a particular policy will have on women, since, conceivably, it might be advantageous for some women and disadvantageous for others. Another fear is that mainstreaming will mean that other strategies to promote equality, such as special programmes to attract women into occupations where they are under-represented, will cease to attract support. In addition, agencies which currently have the task of co-ordinating equal opportunities measures, such as the Equal Opportunities Commission or local authority equal opportunities units, might find their continued existence under threat, on the basis that the promotion of gender equality had become the responsibility of policy makers and service deliverers. As a consequence, there might be a fragmentation of equal opportunities strategies, since gender mainstreaming would operate on a departmental/service provider basis. Nor would there be any guarantee that there would be sufficient resources (in terms of money and personnel) devoted to gender mainstreaming to ensure its effectiveness.

These worries apart, mainstreaming's most problematic features are what the process entails and how it can be made to work. The definitions of mainstreaming quoted earlier refer to a process that 'integrates gender' or that takes 'into account at the planning stage their [policies'] possible effects on the respective situations of men and women'. Put this way, mainstreaming seems little more than a political commitment, rather than a tangible means of promoting equal opportunities. If the strategy is to work, mainstreaming would seem to require the presence of certain essentials – a transparent process for officials to follow and personnel who have an understanding of equality issues. Without these essentials, mainstreaming may simply be regarded as a 'hurdle' that has to be negotiated before a preferred policy can be put into operation. Mainstreaming's prospects of success would, therefore, appear to be inextricably linked with the use of a procedure for measuring gender impact.

GENDER IMPACT ASSESSMENT AS AN ESSENTIAL
FEATURE OF MAINSTREAMING STRATEGY

Gender impact assessment is a process to assess the degree of gender impact a policy proposal may have. It normally consists of a set of questions designed to elicit, at an early stage, the effect the proposed policy will have on men and women, taking into account the current situation between the sexes in terms of, for example, resources.

> Gender impact assessment has its roots in the environmental sector and is a typical example of an existing policy tool that has been adapted for the use of gender mainstreaming. Gender impact assessment allows for the screening of a given policy proposal, in order to detect and assess its differential impact or effects on women and men, so that these imbalances can be redressed before the proposal is endorsed. An analysis from a gender perspective helps to see whether the needs of women and men are equally taken into account and served by this proposal. It enables policy makers to develop policies with the understanding of the socio-economic reality of women and men and allows for policies to take (gender) differences into account.[25]

Some countries[26] already employ what is commonly referred to as gender impact assessment. There are a variety of approaches to this process, since much depends on the administrative and political landscape within which it operates. There are, however, certain general issues that any procedure designed to measure gender impact must address, if it is to be effective. In order to illustrate what these issues are, this chapter will briefly examine two such examples. These are the use in Northern Ireland of PAFT – Policy Appraisal and Fair Treatment – and, in the rest of the United Kingdom, of PAET – Policy Appraisal and Equal Treatment.

---

25 Gender mainstreaming – conceptual framework, methodology and presentation of good practices, *Final Report of Activities of the Group of Specialists on Mainstreaming*, Strasbourg, May 1998, p 22. One example of gender impact assessment given in this report is that of the Flemish Gender Impact Assessment: 'The Flemish Gender Impact Assessment consists of three steps, ie, to trace the gender dimension of a policy proposal, to estimate its size and to formulate alternatives where necessary. In summary, the instrument helps to recognise a problem, to assess its dimension and to find a solution for it.' This example is given on p 45.

26 Eg, The Netherlands. According to the Equal Opportunities Commission's *Briefing on Mainstreaming* (*op cit*, fn 21), mainstreaming and policy appraisal/gender impact evaluation are not the same thing. Their paper describes policy appraisal/gender impact evaluation as a process designed to avoid unnecessary sex discrimination, rather than actively promoting equal opportunities. Whilst it is true that policy appraisal/gender impact assessment screens policy proposals, it does so with the aim of alerting policy makers to the unequal impact of their policies. In this manner, they may well become more sensitive to the different socio-economic situations of men and women. If mainstreaming amounts to nothing more than telling policy makers to integrate gender without a procedure for assessing whether or not this has occurred, it seems doomed to failure.

Both PAFT and PAET originate in an initiative launched in the 1980s by the Ministerial Group on Women's Issues, which encouraged Departments to develop guidelines on equality proofing. Over the years, both PAFT and PAET have been reviewed and amended on several occasions. The latest review of PAFT was as a direct consequence of the Northern Ireland peace process. The Northern Ireland Act 1998 has, as a result, placed a statutory obligation on public authorities to mainstream equality.[27] PAET, too, has recently been reviewed.[28] The account of PAFT and PAET which follows is, therefore, largely based on evidence regarding their operation before these reviews took place.

POLICY APPRAISAL AND FAIR TREATMENT (PAFT)

PAFT is an administrative process, devised by the Northern Ireland Office, which was intended to supplement the anti-discrimination legislation[29] and other social policy initiatives.[30]

> The aim of the PAFT initiative is to ensure that issues of equality and equity inform policy making and action in all spheres and at all levels of Government activity, whether in regulatory and administrative functions or in the delivery of services to the public. The guidelines identify a number of areas where there is potential for discrimination or unequal treatment and outline steps which those responsible for the development of policy and the delivery of services should take to ensure that they do not unjustifiably or unnecessarily discriminate against specified sections of the community.[31]

The areas where there was potential for discrimination identified by PAFT were:

- gender;
- age;
- ethnic origin;
- religious belief or political opinion;
- married and unmarried people;

---

27 See the Northern Ireland Act 1998, Pt VI, s 60, in particular, and Sched 10.

28 The revised guidelines were published in November 1998. They appear to be much vaguer than those they replaced. There is, eg, no specific list of target groups.

29 In Northern Ireland, sex discrimination is dealt with in the Sex Discrimination (NI) Order 1976. Its terms are largely identical to those in the Sex Discrimination Act 1975.

30 Targeting Social Need (TSN) is a strategy aimed at targeting resources in Northern Ireland into areas of greatest need. It has been pointed out, by Hadden, T, Rainey, B and McGreevy, G, in 'Equal but not separate' (1998) 12 Fortnight 371, that the relationship between PAFT and TSN is confused and that the danger exists that policies directed at certain groups in Northern Ireland could be in breach of PAFT.

31 CCRU, *PAFT Annual Report 1996*, 1997, p 3.

- disabled and non-disabled people;
- people with or without dependants;
- people of differing sexual orientation.

The policy appraisal which is at the heart of PAFT required officials from each Department in the Northern Ireland Office to assess whether any of the target groups would be adversely affected by proposed new policies or legislation. The Northern Ireland Office insisted that submissions to ministers on new policies should include a PAFT appraisal indicating whether there were or were not PAFT implications and the reasons for these conclusions. The PAFT guidelines also required officials to take account of 'fair treatment aspects when reviewing existing policies and delivery of services'. This would necessitate an ongoing review programme, with major policies subject to evaluation at regular intervals. What constituted an adverse effect for the purpose of a PAFT appraisal apparently evolved over the years. PAFT appears to have started out as a procedure for identifying direct and indirect discrimination against one of the target groups[32] but developed into a wider appraisal to eliminate unfairness: 'The guidelines, however, extend beyond the sphere of statutory protection [against discrimination], requiring departments to take regard of wider issues of equity, avoiding unjustifiable discrimination, even when the action in question is not illegal.'[33] When a policy was shown to have an unfair, but not illegal, impact on a target group, it was left to the department to determine whether the objectives of the policy in question outweighed this unfairness.

The guidelines describing how PAFT worked indicate that the process was meant to ensure that 'there is no unlawful discrimination or unjustifiable inequality in any aspect of public administration'. As a consequence, PAFT was applied to non-departmental agencies, such as health authorities, which, whilst they are not part of the Northern Ireland Office, are part of the process of public administration. Finally, the PAFT guidelines required the Secretary of State for Northern Ireland to publish an annual report on the action taken to implement PAFT. It is from these reports that details emerge of the steps taken to embed policy appraisal in the public sector. These included the training of officials, the dissemination of good practice and regular meetings of senior officials with responsibility for implementing PAFT.

On the evidence, PAFT emerges as a flawed process which has failed to have a major impact and was in need of reform.[34] Commentators have argued

---

32 CCRU, *PAFT Annual Report 1994*, 1993, p 15.

33 *Op cit*, CCRU, fn 31, p 4.

34 For studies of the PAFT process, see McCrudden, C, *Mainstreaming Fairness – A Discussion Paper on PAFT*, 1996, Belfast: Committee on the Administration of Justice; McCrudden, C, *Mainstreaming Fairness in the Governance of Northern Ireland*, 1998, Belfast: Committee on the Administration of Justice; *op cit*, Hadden, Rainey, and McGreevy, fn 30.

that PAFT should be put on a statutory basis in order to show government commitment to the process and to clarify how exactly the procedure should be conducted.[35] Other ways in which the PAFT process could be strengthened have been suggested, including the provision of adequate training for officials, the need to consult outside bodies in the course of a PAFT appraisal, the importance of monitoring policies and actions post-PAFT to determine whether the PAFT predictions were accurate and the establishment of an independent review body.[36]

POLICY APPRAISAL AND EQUAL TREATMENT (PAET)

Compared with PAFT, very little publicity has been given to PAET.[37] Part of the explanation may relate to the special circumstances in Northern Ireland, where the desire to address issues of inequality, particularly in respect of religion, may have provided the impetus to publicise PAFT. What is apparent is that each government department should possess a set of PAET guidelines. Gaining access to them has, however, not always been easy. One department which has made its PAET guidelines available is the Department for Education and Employment.[38] According to its guidelines, policy appraisal means that '*at every stage* in the life of a policy or programme, the potential impact on different groups of the population is actively considered, and amendments are made where necessary. It applies to reviews of existing legislation, services or policies, as well as to new developments'.[39]

The justification for adopting this procedure is said to be good government, since it will prevent ministers acting in a fashion that is contrary to national or international law. In addition, the guidelines are said to be a recognition of the fact that policies can have different impacts on different groups in society. PAET mainstreams this issue by making it '*everyone's job* to consider the variety of needs amongst the population – rather than relying on special units, such as equal opportunities units, to do this'.[40]

---

35   *Op cit*, McCrudden, 1998, fn 34; Osborne, R, Gallagher, A, Cormack, R with Shortall, S, 'The implementation of the policy appraisal and fair treatment guidelines in Northern Ireland', in McLaughlin, E and Quirk, P (eds), *Policy Aspects of Employment Equality in Northern Ireland*, 1996, Belfast: SACHR.

36   See materials listed in fn 34.

37   Obtaining copies of departmental guidelines, particularly since they are under review, is not easy.

38   Department for Education and Employment, *Equal Opportunities into the Mainstream: Guidance on Policy Appraisal for Equal Treatment*, 1996, London: DfEE.

39   *Ibid*.

40   *Ibid*.

The Department for Education and Employment lists three stages to policy appraisal: identifying, validating and amending. At the identification stage, officials are looking for differential impact on a list of target groups. These are:

- men and women;
- people of different racial groups;
- people of different ages;
- people who have, or have had, a disability compared to other people;
- married and unmarried people;
- people with or without dependants;
- women who are pregnant or on maternity absence;
- people of different religious beliefs or political opinions;
- people of different sexual orientations;
- people with a particular disability or disabilities.[41]

In making this assessment, officials require information, and they are advised that they may need to refer to existing research, to commission new research or to adopt monitoring and evaluation systems to ensure that the relevant data is available. The validation stage then requires officials to determine whether any differential impact is 'legally permissible and, if so, whether it is justified in policy terms'.[42] The advice which follows then sets out examples of what amounts to direct and indirect discrimination[43] and indicates that, if the policy or practice is not legally permissible, it will have to be amended. The guidelines do, however, go on to deal with the situation where the differential impact is legally permissible.

> If the policy or practice is legally permissible, you will, then, want to consider whether the proposal is justified in policy terms. This will require judgments about whether or not it is the right/appropriate course of action; whether the differential impact of the policy is proportionate to the objective which the policy is intended to achieve; costs and benefits considerations; estimations of potential criticism, and so on.[44]

The decision whether, in these circumstances, the particular policy should be pursued is, however, ultimately a question for the minister. The final stage of the appraisal is to consider how to amend policies which are not legally permissible. In doing this, officials are advised that they might find it useful to

---

41 *Op cit*, Department for Education and Employment, fn 38, Annex A.
42 *Op cit*, Department for Education and Employment, fn 38.
43 Annex B contains a list of relevant anti-discrimination measures and descriptions of what amounts to direct and indirect discrimination.
44 *Op cit*, Department for Education and Employment, fn 38, Annex A, para 2.9.

contact organisations whose job is to promote equal opportunities, such as the Equal Opportunities Commission.[45]

With the benefit of these accounts of PAFT and PAET, it now seems appropriate to consider how best to ensure that mainstreaming proves an effective strategy in promoting equal opportunities.

ASSESSING MAINSTREAMING'S POTENTIAL TO SECURE EQUAL OPPORTUNITIES

Any assessment of mainstreaming's potential to promote equal opportunities has to concentrate on two distinct, but related, issues. The first relates to mainstreaming as a strategy: does it have more to offer women than existing devices? If it does, what is the best form for such a procedure to take, in order to secure the maximum impact?

There is a great deal of evidence that the procedures currently in place to eliminate inequality have not succeeded. As one commentator has concluded: 'Substantial inequalities between different groups continue to mar our society. Anti-discrimination legislation cannot bear the full burden of reducing that inequality, though it is a necessary part of the armoury of tools for doing so.'[46] Mainstreaming gender, however, is perceived as a strategy that can take the process of promoting equality a step further. This is because *all* policies are assessed for any negative impact at the time when those policies are in the course of development. Promoting equality becomes everyone's business and decision makers would be forced to confront the needs of women and men.

> Mainstreaming approaches are intended to be anticipatory (rather than essentially retrospective, or relatively late insertions into the policy making process), to be extensively participatory (rather than limited to small groups of the knowledgeable) and to be integrated into the policy making of those primarily involved (rather than external add ons perceived to be external by policy makers).[47]

Yet, whatever its strengths, the adoption of gender mainstreaming should not be used as an excuse to abandon other equality strategies. Anti-discrimination laws still need to be in place to deal with individual examples of sex discrimination by employers or service providers. Positive action and positive discrimination still have a role to play in encouraging individual women to participate fully in public life. Mainstreaming should be part of a concerted effort to promote equality, since it can ensure that all laws and policies,

---

45 *Op cit*, Department for Education and Employment, fn 38, Annex C.
46 *Op cit*, McCrudden (1996), fn 34, p 1.
47 *Op cit*, McCrudden (1996), fn 34, p 4.

including those designed to promote equal opportunities, do not have an adverse impact on women.

The second issue is how best to put mainstreaming into practice. Since this is achieved by assessing in some factual manner gender impact (gender impact assessment), the design of this process is crucial. PAFT and PAET provide vital evidence of the pitfalls associated with gender impact assessment. In the first place, gender impact assessment needs to be a transparent process. PAFT and PAET appraisals both took place 'behind closed doors'. Whether, therefore, the process works well in practice is very difficult to determine. A cynic might conclude that, since both procedures have been in place for a number of years without the position of women improving substantially during this period, the answer must be that it does not. The only evidence available is the very abbreviated accounts of PAFT appraisals in the annual reports. Here, departments listed new policies or reviews of existing policies and indicated the outcome of their appraisal. In the 1994 Annual Report, for example, an Order in Council to 'remove the statutory obstacles to contracting out in central and local government'[48] was said not to have a differential impact on any defined PAFT group. Proposals to replace unemployment benefit and income support for the unemployed with the Jobseekers Allowance and to equalise the State pensionable age at 65 were, also, said to have no differential impact within the PAFT principles.[49] Yet, comment on these proposals predicted that they would have an adverse impact on women.[50] The 1995 Annual Report conceded this point in relation to market testing and contracting out, but went on to justify the lack of action:

> The controversy over market testing and competitive tendering points to the potential for tensions between the philosophy of PAFT and aspects of other government policies. Many forms of discrimination are illegal under Northern Ireland statute and, clearly, cannot be breached by the Government. Other forms of differential treatment are legally permissible and PAFT requires departments to consider carefully the potential for rectifying them. This may, sometimes, involve assessing the competing claims of different policies and this may, ultimately, be a matter for ministerial judgment as to public interest. PAFT seeks to ensure that issues of equality and equity are given full weight in these considerations but it cannot be assumed that PAFT considerations will always predominate.[51]

PAFT's lack of transparency is, however, far outweighed by the obscurity surrounding PAET. No annual reports have been published to demonstrate how the initiative has been implemented by individual ministries. Indeed,

---

48 CCRU, *PAFT Annual Report 1994*, 1995, p 65.
49 *Ibid*, pp 74–75.
50 See, *op cit*, Morris and Nott, fn 5, pp 153–54, 159–60.
51 CCRU, *PAFT Annual Report 1995*, 1996, p 12.

there is no evidence that every ministry has a set of PAET guidelines. The newly formed Women's Unit[52] has assumed responsibility for mainstreaming and, hence, this situation seems set to change. Currently, however, it is impossible to say how successful PAET has been in promoting equal opportunities.

Secondly, both PAFT and PAET clearly demonstrate the need for clear guidance on the timing of a policy appraisal and the bodies obliged to undertake the procedure. Attention has been drawn to the variation in practice which occurred among the Departments in the Northern Ireland Office. This was particularly common in relation to the obligation to review existing policies and programmes as opposed to policy initiatives:

> ... some departments claimed that they were expected to conduct a PAFT appraisal of all major policies and programmes on a five year cycle, while others did not appear to recognise any such obligation and, in effect, combined what PAFT appraisals were carried out with managerial reviews of the effectiveness and financial efficiency of their major programmes.[53]

The extent of the application of the PAFT guidelines was also a source of great variation. An unsuccessful action for judicial review taken by the trade union UNISON against the Down and Lisburn Health and Social Services Trust[54] for failing to apply PAFT revealed that the Trust had not applied the guidelines, since it had not received them.[55] The 1995 Annual Report on PAFT indicates that PAFT guidance should be issued to non-departmental public bodies (NDPBs) and that 'departments use all appropriate measures at their disposal to ensure that NDPBs comply'.[56] In practice, this may have meant little more than issuing the advice to these bodies that they should implement the guidelines.[57]

Since there is no evidence available on how PAET is applied by individual ministries, it is impossible to say whether there were variations in practice. If, however, this occurred within the Northern Ireland Office, it is difficult to imagine that the same was not true of other ministries. Neither is it clear whether the guidelines extended to other agencies. In the light of the role that such agencies now play in providing services to the public at large, this seems to limit considerably the potential of mainstreaming. The Equal Opportunities

---

52 The Women's Unit was set up by the current government to develop policy on the Ministers for Women's priority agenda, brief the ministers, liaise with other departments, ensure the United Kingdom fulfils its international obligations and keep a watch across Whitehall for issues of special concern to women.

53 *Op cit*, Hadden, Rainey and McGreevy, fn 30, p 10.

54 Unreported.

55 As a consequence, the action failed. See *op cit*, CCRU, fn 51, p 10.

56 *Op cit*, CCRU, fn 51.

57 *Op cit*, Hadden, Rainey and McGreevy, fn 30, p 10.

Commission has commissioned research to demonstrate the voluntary use of mainstreaming by local authorities.[58] Clearly, the willingness of some local authorities to comply, whilst welcome, is not a satisfactory basis for effective policy appraisal.

Thirdly, gender impact assessment's effectiveness has been limited by a lack of relevant statistics. There is evidence, in the PAFT Annual Reports, of research being commissioned in order to obtain such data.[59] In *Casey v Department of Education*,[60] however, judicial review was sought because of the Department of Education's failure to carry out a PAFT appraisal. The Department had decided not to award student grants to those who attended colleges in the Irish Republic. It was asserted that this would have a greater impact on Catholic than Protestant students. The Department's reason for not conducting a PAFT appraisal was a lack of reliable, up to date statistics. In the event, the court found in favour of the Department, since the guidelines had no legislative force and it was for the Department, provided it acted reasonably, to conclude whether, realistically, a PAFT appraisal could be undertaken.

Apart from these specific criticisms of PAFT and PAET, a final reservation that some women may have in relation to gender impact assessment is that it is an example of State feminism in action. In other words, rather than women taking the initiative, this is a process whereby officials, many of whom are men, will determine whether a particular policy will have an adverse impact on women. One has only to recall how, in the past, the courts have interpreted the anti-discrimination legislation in a totally unsympathetic fashion to experience doubts over whether civil servants will do better in the context of mainstreaming.

Yet, despite these reservations, mainstreaming does seem to have the potential for moving the equality debate onwards. If, however, this potential is to be realised, the procedure for assessing gender impact has to be satisfactory. Should this not be so, then all mainstreaming will amount to is an expression of good intentions with no positive impact on policy making whatsoever. Anyone setting out to devise a model for gender impact assessment has to consider the following questions. In the first place, should the procedure be put on a statutory basis? The advantage of it being so would be the existence of a clear duty for policy makers to carry out a gender impact assessment. The legislation could set out what that duty required, the form it would take, which bodies would be bound by such a duty and arrangements for reporting the results of such appraisals. This would avoid arguments of

---

58 *Op cit*, Equal Opportunities Commission, fn 20.

59 *Op cit*, CCRU, fn 31, p 14–18.

60 *Op cit*, CCRU, fn 31, pp 11–12.

what an impact appraisal requires, would make it difficult – though not impossible – for a newly elected government, not well disposed towards the concept, to abandon the procedure, and would guarantee the transparency that is vital if women are to have faith in the process. The major disadvantage would be the ability of the judiciary to interpret the legislation, particularly in the context of judicial review. One simply has to recall how restrictively the courts interpreted the Equal Opportunities Commission's power to conduct a formal investigation under s 58 of the Sex Discrimination Act 1975[61] to realise how unsympathetic the courts can be. It is, also, worthwhile remembering that the courts are one institution who will not be asked to assess the gender impact of their judgments. On balance, however, there seem to be more reasons for putting the procedure on a statutory basis than not doing so.

The second factor that an effective model for assessing gender impact has to consider is on what basis an adverse impact will be judged. Both PAFT and PAET refer to differential impact between target groups but resort to concepts such as 'discrimination', which has a specific meaning in the context of the anti-discrimination legislation, or the much vaguer 'unfairness'. McCrudden, in his proposal for a revised PAFT mechanism, refers to the 'significant impact' that a proposed action may have in preventing a public body from fulfilling certain duties.[62] Those duties are the duty not to discriminate 'unfairly, directly or indirectly on any ground such as race, gender, sex, pregnancy, marital status, political or other opinion, ethnic or social origin, colour, sexual orientation, age, disability, religion, conscience, belief, culture, language, birth, nationality, national origin, or other status'.[63] In addition, public authorities are under a duty to promote 'full and effective equality of opportunity between all parts of the community ... in all areas of economic, social, political and cultural life in which the public authority is involved'.[64]

An effective impact assessment must, also, stipulate clearly the bodies which are under an obligation to carry out such an appraisal. If government departments are the only organisations to undertake such assessments, then unfairness can arise when a public body charged with implementing a policy or delivering a service does so in a way that is disadvantageous to women. Mainstreaming must be an inclusive process, if it is to work efficiently.

The next ingredient for effective impact assessment is information and consultation. In order to predict impact, the body in question must have available statistics which are broken down so as to reflect the situation of the

---

61 See, eg, *Re Prestige Group plc* [1984] IRLR 166; *Hillingdon London Borough Council v CRE* [1982] IRLR 424; *CRE v Amari Plastics* [1982] IRLR 252. *Op cit*, Fredman, fn 7, p 371, comments that these cases against the Commission for Racial Equality have trammelled their power of formal investigation with a chain of restrictive procedural requirements. The EOC has almost identical powers and is affected in the same way.

62 *Op cit*, McCrudden, 1998, fn 34, p 27.

63 *Op cit*, McCrudden, 1998, fn 34, p 25.

64 *Op cit*, McCrudden, 1998, fn 34, p 26.

target groups.[65] In addition, it would seem sensible to consult representatives of the target groups when attempting to predict whether a particular measure would have an adverse impact. If impact assessment is to work, it has to ensure that those working in the public service are made fully aware of the difficulties faced by the socially excluded. Consideration should, also, be given to the desirability of having some organisation charged with the responsibility of overseeing the impact assessment process. This might be an internal body whose members are drawn from those who participate directly in the policy making process. Alternatively, or perhaps additionally, there could be an external agency whose members are from the target groups mainstreaming is meant to help.

One of the distinguishing features of PAFT and PAET is that they target a whole range of groups in assessing whether a particular policy will have an adverse impact. There are, undoubtedly, disadvantages to doing this. More resources and effort are required and those with particular concerns over gender equality might worry that the interests of women will suffer, as a consequence. The range of target groups covered by PAFT was such that the fear was expressed that the whole process had become too superficial. It was said that PAFT appraisals were focused on two targets – religion and gender – whilst the remaining six areas were assessed only if the differential impact on them was clear.[66] One reason for this may have been a lack of statistical data relating to certain target groups. In its defence, however, the advantage of an impact assessment scheme that deals with other groups beside women is that it may tackle more effectively the problems experienced by those women who suffer double discrimination.

Finally, if gender impact assessment is to work it also requires that those who are responsible for undertaking impact appraisals are properly trained. This means devoting resources to preparing those individuals and providing them with the information they need to perform this task.

---

65 The Government Statistical Service has agreed to promote the collection and dissemination of statistics broken down by gender. The Office of National Statistics and the Equal Opportunities Commission have produced *A Brief Guide to Gender Statistics*, which was published in March 1998. A Gender and Statistics Users Group has, also, been launched by the government. The group Engender, which is an information, research and networking organisation for women in Scotland, is a source of disaggregated statistics: http://www.engender.org.uk/engender/gender_audit/index.html

66 The Annual Reports can be very vague on whether all of the target groups have been considered when a PAFT appraisal has been conducted. See *op cit*, Hadden, Rainey and McGreevy, fn 30, p 10.

CONCLUDING REMARKS:
MAINSTREAMING'S IMPACT IN THE WORKPLACE

Mainstreaming is a strategy that could tackle some of the factors that currently work against women. It could begin the process of 'feminising' laws and legal systems and breaking down the public/private divide that has been a long-standing barrier to promoting equality. More specifically, it could have an impact on employment law and force law and policy makers to take account of women's needs, particularly the need to combine work and family life. The current anti-discrimination legislation places its emphasis on the individual and whether they have suffered discrimination in the workplace. Its insistence that men and women are treated in the same fashion does little to force employers to adapt their practices to suit women's needs. Mainstreaming's emphasis is on what would be in the best interests of women (or, indeed, other target groups) and, hence, might promote a different (holistic) approach to achieving equality in the workplace. There are, however, limits to just how far-reaching mainstreaming's effects would be.

In the first place, mainstreaming cannot compel governments to adopt laws and policies that are advantageous to women in general, and working women in particular, such as the provision of better funded child care facilities. A government's ability to 'pick and choose' its policies may, in its eyes, be severely limited. Mainstreaming can ensure that gender impact informs the debate when policy is formulated. It can insist on an audit of those laws and policies that governments have the political will to implement. It can expose the unfairness to women of laws that purport to be gender neutral. It is another issue whether governments will be prepared to modify their laws and policies to correct any adverse impact.

Secondly, mainstreaming focuses on public bodies and cannot force employers to organise their workplaces in a more woman friendly fashion nor does it place them under a duty to appraise the impact of their managerial policy. This is not to say that mainstreaming cannot work on the shop floor. There is little, if any, evidence that employers would be prepared to 'audit' their work practices for gender impact.[67] Without the involvement of the private sector the ability of mainstreaming to achieve real change may be limited.

---

67 Some public sector employers, eg, are committed to a balanced workforce where men, women and ethnic minorities are represented.

CHAPTER 11

EQUAL PAY:
THEORY AND PRACTICE IN TWO COUNTRIES

Suzanne Jamieson

INTRODUCTION

It is the contention of this chapter that the presence or absence of equal pay legislation, no matter how cleverly worded, will (and can only) have marginal effects upon the achievement of equal pay for individual women or for pay equity across any national labour force. This is because of the limited nature of liberal legal strategies based largely on individual remedies, because of the nature of wage bargaining structures and because of apparently intractable segregation issues in any national labour market. In this paper, those national labour markets are Australia and the Republic of Ireland. I have argued elsewhere[1] that these individual remedies were introduced in Australia at a time of labour market deregulation and increasingly decentralised bargaining, in an attempt to deflect the criticism of vocal women's groups. In the Republic of Ireland, these remedies were the result of external forces (namely, Ireland's entry into the European common market) and domestic calls for equality for women.[2] In both cases, the role of the State has been problematic and demanding of some theorisation for our purposes. This must be linked to an attempt to theorise law from a feminist perspective. Such is the power of law that very rarely do we question its ability to achieve our law reform aims.[3] The political problem for feminists involved in the legal project, then, becomes one of whether we continue our political support for remedies of dubious value, which implies that the State has dealt with the 'problem', or stand outside the process, waiting for a more complete solution. Nicola Lacey has argued recently that we remain 'inside':

> Given its social power, we simply cannot afford to abandon the legal process as a site for political action ... We must try to alter law, so as to make it more

1   Jamieson, S, 'Equity in the workplace', in Hogan, M and Dempsey, K (eds), *Equity and Citizenship Under Keating*, 1995, Sydney: PARC.

2   Shannon, E, 'Comparing feminisms: utilising Sabatier's advocacy coalition framework for international policy analysis' (1995), paper presented to the Public Policy Network annual conference, 2–3 February, Australian National University, Canberra; Shannon, E, 'The influence of feminism on public policy' (1996), paper presented to Women's Electoral Lobby national conference, 26–28 January, Sydney; Curtin, D, *Irish Employment Equality Law*, 1986, Dublin: Round Hall, p 96.

3   Kirkby, D (ed), *Sex, Power and Justice: Historical Perspectives on Law in Australia*, 1995, Melbourne: OUP, p xi.

receptive to the arguments of the powerless, so as to stop it silencing their voices: we should not completely discount law as an area for consciousness raising as well as material political advance.[4]

In endeavouring to engage in a little 'material political advance', I turn, below, to a brief examination of possible ways of conceptualising the State and the law from a feminist perspective and then I examine more closely the legislation and decided cases which should suggest improved remedies or other strategies. First, however, a little needs to be said of law and comparative method.

My concern is not with comparative law as a tool of research or as a tool of education but with comparative law as a tool of law reform.[5]

While our current project might, broadly, be defined as one of law reform, Kahn-Freund was conscious that legal scholars and reformers should not use a study of comparative law as an ideological bludgeon. He was, too, conscious of the specificity of local conditions in law making and referred to Montesquieu's First Book of *The Spirit of the Laws* to substantiate his point.[6] The aim of this chapter is not to show that the Australian or Irish equal pay laws are better than others (indeed, they are both deficient) but to examine how two different States have responded to a similar problem in very different environments.

This project began in the early 1990s, before Australia had any national equal pay laws. Originally, the goal was to compare a legislative regime for equal pay (the Republic of Ireland) with a regime of industrially negotiated or awarded pay outcomes (Australia). At that time, the so called 'equal pay decisions' of Australia's unique conciliation and arbitration system were about 20 years old and men's and women's average hourly wage rates were still converging, women's rates being at 92% of men's,[7] while, in the Republic of Ireland, women's pay was stuck at 68% of men's hourly earnings.[8] In the Republic of Ireland, they remain unchanged, although this may alter in the light of 'low pay' strategies. In Australia, they are beginning to diverge. Whitehouse[9] had published a comparative study of various OECD countries, in which the nature of the bargaining system and economic environment seemed to be the most important determinant of the quantum of women's wages. It was, nevertheless, considered important to be able to measure, at

---

4   Lacey, N, *Unspeakable Subjects – Feminist Essays in Legal and Social Theory*, 1998, Oxford: Hart, p 44.

5   Kahn-Freund, O, 'On uses and misuses of comparative law' (1974) 37 MLR 1.

6   *Ibid*, Kahn-Freund, p 6.

7   Human Rights and Equal Opportunity Commission, *Just Rewards: A Report of the Inquiry into Sex Discrimination in Overaward Payments*, 1992, Canberra: AGPS, p 35.

8   Irish Congress of Trade Unions, *Mainstreaming Equality*, 1993, Dublin: ICTU, p 4.

9   Whitehouse, G, 'Legislation and labour market gender equality: an analysis of OECD countries' (1992) 6 Work, Employment and Society 65.

least in a broad way, how equal pay legislation might affect aggregate national wage outcomes. The answer, as shall be seen below, is, probably, not at all. As time has moved on, however, my goal has shifted slightly and I have become more concerned with theoretical explanations as to why things happen as they do, while participating, on a practical level, as an activist in some of the events I describe.

Australia and the Republic of Ireland were chosen because of their shared legal culture in the common law world and because both have written constitutions to which their national Parliaments are subordinate. Both countries, at the time, enjoyed a reasonably positive atmosphere for the existence of trade unions. The two countries also shared high levels of sex based occupational and industrial segregation at the workplace, both countries witnessed a growing services sector where women played an important role and, in both countries, levels of atypical employment were growing, as were various flexibility initiatives.[10] Great dissonances between the two comparator countries also exist, beyond the obvious differences of size and nature of the populations (and workplaces) and the nature and size of the national economies and markets within which they were, and are, active. As will be seen below, industrial and political arrangements in the two countries are also different and, while the current industrial relations situation in Ireland has been described as 'bargained corporatism', the heavily corporatist arrangements in Australia during the Labour Party-unions accord years of 1983–96 now appear to be rapidly unravelling. Ultimately, however, the greatest difference between the two nations is to be found in Ireland's membership of the European Union, which it joined in 1973, and which has significant implications for any examination of the law relating to equal pay for women.[11]

LAW AND STATE: THEORISING THE STATE

The way in which the State is theorised has taken a huge intellectual battering in the past 20 years, just as some of the other great explanatory theoretical frameworks have come under attack from feminists, postmodernists and post-structuralists. I will argue that the State is not only central to feminist jurisprudence but is, also, central, on a practical level, to the equal pay matters that are investigated below and to many other areas of women's lives. I take

10 See Gunnigle, P, McMahon, G and Fitzgerald, G, *Industrial Relations in Ireland – Theory and Practice*, 1995, Dublin: Gill and Macmillan; and, generally, Gardner, M and Palmer, G, *Employment Relations – Industrial Relations and Human Resource Management in Australia*, 1997, Melbourne: Macmillan.

11 While this is enormously significant, I will not devote much space to this issue but see, also, Morris, Chapter 9, this volume.

the State as my starting point, as I do not believe one can build a sensible feminist jurisprudence from another starting point. Some writers have suggested that attempting to theorise the State at all is a waste of time.[12] While a link may have been identified between unsuccessful attempts to theorise the State and the work of early Marxist feminists, Marx himself was never concerned to subject the State to any close theoretical analysis. While Jessop lists six ways in which Marx did look at the State, his most common approach was to see it as a 'superstructure' of law and politics based on an 'infrastructure' of economics.[13] More popularly, he saw the State as an instrument of class rule by the economically dominant class.[14] This approach has obvious problems for any feminist analysis.

Nicos Poulantzas[15] has argued that the State was more than its juridical arm, but the major feminist encounter with the State reduces the State to the law. Catharine MacKinnon, in *Toward a Feminist Theory of the State*, sees the law as the State – and both as being male. Male supremacist jurisprudence, as she terms it,[16] *is* the legal system, dominating by men, of men and for men. The State is male, and men, as a group, dominate women, as a group. I will link this, below, to other ways of theorising the law from a feminist point of view.

Nicola Lacey, however, observes that the State is not monolithic – 'it is, rather, a set of diverse institutions'.[17] She adopts Foucauldian language to describe it as consisting of 'many interlocking institutions and practices'.[18] While agreeing with Allen that 'the State' is 'too blunt an instrument' to be of much analytical assistance, Lacey presents us with the seeds of a useful approach, that allows us to look at the ways in which the State acts in a non-monolithic, various, sometimes incoherent and, occasionally, contradictory way.

In arguing that the concept of the State is still a useful one, Pringle and Watson also reject the views of Allen (discussed above) and advocate a post-structuralist approach to this concept.[19] Drawing on Foucault, Pringle and Watson note that the famous French historian of power saw power as

---

12 Allen, J, 'Does feminism need a theory of the State?', in Watson, S (ed), *Playing the State: Australian Feminist Interventions*, 1990, Sydney: Allen & Unwin.

13 Jessop, B, *State Theory – Putting Capitalist States in their Place*, 1990, University Park: Pennsylvania State UP, p 26.

14 *Ibid*, p 27.

15 *Ibid*, p 68.

16 MacKinnon, C, *Toward a Feminist Theory of the State*, 1989, Cambridge, Mass: Harvard UP, p 237.

17 *Op cit*, Lacey, fn 4, p 76.

18 *Op cit*, Lacey, fn 4, p 73.

19 Pringle, R and Watson, S, '"Women's interests" and the post-structuralist State', in Barrett, M and Phillips, A (eds), *Destabilizing Theory – Contemporary Feminist Debates*, 1992, Cambridge: Polity, p 67.

relational; that is, not something owned and exercised from above.[20] Foucault argued that the State was an effect of these relations and was not – this approach contrasting sharply with the traditional Marxist view – something that acted in a coherent fashion as the creature of one of the power groups (for example, the economically dominant class). Pringle and Watson extrapolate from his work on governmentality that many of the domains of the modern State are, in fact, clearly masculine. They do not, however, agree with Catharine MacKinnon (see above) that the State is simply male[21] but that 'what feminists are confronted with is not a state that represents "men's interests", as against women's, but government conducted as if men's interests are the only ones that exist'.[22] The State, they argue, is historically specific, 'not structurally "given"'[23] and, in the constant competition between the different forces or groupings, the State may, at times, appear to act in a contradictory manner. Finally, in arguing for a radical democracy that does not concern us here, Pringle and Watson assert that reconceptualising the State 'requires a shift away from seeing the State as a coherent, if contradictory, unity. Instead, we see it as a diverse set of discursive arenas which play a crucial role in ongoing relations of power'.[24] This post-structuralist view of the State will be tested, below, in looking at the way in which the State deals with the problem of equal pay for women in Australia and in the Republic of Ireland.

LAW AND STATE: THEORISING THE LAW

There are many ways of categorising feminist legal theory. Nicola Lacey[25] divides feminist jurisprudence into two approaches. First, she writes of the liberal, or equality, approach which 'is committed, as is mainstream legal theory, to the ideals of gender neutrality and equality before the law. Its focus is primarily instrumental, seeing law as a tool of feminist strategy, and the impact of law as a basis for feminist critique'.[26] For Lacey, the second major form of feminist jurisprudence and, indeed, the one she grew into from an initially liberal position is difference feminism, which she contrasts as being:

---

20 *Op cit*, Pringle and Watson, fn 19, p 55.
21 *Op cit*, Pringle and Watson, fn 19, p 62.
22 *Op cit*, Pringle and Watson, fn 19, p 57.
23 *Op cit*, Pringle and Watson, fn 19, p 63.
24 *Op cit*, Pringle and Watson, fn 19, p 79.
25 *Op cit*, Lacey, fn 4, pp 3–4.
26 *Op cit*, Lacey, fn 4, p 3.

... sceptical about the possibility of neutrality; it has an implicit commitment to ... a more complex idea of equality which accommodates and values, whilst not fixing, women's specificity 'as women' and it has a focus on the symbolic and dynamic aspects of law and not just on its instrumental aspects.[27]

Carol Smart, the British sociologist of law, has theorised the law in a three phase typology. As a Foucauldian, one of her aims has been to deconstruct the law and the gendered construction of Women as legal objects. In some of her more recent work, she has made some interesting observations about the juridification of Women by the English legal system in the 18th and 19th centuries.[28] Her essential point, in *Feminism and the Power of Law*, is that law has been allowed by feminists to occupy too central a place in feminist theory and activities. She is particularly critical of writers, such as American lawyer and activist, Catharine MacKinnon, whom she believes have argued that the law (and the State), are male and, as such, inevitably opposed to the interests of women (or dedicated consciously to the organised oppression of women as a group), on one hand, but have actively pursued a vigorous programme of litigation and legislative reform on issues such as pornography, on the other, seemingly in contradiction in their primary view of the law as male.[29]

Smart argues:

It is the work of feminism to deconstruct the naturalist, gender blind discourse of law by constantly revealing the context in which it has been constituted and drawing parallels with other areas of social life. Law is not a free floating entity, it is grounded in patriarchy, as well as in class and ethnic divisions.[30]

She goes on to cast doubt on the usefulness of developing a whole new feminist jurisprudence, as this assists in the fetishising of the law and, ultimately, may seem to 'replace one hierarchy of truth with another'.[31] This, Smart argues, will not de-centre law, although she does not dismiss attempts at law reform as a short term strategy to improve the position of women.[32]

While Smart holds to this view of law as a gendered discourse, she also discusses other feminist approaches, which may be conveniently entitled 'law is sexist'. As mentioned above, 'law is sexist' is the classic liberal formulation and analysis of women's disadvantaged position in legal terms; that is, women are disadvantaged in law because they are differentiated from men. This view of law, which is the dominant premise supporting the establishment of anti-discrimination laws in Australia, Ireland, Great Britain and the United States, tends to see men as the standard against which women

---

27 *Op cit*, Lacey, fn 4, pp 3–4.
28 Smart, C, *Law, Crime and Sexuality*, 1995, London: Sage, pp 36–39.
29 Smart, C, *Feminism and the Power of Law*, 1989, London: Routledge, pp 70–71.
30 *Ibid*, Smart, 1989, p 88.
31 *Ibid*, Smart, 1989, p 89.
32 *Ibid*, Smart, 1989, p 114.

will be measured. Essentially, in law reform terms, 'law is sexist' means that discrimination and disadvantage may be eliminated as soon as different treatment of men and women is proscribed. An obvious criticism of this approach is that it is not possible to create equality (if that, indeed, is our goal) merely by outlawing discrimination. Nor does this approach address the problem of whether disadvantage is the product of discrimination. This criticism holds whether we are discussing sex, race or other kinds of discrimination.

Smart also rejects the 'law is male' school of thought that is best characterised by the work of Catharine MacKinnon and Mary Jane Mossman. This view, essentially, asserts that, while men physically and practically dominate the legal world as academics, legislators, practitioners and judges, their values have become the standard legal values, while, at the same time, these standards appear to be value-neutral.[33] The end result of this analysis can be despair or paralysis – the pessimistic view that a feminist agenda cannot be accommodated at all within male legal culture. MacKinnon[34] speaks of constructing a whole new feminist jurisprudence while, at the same time, engaging the male legal establishment in her (admirable) anti-pornography campaign. As noted, above, by Smart, this would appear to be contradictory. Smart argues that this approach leads to several problems beyond that of the impossibility of setting up an alternative female/feminist legal culture. These problems include ascribing to law a unity and consistency that it, clearly, does not possess, that is, law does not, at all times and in all circumstances, defend, build and uplift the rights of all men (see Lacey, above). In the Australian context, the situation of Aboriginal men is an obvious example. In Australia and Ireland, issues of class divide the hegemonic white Anglo-Celtic group of men itself. While Smart eschews 'grand theory' from her Foucauldian point of view,[35] she, nevertheless, rejects the 'law is male' view as a stand alone approach because of its implications for practical action and because it, finally, fails to explain the very issues it criticises.

What, then, is meant by *gendered* law? Smart asserts that the 'law as gendered' view does not require the wholesale rejection of all the insights provided by the 'law is male' approach. She writes:

> But, while the assertion that 'law is male' effects a closure in how we think about law, the idea of it as gendered allows us to think of it in terms of processes which will work in a variety of ways and in which there is no

---

33   *Op cit*, MacKinnon, fn 16, p 238.
34   *Op cit*, MacKinnon, fn 16, p 238.
35   *Op cit*, Smart, fn 28, p 163.
36   *Op cit*, Smart, fn 28, p 190.

relentless assumption that whatever it does exploits women and serves men.[36]

This must be read, according to Smart, with the observation that law also acts to produce gender – that is, it produces a gendered subject.

The notion of *woman*, as opposed to *women*, is at the centre of the 'law as gendered' approach and it is precisely this recognition that there is no single category *woman*, who is uniformly, and at all times, oppressed, exploited and debased by law or any other technology of gender, that distinguishes this approach from MacKinnon's 'law is male' approach.

Now, we have reached a point where our chosen feminist legal theory challenges the very gender neutrality which sits at the centre of the traditional liberal formulation of law. Law is gendered and does not impinge on the lives of men and women in the same way and, further, it does not impinge on the lives of all women in the same way. This is, precisely, one form of the 'difference' feminism to which Nicola Lacey referred at the beginning of this short examination of feminist legal theory.[37]

The varied experience of woman/women before the law, and the agencies of the State that administer that law, suggest that liberal notions of equality – the de-sexing of the law – do not inevitably result in practical equality. This differential experience, it should also be said, does not suggest that a patriarchal legal system (or State) oppresses all women at all times. Both the law and the State consist of too many different sites, arenas and practices to operate in a single, conscious fashion, in relation to all persons, at all times. Similarly, different discourses adopted by the State in Australia and the Republic of Ireland, for different purposes, at different times, will constitute a different legal experience for women. Below, I will examine the way in which the two States in question have adopted an 'equality' approach to the law, whereby equal pay is to be achieved by means of the classic liberal individual remedy but where those States act according to the variety, inconsistency and incoherence described, above, by Lacey and Pringle and Watson.

EQUAL PAY LEGISLATION AND ITS ORIGINS

Equal pay legislation has its genesis in the Convention on Equal Pay, adopted by the International Labour Organisation in 1950–51, which had ancestors going back (at least) to clauses within the Treaty of Versailles of 1919. Neither Australia nor the Republic of Ireland had rushed to do much with the Equal

---

37 *Op cit*, Lacey, fn 4, p 3.

Pay Convention, although, as early as 1958, one Australian State (New South Wales) had included the equal pay provisions into its mainstream industrial relations legislation, though it was to remain something of a dead letter for most of the next 40 years. Before I turn to these developments, however, it is useful to survey where women fit into the Australian and Irish wage setting frameworks.

Wage fixation in Australia

The nature of arbitration

It is a commonplace that arbitration, while not coterminous with Australian industrial relations, has certainly dominated it. This is because the system of compulsory arbitration of labour disputes has been supported by State policy, because the system has provided a structure of orders, awards and agreements (including, more recently, enterprise agreements) which regulate most workers' conditions of employment, because these issues are intimately tied to national industrial and economic policy, because the arbitration system has played, until recently, a major role in settling most important labour disputes, because industrial relations, generally, are conducted in the full knowledge that the resources of arbitration are available, if necessary, and, finally, because most trade unions and many employer associations are registered as legal participants within the system.

The most popular view of conciliation and arbitration is that it was put forward, by the Labour movement in the 1890s, as a way of protecting the growing trade union movement from the ravages of expanding capitalism, which, during the great strikes of the period 1890–94, had been openly aided by the institutions of the State. Arbitration saw the State itself provide a protective structure for trade unions, which could provide wider advantages for a peaceful society. Under the second President of the Commonwealth Court of Conciliation and Arbitration, the Irish born Henry Bournes Higgins, arbitration would, also, come to be a crucial player in national economic policy, through the establishment of national minimum wage rates. Arbitration was adopted nationally (having already been adopted by some pre-Federation colonial governments, such as New South Wales) at a crucial time in Australia's history, when other important social, political and cultural patterns were established as recognisably Australian creations. What, however, has arbitration signified for women workers?

Women and wage fixation

The chronology of the interface between women and the arbitration system is well known and documented in many places.[38] In the first successful National Wage case, known popularly as the *Harvester* decision, Mr Justice Higgins, President of the then Arbitration Court, established a rate of pay for male labourers that was designed to provide 'frugal comfort' for a man, his wife and three children.[39] This rate was struck by Higgins on the basis of evidence, provided by Melbourne working class housewives, as to the cost of living. The decision effectively set a pattern for the centralised setting of wage levels that is only now, in the 1990s, under serious challenge. The decision was, apparently, blind to the fact that many women supported families, that many families were not structured according to Higgins' hypothetical working class family and, perhaps more importantly, that probably 45% of all men were single. Simply, Higgins decided that the industrial labourer was a married man with dependents. In the *Fruit Pickers* case of 1912, Higgins actually awarded equal pay rates for women fruit pickers, because it appears that men's jobs were seriously threatened by women, who, without intervention by the Arbitration Court, could well have forced men out of the industry if employers could legally pay them less. In 1919, in the *Clothing* case, Higgins, then not long before his retirement, established what was, effectively, a national minimum rate for women of 54% of the male wage rate. This was increased to 75% in the 1950–51 National Wage case.

In 1969, the successor to the court, the Australian Conciliation and Arbitration Commission, brought down a decision on equal pay for equal work in response to a claim by the Australian Council of Trade Unions. The decision was to be phased in over three years for economic reasons. However, the decision only extended to work performed 'essentially or usually' by females and, given the traditional high levels of segregation in Australian industry,[40] the decision never covered more than 18% of women workers. In 1972, a further test case was mounted, resulting in a decision of equal pay for work of equal value, which was to apply by way of 'consideration of the work performed, irrespective of the sex of the worker'. This was to be achieved using the mechanism of work value comparisons. An attempt was made, in

---

38 Eg, Bennett, L, 'Equal pay and comparable worth and the Australian Conciliation and Arbitration Commission' (1988) 30 Journal of Industrial Relations 533, pp 533–45; *op cit*, Gardner and Palmer, fn 10; *op cit*, Human Rights and Equal Opportunity Commission, fn 7.

39 *Ex p HV McKay* (1907) 2 CAR 1.

40 *Op cit*, Human Rights and Equal Opportunities Commission, fn 7.

1985, to import the notion of comparable worth from North America into an Australian Council of Trade Unions case run on behalf of nurses. While there was no serious attempt to compare the work of women with that of men, the Commission rejected the concept. It has long been felt that women's work has traditionally been undervalued in relation to men's work and, while Justice Higgins' concept of the 'family wage' has no legal standing in Australia today, it is one of the factors which continues to affect the way women's work is valued.

The 1985 *Nurses* case was complicated by the existence of the (Prices and Incomes) Accord, which had been struck between the Australian Council of Trade Unions and the Australian Labor Party in February, 1983, one month before that party won national government. The Accord was a compact which saw the trade union movement trade off wages increases for other social benefits, such as tax relief, social programmes, health insurance and policy initiatives in training, occupational health and safety and trade union reform. The Accord was regularly renegotiated in the light of changed economic circumstances and came to an end with the election of a Conservative Government, in March 1996.

The move, recently, towards greater decentralisation of wage fixing through the adoption of workplace, company or plant level bargaining has marked wages policy in both Labor and Conservative governments across Australia. There is evidence that this deregulation is not restricted to Australia. Nor is it the first time some decentralisation has occurred within the Australian system. However, the institutional support given to the move away from a decentralised system by the central government in the way of redrafted legislation (for example, the Industrial Relations Reform Act 1993) was truly unprecedented.

It was in that climate that the equal pay provisions first saw the light of day in Federal industrial legislation. These provisions remained in the redrafted legislation, the Workplace Relations Act 1996, after concentrated lobbying of the minister and the minority parties in the Australian Senate and after the rigours of a full Senate inquiry. This must be seen in the light of the fact that the gender wage gap in Australia in the 1990s is widening again.[41]

WAGE FIXATION IN IRELAND

Ireland, of course, shares a legislative history with the United Kingdom up to

---

41   Probert, B, Ewer, P and Whiting, K, *Gender Pay Equity in Australian Higher Education*, 1998, Melbourne: National Tertiary Education Union, p 5.

1922. The landmark legislation, such as the Trade Union Act 1871, the Trade Disputes Act 1906 and the Trade Union Act 1913 were operative on both sides of the Irish Sea. The kind of large scale intervention by the State, as in the Australian system of conciliation and arbitration, described above as a settlement between capital and labour, did not occur. The general environment for collective bargaining was, for trade unions, a relatively agreeable one up until the Second World War.[42] The relative lack of State intervention and the greater reliance on decentralised bargaining in Ireland over the 20th century has led to a greater disparity between men's and women's wages than is seen in Australia. Drawing on a range of other writers, Gunnigle *et al* describe a shift in Irish industrial relations across the 20th century from market individualism to liberal collectivism, in which the State increasingly attempted to exert what might be described as corporate control. This expressed itself in tripartite programmes, such as the Programme for National Recovery, the Programme for Economic and Social Progress, the Programme for Competitiveness and Work and Partnership 2000. In line with its obligations under the instruments setting up the European Union, in the summer of 1997, it established a National Minimum Wage Commission, which reported in April 1998. Its recommendations are to be implemented in April 2000. Concurrently, the Blair Labour Government in the United Kingdom had established the Low Pay Commission. While neither of these initiatives was directed solely at women, given that women make up a significant cohort in the low paid across the world, these measures may, in the future, have an effect on women's aggregate levels of pay, where the individual remedies of the equal pay legislation, as seen below, have had no measurable effect.

The legislation

The Australian legislation in the Workplace Relations Act of 1996 merely repeats the provisions of 1993 and provides no real guidance as to the way in which the Australian Industrial Relations Commission is to go about establishing what is equal remuneration or how it might be implemented.

Part VIA – Minimum entitlements of employees

Division 2 – Equal remuneration for work of equal value

170BA Object

The object of this division is to give effect, or further effect, to:

(a)   the Anti-Discrimination Conventions;

(b)   the Equal Remuneration Recommendation, 1951, which the General

---

42   *Op cit*, Gunnigle, McMahon and Fitzgerald, fn 10, p 53.

Conference of the International Labour Organisation adopted on 29 June 1951, and is also known as Recommendation No 90; and

(c) the Discrimination (Employment and Occupation) Recommendation, 1958, which the General Conference of the International Labour Organisation adopted on 25 June 1958, and is also known as Recommendation No 111.

170BB Equal remuneration for work of equal value

A reference in this division to equal remuneration for work of equal value is a reference to equal remuneration for women and women workers for work of equal value.

An expression has, in sub-s (1), the same meaning as in the Equal Remuneration Convention.

Note: Art 1 of the Convention provides that the term *equal remuneration for men and women workers for work of equal value* refers to rates of remuneration established without discrimination based on sex.

170BC Orders requiring equal remuneration

Subject to this division, the Commission may make such orders as it considers appropriate to ensure that, for employees covered by the orders, there will be equal remuneration for work of equal value.

(2) Without limiting sub-s (1), an order under this division may provide for such increases in rates (including minimum rates) of remuneration (within the meaning of the Equal Remuneration Convention) as the Commission considers appropriate to ensure that, for employees covered by the order, there will be equal remuneration for work of equal value.

The Irish Anti-Discrimination (Pay) Act 1974 has no up front objectives but states:

2 (1) Subject to this Act, it shall be a term of the contract under which a woman is employed in any place that she shall be entitled to the same rate of remuneration as a man who is employed in that place by the same employer (or by an associated employer if the employees, whether generally or of a particular class, of both employers have the same terms and conditions of employment) if both are employed on like work.

(2) For the purpose of this section, two employers shall be taken to be associated if one is a body corporate, of which the other (whether directly or indirectly) has control or if both are bodies corporate, of which a third person (whether directly or indirectly) has control.

3 Two persons shall be regarded as employed on like work:

(a) where both perform the same work under the same or similar conditions, or where each is, in every respect, interchangeable with the other in relation to the work; or

(b) where the work performed by one is of a similar nature to that performed by the other and any differences between the work performed, or the conditions under which it is performed, by each, occur only infrequently or are of small importance in relation to the work as a whole; or

(c)   where the work performed by one is equal in value to that performed by the other in terms of demands it makes in relation to such matters as skill, physical or mental effort, responsibility and working conditions.

In the first instance, applications are to be made to an Equality Officer of the Labour Court (s 6) who is to investigate the matter and who may issue a recommendation. Disputes arising from recommendations are to be heard by the Labour Court (s 8).

As indicated above, both pieces of legislation are imperfect. Just how imperfect the Australian legislation may prove to be, in practice, is difficult to tell, as only one case has been litigated under the legislation, which has been on foot since 31 March 1994. While more will be said about this below, the fact that, in Australia, only one case has been prosecuted, one case withdrawn and two settled would suggest that potential claimants (and their unions) have some good reason for not filing applications.

The form of the Irish legislation was the subject of considerable debate in the Dail and Seanad during the whole of 1974. A study of that debate must wait for another time, as must the debate surrounding the cognate Employment Equality Act 1977, which was under discussion in various forms from 1975 to 1977 and which aims to provide the classic liberal prescriptions for equality, including protection against direct and indirect discrimination at work and discrimination arising out of pregnancy. Compared to other national legislative instruments concerning discrimination generally, the Irish position of singling out sex discrimination only at work seems very narrow.

All of this must, of course, be seen in the light of the way in which the Constitution of Ireland itself views gender and the effect Ireland's membership of the European Union has had on the creation of the legislation and the development of equal pay jurisprudence. The Constitution of 1937 states:

Article 40.1

All citizens shall, as human persons, be held equal before the law.

And, in other, rather remarkable, terms, goes on to declare:

Article 41.2

1   In particular, the State recognises that, by her life within the home, woman gives to the State a support without which the common good cannot be achieved.

2   The State shall, therefore, endeavour to ensure that mothers shall not be

> obliged, by economic necessity, to engage in labour, to the neglect of their duties in the house.

There are no similar prescriptions or guarantees of any identifiable human rights in the Australian Constitution of 1900.

Article 119 of the Treaty of Rome, which established the common European market, states that each Member State must 'ensure and, subsequently, maintain the application of the principle that men and women should receive equal pay for equal work'. In the landmark case *Defrenne v Sabena* [1976] ECR 455, the European Court declared:

> ... the aim of Art 119 is to avoid a situation in which undertakings established in States which have actually implemented the principle of equal pay suffer a competitive disadvantage in intra-Community competition, as compared with undertakings established in States which have not yet eliminated discrimination against women workers as regards pay. Secondly, this provision forms part of the social objectives of the Community, which is not merely an economic union but is, at the same time, intended, by common action, to ensure social progress and seek the constant improvement of the living and working conditions of their peoples, as emphasised by the Preamble to the Treaty (p 472).

Clearly, non-compliance with the supra-national law was not an option. Below, I will examine cases which throw into sharp relief the way in which the State, constituted as a series of separate arenas, has engaged with the concept of equal pay. Those arenas might be labelled the legislature, the judiciary (national and supra-national), the executive and the State as employer. In both the Irish and Australian cases, it will be seen that the State does not act as a monolith but in a various, inconsistent and, sometimes, incoherent way.

THE LEGISLATION IN COURT

By the end of 1998, it would seem that the equal pay legislation in Australia and the Republic of Ireland had not resulted in changes to the ratio of women's to men's wages, although there is evidence that, initially, the Irish legislation did have an effect on aggregate wages.[43] Perhaps we are guilty of what Carol Smart may call putting the law too much at the centre of social debate and feminist demands. On the other hand, it is impossible to measure whether the mere existence of the legislation has prevented the gender wage gap from widening or, in the case of Australia in the second half of the 1990s, widening at a faster rate. In the Australian case, the increasing

---

43   von Prondzynski, F, *Employment Law in Ireland*, 1989, London: Sweet & Maxwell, p 82.

decentralisation of wage fixation has coincided almost exactly with the existence of the legislation. One cannot measure the possible 'deterrent' effect any piece of legislation may exert. Putting these difficult questions to one side, I now turn to a very brief examination of some of the cases and how they might fit into the explanatory framework posited above.

Ireland

Interview evidence gathered in Ireland, in 1993 and 1997, from trade union officials, employer representatives and Equality Officers indicated that the logistic difficulties in proving matters under s 8 of the 1974 Act are not inconsiderable. From a union point of view, women workers must know that there is a problem and that there is a complaint mechanism. Alternatively, union officials must observe an anomaly. The fact that s 2 of the 1974 Act requires that the 'comparator' male employees must be employed by the same employer, at the same place, seems to ignore the realities of a segregated labour market. The fact that the women complainants and the male comparators may belong to the same union could, clearly, also cause further problems. All parties interviewed believed that the process itself of problem identification, evidence collection, investigation and determination was resource intensive and not conducive to the mounting of many cases. Union interviews indicated that many unions simply did not have the technical resources, or the political will to develop the technical resources, necessary to mount successful applications under the 1974 Act. All parties agreed that, after the implementation of the legislation in 1975, early successes were drawn from situations that were, in fact, relatively easy to establish and that, as time went on, only the more difficult cases remained. Labour Court Annual Reports from 1989–96 also seem to suggest that something of a backlog of cases accumulated in the Equality Officers' in trays which, from interview evidence, would seem to be the result of under-resourcing.

What has the State had to do with all of this? Clearly, the State has created the legislation within a fairly broad framework, established by the Treaty of Rome. It administers the legislation through the Equality Officers and the Labour Court and the appellate courts above the Labour Court. Finally, in a number of determinations issued by the Labour Court (an appeal from the Equality Officers), the State has also, in one guise or another, been the employer resisting the equal pay claims of women workers. As recently as 1996, the Department of Agriculture, Food and Forestry was successful in defeating a union claim under s 8 of the 1974 Act. In fact, during the period 1991–96, only in 1994 were there no determinations of the Labour Court involving State employers and, in the period 1991–96, State employers were involved in 10 of 35 determinations before the Labour Court. This may be the result of sectoral differences and gender concentrations but may also suggest a degree of tenacity on the part of public sector employers to defend these actions.

State employers are not unknown in the reported decisions of the Labour Court and the appellate courts. Perhaps the most notorious case, in this respect, is *Murphy and Others v An Bord Telecom Eireann*.[44] This case has been much discussed elsewhere.[45] Briefly, 28 women, engaged in dismantling, cleaning, oiling and reassembling telecommunications equipment, sought to be paid the same as a male comparator, a more generously remunerated stores labourer, who was engaged in cleaning, collecting and delivering equipment and components. The Equality Officer, not surprisingly, found this work to be of higher value than the male comparator's work and, therefore, not deserving of a remedy under the 1974 Act. This was solemnly confirmed by the Labour Court and the High Court of Ireland. The European Court of Justice, again, not surprisingly, gave this approach short shrift, a literal interpretation seemingly resulting in the Irish Parliament having legislated in obvious contravention of Community law.

The role of the State here (that is, the Republic of Ireland and the European Community, as it was then styled) may be characterised as various, contradictory and incoherent when seen operating within separate arenas – that is, legislature, judiciary, executive and employer.

Australia

In Australia, there is very little jurisprudence under s 170BA of the 1993 and 1996 Acts to discuss. One early case, lodged by a public sector union in 1995, was withdrawn (allegedly at the request of the Australian Council of Trade Unions). In December 1995, three new claims were jointly filed by the union congress and the Australian Manufacturing Workers' Union. Two were eventually settled. In respect of the third matter, women who were employed to assemble and pack small electrical and electronic components claimed parity with male general hands and storemen. The general hands earned between $13 and $53 per week more than the women workers. The initial case

---

44 [1986] ILRM 483 and IRLR 267.
45 Curtin, D, *Irish Employment Equality Law*, 1989, Dublin: Round Hall, pp 51–52; *op cit*, von Prondzynski, fn 43, p 93; Fennell, C and Lynch, I, *Labour Law in Ireland*, 1993, Dublin: Gill and Macmillan, p 168.

concluded, in early 1998, with no real result and was immediately refiled by the union as a work value case. The case is being heard as I write. The matter is being vigorously defended by the employer (a private manufacturer) who, also, eventually sacked all the general hand comparators. The union case is supported by women's organisations which have been afforded standing to intervene. The Commonwealth Government is also a party but is saying virtually nothing and openly standing at arm's length. Previous Commonwealth governments (for example, in the 1972 case mentioned above) have been active in seeking redress for women on the issue of equal pay. The current Commonwealth Government had also proposed in 1996 that the equal pay legislation should be abandoned.

CONCLUSIONS

It is doubtful that an individual complaint remedy can have an effect on aggregate wages in an economy. In any event, access to equality rather than outcomes has been the driving force behind most anti-discrimination legislation, including the equal pay legislation of Australia and the Republic of Ireland which has been examined here. That individual women have benefited (at least under the Irish legislation) is documented in the law reports. Group disadvantage appears not to have been dented at all.

Our attempts to theorise the State at the outset of this paper have ignored the existence of a supra-national State in the European Union. In dealing with the national States under examination and the law of equal pay, the State has been seen to take on many different roles. We have, also, seen it act in different ways at different times. Two examples, however, do not prove the correctness of any theory; but it would seem that our explanatory framework of state and law may provide some useful insights into the way in which the equal pay laws operate in Australia and the Republic of Ireland. What

INDEX